30 DAYS TO UNDERSTANDING THE BIBLE

30 DAYS TO UNDERSTANDING THE BIBLE in 15 MINUTES A DAY!

MAX ANDERS

Publishers Since 1798

THOMAS NELSON PUBLISHERS
NASHVILLE

30 DAYS TO UNDERSTANDING THE BIBLE IN 15 MINUTES A DAY

Library of Congress Cataloging-in-Publication Data

Anders, Max E., 1947–
   30 days to understanding the Bible in 15 minutes a day / Max Anders.
      p.   cm.
   Expanded ed. of: 30 days to understanding the Bible. c1994.
   ISBN 0-7852-1423-2
   1. Bible—Introductions. I. Anders, Max E., 1947– 30 days to understanding the Bible. II. Title.
   BS475.2.A53   1998
   220.6'1—dc21   98-14122
                                        CIP

7 03 02

Printed in the United States of America

To Jake and Wilma,
my spiritual mentors and dear friends

If you are interested in having Max Anders speak to your church, organization, or special event, please contact:

interAct Speaker's Bureau
P.O. Box 1022
Dickson, TN 37056
Telephone: (615) 446-2837
Facsimile: (615) 446-7818

CONTENTS

SECTION 3: General Overview of the Bible

Appendix

ACKNOWLEDGMENTS

This book was much harder to write than I imagined. In fact, it would not have been completed if it had not been for the timely and providential contributions made by many people. Had it not been for the considerable knowledge and creative input of Bob Roland and Art Vander Veen, I would not even have started. Dr. Steve Grill supplied the information for the United States history charts. Anne Cundiff did much of the thinking and artwork on the original illustrations. Gary McKnight did the research and first draft for chapters 20 through 27 in this revised edition. His skillful work under close deadlines was extremely valuable and greatly appreciated. Roxanne Brooks typed and edited the new material in the revised manuscript.

My thanks to those who field-tested the original manuscript and made many valuable contributions: Lara and Richard Anders, Ken Axt, Dr. Ken Boa, Eric Frank, Garlen Howington, Jerome King, Marcia Price, David Rogers, and Lynn Tarleton. Lara and Richard Anders, Marcia Price, and Lynn Tarleton are all members of my family. Bless you! Thanks to Judy Lunsford, who not only field-tested the manuscript but gave it many hours of skillful editorial evaluation.

Special thanks to my wife, Margie, whose meticulous frontal assault on my original fuzzy thinking raised the manuscript a full stratum above its original level. Her razor logic and editorial insights made this a much better book than it would have been otherwise.

And finally, thanks to the Lord for His providential oversight in my life in prompting and enabling me to write the book. To God be the glory!

INTRODUCTION

Let's make a bargain.

If you'll give me *fifteen minutes* a day for *thirty days,* I'll give you an understanding of the Bible, the most widely distributed publication in history (approximately three *billion* copies!).

In one month, you will learn . . .

all the major men and women,

all the major events, and

all the major points of geography.

You will be able to put these people and facts together in their proper chronological order and trace the geographical movement as you think your way through the entire Bible! You will know the story of the Old Testament and the story of the New Testament.

Yet the Bible is more than history. In order to understand the history more fully, it is very helpful to understand such things as why there are four Gospels, why Jesus spoke in parables, how we can comprehend the miracles and the prophecies in the Bible, and so on.

No attempt has been made to interpret the Bible for you. The information is presented at face value as it is found in the text. No previous knowledge is taken for granted. A new Christian won't be intimidated, nor will the student interested in refreshing his or her memory. Frequent self-tests are found throughout the text to help you commit the information to memory. These tests highlight areas that might require another read-through.

This is the first book in a series of books in the "30 Days" series. These books are rooted in a deep conviction that much learning is self-generated. Therefore, we must teach the basics and teach them well so the learner is positioned to go on to self-directed advanced learning. When laying the foundation of any body of learning, teaching less is teaching more. It is better to learn all of a little rather than none of a lot. It is my earnest desire and prayer that this book will give you a better understanding of the Great Book of the Ages and an increased capacity to read it with profit for yourself.

The Bible is an enormous book covering many subjects of profound significance, and it is not possible that you will learn *everything* about it in thirty days. But you will gain a beginning knowledge, an overview, that you can use to build a more complete understanding in the years ahead. In just fifteen minutes a day for thirty days you can gain a foundational grasp of the most important book ever written.

THE
STORY
OF THE
OLD
TESTAMENT

O N E

THE STRUCTURE OF THE BIBLE

 Charles Steinmetz was an electrical engineer of towering intellect. After retiring, he was asked by a major appliance manufacturer to locate a malfunction in their electrical equipment. None of the manufacturer's experts had been able to locate the problem. Steinmetz spent some time walking around and testing the various parts of the machine complex. Finally, he took out of his pocket a piece of chalk and marked an X on a particular part of one machine. The manufacturer's people disassembled the machine, discovering to their amazement that the defect lay precisely where Steinmetz's chalk mark was located.

Some days later, the manufacturer received a bill from Steinmetz for ten thousand dollars. They protested the amount and asked him to itemize it. He sent back an itemized bill:

Making one chalk mark .... $ 1
Knowing where to place it $9,999

If you know where the chalk marks go, the most overwhelming tasks are easily solved. If you don't, even simple tasks can be impossible.

Learning about the Bible can be much the same. If you don't know much about it, it can be like trying to cross the Sahara Desert blindfolded. Yet if you learn where a few of the major chalk marks go, the Bible can be at the very least an interesting and valuable source of information and inspiration.

My own experience bears this out. Many years ago, I decided I was going to master the Bible. I was going to begin with

Genesis, read to Revelation, and I wasn't going to put it down until I understood it. I soon became hopelessly entangled in a jungle of fantastic stories, unpronounceable names, broken plots, unanswered questions, and endless genealogies. I stubbed my toe on Leviticus, sprained my ankle on Job, hit my head on Ecclesiastes, and fell headlong into the mud on Habakkuk.

I was defeated. I threw my Bible down. One thing seemed clear: The Bible was a series of unrelated stories put together in random order!

Then one day I discovered a key. With this key, the fog that enshrouded my understanding of the Bible began to lift. Not that things came into sharp focus, but I began to see shapes on the horizon.

The key: *Learning the structure of the Bible.* If you want to learn architecture, you must first learn how buildings are put together. If you want to learn sailing, you must first learn how ships are put together. And if you want to learn to understand the Bible, you must first learn how the Bible is put together.

The Old and New Testaments

The Bible has two major divisions: the Old Testament and the New Testament. The Old Testament begins with creation, and tells the story of the Jewish people up to the time of Christ. It is made up of *thirty-nine* individual "books" (the Book of Genesis, the Book of Exodus, etc.) written by twenty-eight different authors and spans a period of over two thousand years.

The New Testament is the record of the birth of Jesus, His life and ministry, and the ministry of His disciples, which was carried on after Jesus was crucified. The New Testament is composed of *twenty-seven* books written by nine different authors and covers a time period of less than one hundred years. The total number of books in the entire Bible is *sixty-six*.

Self-Test

How many?   _____ books in the Old Testament
                 _____ books in the New Testament
                 _____ books in the whole Bible

Old Testament Books

Genesis	2 Chronicles	Daniel
Exodus	Ezra	Hosea
Leviticus	Nehemiah	Joel
Numbers	Esther	Amos
Deuteronomy	Job	Obadiah
Joshua	Psalms	Jonah
Judges	Proverbs	Micah
Ruth	Ecclesiastes	Nahum
1 Samuel	Song of Solomon	Habakkuk
2 Samuel	Isaiah	Zephaniah
1 Kings	Jeremiah	Haggai
2 Kings	Lamentations	Zechariah
1 Chronicles	Ezekiel	Malachi

New Testament Books

Matthew	Ephesians	Hebrews
Mark	Philippians	James
Luke	Colossians	1 Peter
John	1 Thessalonians	2 Peter
Acts	2 Thessalonians	1 John
Romans	1 Timothy	2 John
1 Corinthians	2 Timothy	3 John
2 Corinthians	Titus	Jude
Galatians	Philemon	Revelation

The Old Testament

"The used key is always bright." Benjamin Franklin

Here is the key to understanding the Old Testament. Of the thirty-nine books in the Old Testament, *there are three different kinds of books:* Historical Books, Poetical Books, and Prophetical Books.

What kind of information would you expect to find in the Historical Books? .... *history!*

What kind of information would you expect to find in the Poetical Books? .... *poetry!*

What kind of information would you expect to find in the Prophetical Books? .... *prophecy!*

If you know what kind of book you are reading, then you will know what kind of information to expect, and you can easily follow the logical flow of the Old Testament!

In the Old Testament:

> . . . the first seventeen books are historical,

> . . . the next five books are poetical, and

> . . . the next seventeen books are prophetical!

The Three Kinds of Books in the Old Testament

Historical	*Poetical*	*Prophetical*
Genesis	Job	Isaiah
Exodus	Psalms	Jeremiah
Leviticus	Proverbs	Lamentations
Numbers	Ecclesiastes	Ezekiel
Deuteronomy	Song of Solomon	Daniel
Joshua		Hosea
Judges		Joel
Ruth		Amos
1 Samuel		Obadiah
2 Samuel		Jonah
1 Kings		Micah
2 Kings		Nahum
1 Chronicles		Habakkuk
2 Chronicles		Zephaniah
Ezra		Haggai
Nehemiah		Zechariah
Esther		Malachi

If you want to read the story of the Hebrew nation in the Old Testament, you must read the first seventeen books. These books compose a historical time line for the nation of Israel.

If you want to read the poetry of Israel, you must read the next five books of the Old Testament.

If you want to read about the prophecy of Israel, you must read the final seventeen books.

This is somewhat oversimplified, for there is some poetry in the Historical Books, and some history in the Prophetical Books, etc. The point is, however, that each of the books fits into a primary category. If you keep this structure in mind, the Old Testament will begin to take shape for you.

My mistake was in assuming that the whole Old Testament was one long, unbroken story and that the history would flow evenly and consistently out of one book into the next until they were all finished. Now I know the story line is contained in the first seventeen books.

Of the seventeen Historical Books, eleven are *primary* Historical Books and six are *secondary* Historical Books. The history of Israel is advanced in the eleven primary books and repeated or amplified in the six secondary books. The Poetical and Prophetical Books were written during the time period that is constructed in the first seventeen books.

Let's take a look at the historical time line of the Old Testament in chart form:

Time Line of the Old Testament

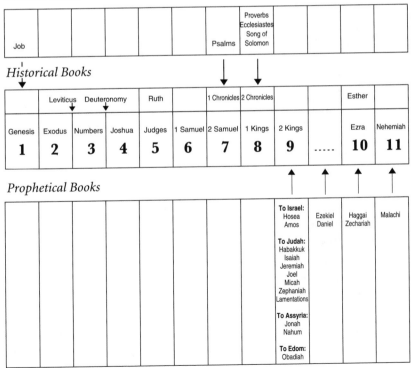

Poetical Books

							Proverbs Ecclesiastes Song of Solomon			
Job					Psalms					

Historical Books

	Leviticus	Deuteronomy		Ruth		1 Chronicles	2 Chronicles		Esther	
Genesis	Exodus	Numbers	Joshua	Judges	1 Samuel	2 Samuel	1 Kings	2 Kings	Ezra	Nehemiah
1	**2**	**3**	**4**	**5**	**6**	**7**	**8**	**9**	----- **10**	**11**

Prophetical Books

						To Israel: Hosea Amos **To Judah:** Habakkuk Isaiah Jeremiah Joel Micah Zephaniah Lamentations **To Assyria:** Jonah Nahum **To Edom:** Obadiah	Ezekiel Daniel	Haggai Zechariah	Malachi

As you can see, Job was written during the time period of the Book of Genesis, and Psalms during the time of 2 Samuel, while Proverbs, Ecclesiastes, and Song of Solomon were written during the time of 1 Kings, and so on.

To use an analogy, we constructed a similar chart for U.S. history. Imagine that you read an American history book for the main story line. The history book would give you the major periods in U.S. history. Some of these periods might be associated with a major poet or writer and a major philosopher. The poets would correspond to the poets of Israel, and the philosophers would correspond to the biblical prophets.

Time Line of U.S. History

Poets / Writers

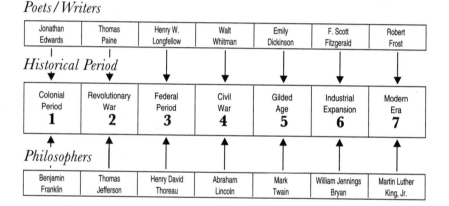

Jonathan Edwards	Thomas Paine	Henry W. Longfellow	Walt Whitman	Emily Dickinson	F. Scott Fitzgerald	Robert Frost

Historical Period

Colonial Period **1**	Revolutionary War **2**	Federal Period **3**	Civil War **4**	Gilded Age **5**	Industrial Expansion **6**	Modern Era **7**

Philosophers

Benjamin Franklin	Thomas Jefferson	Henry David Thoreau	Abraham Lincoln	Mark Twain	William Jennings Bryan	Martin Luther King, Jr.

The New Testament

Of the twenty-seven books of the New Testament, *there are also three different kinds of books:* Historical Books, Pauline Epistles, and General Epistles. The Historical Books are the four gospels and the Acts of the Apostles. The Epistles were letters written to various individuals and church congregations. The Pauline Epistles were letters written by the apostle Paul. The General Epistles were letters written to individuals and congregations by a number of different people, hence the rather generic name General Epistles. The primary content in all the Epistles is instruction on Christian doctrine and lifestyle.

What kind of information would you expect to find in the Historical Books? .... *history!*

What kind of information would you expect to find in the Pauline Epistles? .... *instruction!*

What kind of information would you expect to find in the General Epistles? .... *instruction!*

In the New Testament:

> . . . the first five books are Historical Books,
>
> . . . the next thirteen books are Pauline Epistles, and
>
> . . . the next nine books are General Epistles!

The Three Kinds of Books in the New Testament

Historical	*Pauline*	*General*
Matthew	TO CHURCHES:	Hebrews
Mark	Romans	James
Luke	1 Corinthians	1 Peter
John	2 Corinthians	2 Peter
Acts	Galatians	1 John
	Ephesians	2 John
	Philippians	3 John
	Colossians	Jude
	1 Thessalonians	Revelation
	2 Thessalonians	
	TO INDIVIDUALS:	
	1 Timothy	
	2 Timothy	
	Titus	
	Philemon	

If you want to read the story of Jesus and the Church He established, you must read the first five books of the New Testament. These five books form the historical framework for understanding the entire New Testament!

If you want to read the apostle Paul's instruction to churches and individuals, you must read the next thirteen books.

If you want to read the instruction to churches and individuals by men like the apostles Peter and John, you must read the final nine books of the New Testament.

References

To find something in the Bible, you use a standard reference system. This consists of the name of the book of the Bible, the chapter number followed by a colon, and the verse number (each chapter is divided into numbered verses). For example:

Genesis 1:1 =   Genesis   1:   1
                (book)   (chapter) (verse)

When you see a reference such as Joshua 1:21, you will either have to memorize the books of the Bible to know where Joshua is, or you can look it up in the table of contents. It is well worth the time to memorize the books, and if you do, it is easiest to memorize them according to their categories.

For example, you now know that there are three types of books in both the Old Testament (Historical, Poetical, and Prophetical) and the New Testament (Historical, Pauline Epistles, and General Epistles), and how many books are in each section. Memorize the first seventeen Historical Books. Then, when you have these memorized, learn the five Poetical Books, and so on. This system is much easier than attempting to memorize an unbroken list of sixty-six books.

There is no substitute for reading the whole book for yourself, of course, but it is possible to offer a quick overview. To read "The Story of the Bible in 1,000 Words," turn to the Appendix.

Summary

1. There are 39 books in the Old Testament.
   There are 27 books in the New Testament.
   There are 66 books in the whole Bible.

2. The Old Testament is the story of God and the Hebrew people, their poets, and prophets.

There are 3 kinds of books in the Old Testament:

   17 Historical Books,
    5 Poetical Books, and
   17 Prophetical Books.

3. The New Testament is the story of Jesus of Nazareth, the Church He founded, and its growth under the leadership of His apostles after His death.

There are 3 kinds of books in the New Testament:

    5 Historical Books,
   13 Pauline Epistles, and
    9 General Epistles.

Self-Test

The Bible:

How many?   _____ books in the Old Testament
                _____ books in the New Testament
                _____ books in the whole Bible

The Old Testament:

The Old Testament is the story of G_____ and the H_____ people, their poets, and prophets.

There are 3 kinds of books in the Old Testament:

    H _____ Books,
    P _____ Books, and
    P _____ Books.

There are _____ Historical Books.
There are _____ Poetical Books.
There are _____ Prophetical Books.

The New Testament:

The New Testament is the story of J_____, the C_____ He founded, and its growth under the leadership of His a_____s after His death.

There are 3 kinds of books in the New Testament:

      H _____ Books,
      P _____ Epistles, and
      G _____ Epistles.

There are _____ Historical Books.
There are _____ Pauline Epistles.
There are _____ General Epistles.

Congratulations! You are off to a fine start. As we move from the general to the specific, you can build your knowledge of the Bible like rows of brick on a house, and in twenty-nine more days, your house will be finished.

THE GEOGRAPHY OF
THE OLD TESTAMENT

 The size of our solar system is beyond comprehension. To get some perspective, imagine you are in the middle of the Bonneville Salt Flats with nothing but tabletop flat ground around you for miles and miles. There you put down a beachball two feet in diameter, which you use to represent the sun. To get a feel for the immensity of the solar system, walk about a city block and put down a mustard seed for the first planet, Mercury. Go another block and for Venus put down an ordinary BB. Mark off yet another block and put down a green pea to represent Earth. A final block from there, put down a mustard seed to represent Mars. Then sprinkle some grass seed around for an asteroid belt.

We have now walked about four blocks, and we have a beachball (sun), mustard seed (Mercury), BB (Venus), pea (Earth), mustard seed (Mars), and grass seed (asteroid belt). Now things begin to stretch out.

Continue for another quarter of a mile. Place an orange on the ground for Jupiter. Walk another third of a mile and put down a golf ball for Saturn.

Now lace up your tennis shoes and check their tread. Then step off another mile and, for Uranus, drop a marble. Go another mile and place a cherry there for Neptune. Finally, walk for another two miles and put down another marble for Pluto.

At last, go up in an airplane and look down. On a smooth surface almost ten miles in diameter we have a beachball, a mustard seed, a BB, a pea, another mustard seed, some grass seed, an orange, a golf ball, a marble, a cherry, and another marble.

To understand our replica of the solar system even better, use another beachball to represent Alpha Centauri, the next-nearest star to our sun. You would have to go another 6,720 miles and put it down in Japan!

Understanding the size and location of things and the relationships and distances between them gives us perspective. Just as this example gives us perspective about the solar system, a knowledge of geography can give perspective about the events of the Bible. It is helpful to know the names, locations, and distances between important geographical locations. Otherwise, we skim over information without comprehension or visualization, and the Bible is less interesting and less easily understood.

The one who is ignorant of geography cannot know history. The Bible is largely history. So to begin our mastery of the history of the Bible, we must start with the geography of the Bible.

Bodies of Water

The primary anchor points for mastering the geography of the Bible are the bodies of water. *(As you read each description, go to the Work Map and insert the name of the body of water beside the matching number.)*

1. The Mediterranean Sea

The land of the Old Testament lies east of this beautiful blue body of water.

2. The Sea of Galilee

To call this body a sea seems to be an overstatement. It is a fresh-water lake that is seven miles wide and fourteen miles long. It lies inland from the Mediterranean about thirty-six miles.

3. The Jordan River

Flowing south out of the Sea of Galilee, the Jordan River travels for sixty-five miles, as the crow flies, to empty into the Dead Sea. Many are surprised at how much history has revolved around such a small (by many standards) river.

4. The Dead Sea

Shaped like a giant hot dog with a bite out of the lower third, the Dead Sea lies at the "bottom of the world." It is the lowest point on land, almost three thousand feet below sea level at its lowest point, so that water flows into it, but no water flows out of it. As a result, the water has developed very high mineral deposits and does not support normal plant or animal life. Hence the name Dead Sea.

5. Nile River

Perhaps the most famous river in the world, the Nile flows through the heart of Egypt, spreads out like so many fingers, and empties into the waiting arms of the Mediterranean.

6. Tigris and (7.) Euphrates Rivers

These twin rivers flow for almost a thousand miles each before they join hands and deposit their treasure into the Persian Gulf.

8. Persian Gulf

These last three bodies of water, the Tigris, the Euphrates, and the Persian Gulf, form the easternmost boundary for the lands of the Old Testament. The Tigris and Euphrates flow through present-day Iraq, while the Persian Gulf separates Iran from Saudi Arabia.

Work Map
Bodies of Water of the Old Testament

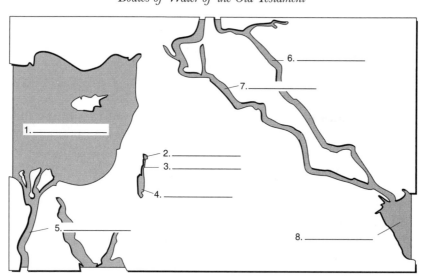

Locations

With the geographical framework offered by the bodies of water, we can establish the locations that are relevant to the Old Testament. *(As you read the description of each location, insert its name beside the appropriate letter on the Location Work Map that follows.)*

A. The Garden of Eden

The exact location of the Garden of Eden, where everything began, is impossible to pinpoint. However, it was near the convergence of four rivers, two of which were the Tigris and Euphrates.

B. Canaan/Israel/Palestine

This smallish piece of real estate, which lies between the Mediterranean coast and the Sea of Galilee-Jordan River-Dead Sea, changes names throughout the Old Testament. In Genesis it is called *Canaan.* After the Hebrew people establish themselves in the land in the Book of Joshua, it becomes known as *Israel.* Thirteen hundred years later, at the beginning of the New Testament, it is called *Palestine.*

C. Jerusalem

Located just off the northwestern shoulder of the Dead Sea, this city, nestled in the central mountains of Israel, is so central to the story of the Old Testament that it must be singled out and identified. It is the capital of the nation of Israel.

D. Egypt

The *grande dame* of ancient civilization, Egypt plays a central role in the history of the Old Testament.

E. Assyria

Located at the headwaters of the Tigris and Euphrates, this great world power is notable in the Old Testament for conquering the Northern Kingdom of Israel and dispersing her people to the four winds.

F. Babylonia

Another gigantic historical world power, this fabulous, albeit short-lived, nation conquered Assyria. It also conquered the Southern Kingdom of Judah 136 years after Assyria conquered the Northern Kingdom of Israel. It is found in Mesopotamia, between the Tigris and Euphrates. (Mesopotamia means "in the middle of" [meso]—"rivers" [potamus].)

G. Persia

The final historical superpower of the Old Testament is located at the north bank of the Persian Gulf. Persia comes into play by conquering Babylonia and by allowing the Hebrews to return from captivity in Babylonia to rebuild the city of Jerusalem and reinstate temple worship.

If these historical notes are foreign to you, don't worry about it now. Instead, content yourself with learning these locations so that, as the story unfolds, the names of these locations will mean something to you.

Location Work Map
Locations of the Old Testament

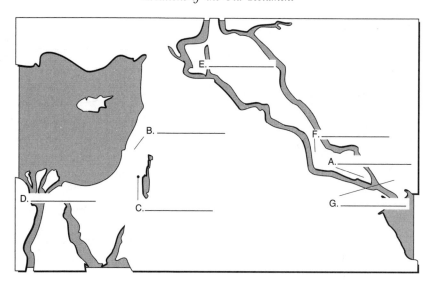

Now compare the ancient map you have just filled in with the contemporary map of the same region on the next page.

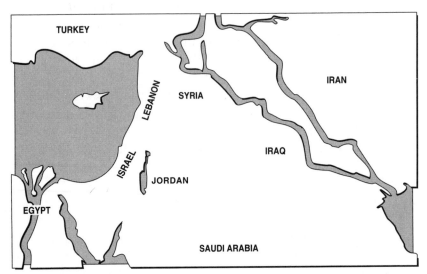

It might also help to get this Old Testament information into perspective by seeing how the map of the Old Testament compares with an overlay of a map of the state of Texas.

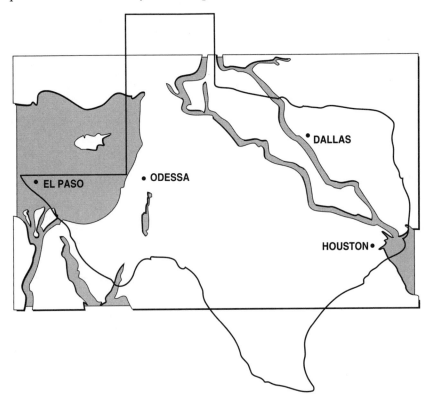

The entire land of the Old Testament is approximately the same size as the state of Texas. Traveling from the Persian Gulf to Israel would be like going from Houston to Odessa. Traveling from Israel to Egypt would be like going from Odessa to El Paso. If you keep this in mind as the story of the Bible unfolds, it will help you keep geographical perspective.

Review

The Geography of the Old Testament

Review both the eight bodies of water and the seven locations by placing the numbers and letters by the appropriate names below.

BODIES OF WATER		LOCATIONS	
_____	Mediterranean Sea	_____	Eden
_____	Sea of Galilee	_____	Israel
_____	Jordan River	_____	Jerusalem
_____	Dead Sea	_____	Egypt
_____	Nile River	_____	Assyria
_____	Tigris River	_____	Babylonia
_____	Euphrates River	_____	Persia
_____	Persian Gulf		

Self-Test
The Geography of the Old Testament

As the final exercise, fill in the blanks from memory. (Remember, the blanks with numbers are bodies of water, and the blanks with letters are locations.)

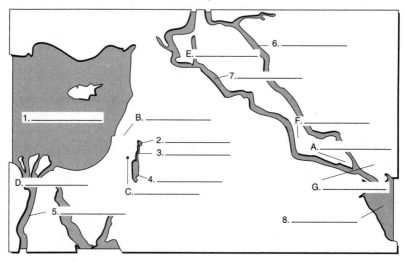

Excellent! Your knowledge of the geography of the Old Testament will enable you to understand and envision the history that unfolds from it. You have just mastered an important section.

Answers
The Geography of the Old Testament

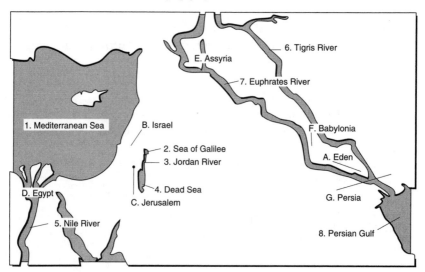

THREE

THE HISTORICAL BOOKS

On the flight from Los Angeles to Portland, one flies over the entire length of the Cascade Mountains. From thirty-five thousand feet it is difficult to get the perspective to determine which are the higher mountain peaks.

One day in late October as I was making that flight, the air was crisp and clear after a light snowfall and the puzzle of how to differentiate the higher from the lower peaks was answered. The snow only fell on elevations of about seven thousand feet and higher. As we flew over them, regardless of how close or far away they were, the highest peaks were easy to determine: They were the ones with snow on them.

As we begin to look into the stories of the Old Testament, we will only look at the highest peaks, the ones with snow on them.

To do so, it will be helpful to continue the analogy with the story of the United States. If you were going to condense just the story of the United States, omitting the poets and philosophers, you would take the main periods of history, link them with the central historic figure of the era, and add the primary location. In chart form, it might look like this:

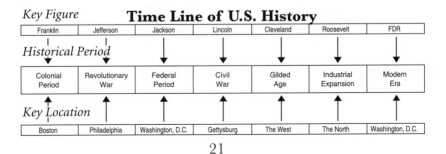

Time Line of U.S. History

Key Figure

Franklin	Jefferson	Jackson	Lincoln	Cleveland	Roosevelt	FDR

Historical Period

Colonial Period	Revolutionary War	Federal Period	Civil War	Gilded Age	Industrial Expansion	Modern Era

Key Location

Boston	Philadelphia	Washington, D.C.	Gettysburg	The West	The North	Washington, D.C.

21

Include a brief story-line summary of the era, and the story of the United States could be overviewed in a chart, such as the following:

Story of the United States

KEY ERA	KEY FIGURE	LOCATION	STORY LINE
Colonial	*Franklin*	*Boston*	As the thirteen colonies long for independence, Franklin leads in the formulation of necessary strategy.
Revolution	*Jefferson*	*Philadelphia*	Jefferson forges the Declaration of Independence.
Etc.	*Etc.*	*Etc.*	Etc.

This same approach can be used in condensing the story of the Bible, charting the main periods (or eras), the central figures, the main locations, and a summary story line. The story line of the Bible can be divided into twelve main eras, with a central figure and main location for each era. Nine of the eras are found in the Old Testament, and three are found in the New Testament.

In this chapter, we will deal with only the Old Testament and will complete only the first three aspects of the chart: the main eras, the central figures, and the main locations. The summary story line and the New Testament events will be added in the following chapters.

The Nine Main Eras of the Old Testament

1. Creation
The *creation* of the world and man, and early events.

2. Patriarch
The birth of the Hebrew people through a family of *patriarchs*, covering a period of two hundred years.

3. Exodus

The *exodus* of the Hebrew people as they are delivered out of four hundred years of slavery in Egypt.

4. Conquest

The *conquest* of the Promised Land by the Hebrew people upon their return from Egypt.

5. Judges

A four-hundred-year period during which Israel is governed by rulers called *judges*.

6. Kingdom

An additional four-hundred-year period during which Israel becomes a full-fledged nation ruled by a *monarchy*.

7. Exile

A seventy-year period during which Israel's leaders live in *exile*, having been conquered by foreign countries.

8. Return

The *return* of exiled Jews to Jerusalem to rebuild the city and the temple.

9. Silence

A final four-hundred-year period between the close of the Old Testament and the opening of the New Testament.

Following the pattern of the chart for the Story of the United States, let's begin to chart the Story of the Old Testament.

Story of the Old Testament

ERA	FIGURE	LOCATION	STORY LINE
Creation *Patriarch* *Exodus* *Conquest* *Judges* *Kingdom* *Exile* *Return* *Silence*	To be supplied later.	To be supplied later.	To be supplied later.

Another way to help us remember the historical story line of the Bible is to visualize the main eras with symbols, such as in the Arc of Bible History.

Arc of Bible History

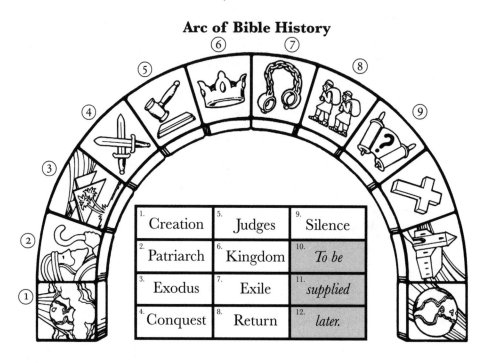

1. Creation	5. Judges	9. Silence
2. Patriarch	6. Kingdom	10. *To be*
3. Exodus	7. Exile	11. *supplied*
4. Conquest	8. Return	12. *later.*

Review

Write in the correct era on the line matching the description.

OPTIONS:	ERA:	DESCRIPTION:
Exile	_____	The *creation* of the world and man, and early events
Judges		
Creation	_____	The birth of the Hebrew people through a family of *patriarchs,* covering a period of two hundred years
Kingdom		
Patriarch		
Conquest		
Return	_____	The *exodus* of the Hebrew people as they are delivered out of four hundred years of slavery in Egypt
Silence		
Exodus		

ERA:	DESCRIPTION:
_____	The *conquest* of the Promised Land by the Hebrew people upon their return from Egypt
_____	A four-hundred-year period during which Israel is governed by rulers called *judges*
_____	An additional four-hundred-year period during which Israel becomes a full-fledged nation ruled by a *monarchy*
_____	A seventy-year period during which Israel's leaders live in *exile,* having been conquered by foreign countries
_____	The *return* of the exiled Jews to Jerusalem to rebuild the city and the temple
_____	A final four-hundred-year period between the close of the Old Testament and the opening of the New Testament

The Nine Central Figures of the Old Testament

ERA:	FIGURE:	DESCRIPTION:
Creation	Adam	The first *man*
Patriarch	Abraham	The first *patriarch*
Exodus	Moses	The leader of the *exodus*
Conquest	Joshua	The leader of Israel's *army*
Judges	Samson	The most famous *judge*
Kingdom	David	The most well-known Israelite *king*
Exile	Daniel	The major exilic *prophet*
Return	Ezra	The central *return* leader
Silence	Pharisees	The *religious* leaders

Review

(Fill in the blank.)

ERA:	FIGURE:	DESCRIPTION:
Creation	Adam	The first _____
Patriarch	Abraham	The first _____
Exodus	Moses	The leader of the _____
Conquest	Joshua	The leader of Israel's _____
Judges	Samson	The most famous _____
Kingdom	David	The most well-known Israelite __
Exile	Daniel	The major exilic _____
Return	Ezra	The central _____ leader
Silence	Pharisees	The _____ leaders

(Match the era with the key figure.)

ERA:	FIGURE:	OPTIONS:
Creation	_____	*Moses*
Patriarch	_____	*Daniel*
Exodus	_____	*Abraham*
Conquest	_____	*Joshua*
Judges	_____	*Pharisees*
Kingdom	_____	*Ezra*
Exile	_____	*David*
Return	_____	*Samson*
Silence	_____	*Adam*

Now we will add the central figure to our story-line chart.

Story of the Old Testament

ERA	FIGURE	LOCATION	STORY LINE
Creation	Adam	To be	To be
Patriarch	Abraham	supplied	supplied
Exodus	Moses	later.	later.
Conquest	Joshua		
Judges	Samson		
Kingdom	David		
Exile	Daniel		
Return	Ezra		
Silence	Pharisees		

Our final task is to identify the general or primary geographic location of the events of the main eras of the Old Testament. Beginning with Creation and Adam, as an exercise in memory, write in each main era and central historical figure as you read the description of the location of each of the eras.

The Nine Main Locations of the Old Testament

ERA:	FIGURE:	LOCATION:	DESCRIPTION:
1. _____	_____	Eden	The garden of Eden, where Adam is created. Near the convergence of the Tigris and Euphrates Rivers.
2. _____	_____	Canaan	Abraham migrates from Ur, near Eden, to Canaan, where he and the other patriarchs live until the time of slavery in Egypt.
3. _____	_____	Egypt	During a severe famine, the Israelites migrate to Egypt and are enslaved four hundred years before their exodus to freedom.
4. _____	_____	Canaan	Joshua leads the conquest of the Promised Land in Canaan.
5. _____	_____	Canaan	The Israelites live in Canaan under a loose tribal system ruled by judges for the next four hundred years.
6. _____	_____	Israel	With the formation of a formal monarchy, the land is now referred to by the national name of *Israel*.

ERA:	FIGURE:	LOCATION:	DESCRIPTION:
7. _____	_____	Babylonia	Because of judgment for national moral corruption, Israel is conquered by foreign nations, finally forcing her leaders into seventy years of exile in Babylonia.
8. _____	_____	Jerusalem	The exiled Israelites are allowed to return to Jerusalem to rebuild the city and temple, though they remain under the dominion of Persia.
9. _____	_____	Jerusalem	Though dominion of the land changes from Persia to Greece to Rome, Israel is allowed to worship in Jerusalem without disruption for the next four hundred years of "silence."

Along with the main era and the central figure, we are now able to add the main location to our chart.

Story of the Old Testament

ERA	FIGURE	LOCATION	STORY LINE
Creation	Adam	Eden	To be
Patriarch	Abraham	Canaan	supplied
Exodus	Moses	Egypt	later.
Conquest	Joshua	Canaan	
Judges	Samson	Canaan	
Kingdom	David	Israel	
Exile	Daniel	Babylonia	
Return	Ezra	Jerusalem	
Silence	Pharisees	Jerusalem	

Arc of Bible History

(Fill in the names of the eras. To check your answers, see the Appendix.)

1. C_____	5. J_____	9. S_____
2. P_____	6. K_____	10.
3. E_____	7. E_____	11.
4. C_____	8. R_____	12.

Review

On the following map draw arrows to show the movement during the major Eras of the Old Testament that we have just learned. Begin at Eden and draw an arrow to the next location as it changes: Eden to Canaan, to Egypt, to Canaan, to Babylonia, to Jerusalem.

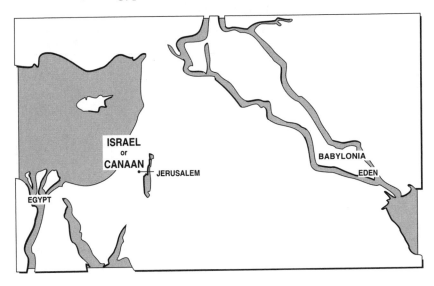

In its most basic form, your map should look something like this:

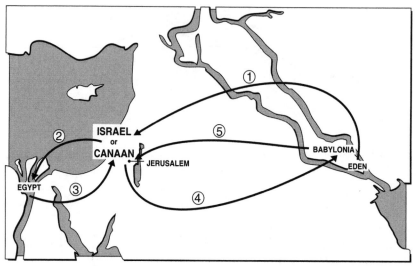

From the options given, fill in the blanks in the following chart, matching the location to the era and central figure. (A location may be used more than once.)

Babylonia   Eden   Israel
Canaan   Egypt   Jerusalem

Story of the Old Testament

ERA	FIGURE	LOCATION	STORY LINE
Creation	Adam	_____	To be
Patriarch	Abraham	_____	supplied
Exodus	Moses	_____	later.
Conquest	Joshua	_____	
Judges	Samson	_____	
Kingdom	David	_____	
Exile	Daniel	_____	
Return	Ezra	_____	
Silence	Pharisees	_____	

You are now ready to begin final mastery of a very critical chart. Once you master this chart, you have come a long way in understanding the overview of the Old Testament. Fill in the blanks.

Story of the Old Testament

ERA	FIGURE	LOCATION	STORY LINE
Creation	Adam	_____	To be
Patriarch	_____	Canaan	supplied
_____	Moses	Egypt	later.
Conquest	Joshua	_____	
Judges	_____	Canaan	
_____	David	Israel	
Exile	Daniel	_____	
Return	_____	Jerusalem	
_____	Pharisees	Jerusalem	

Self-Test

Finally, fill in the following chart from memory. It might be easiest to fill in the eras, then go back and fill in the central figures and main locations. (To check your answers see the Appendix for a completed Story of the Bible chart.)

Story of the Old Testament

ERA	FIGURE	LOCATION	STORY LINE
_____	_____	_____	To be
_____	_____	_____	supplied
_____	_____	_____	later.
_____	_____	_____	
_____	_____	_____	
_____	_____	_____	
_____	_____	_____	
_____	_____	_____	
_____	_____	_____	

Congratulations! You have just taken a major step toward mastering an overview of the Old Testament. From now on, we will become more and more specific, but you have laid a good foundation that can be built upon in successive chapters.

F O U R

THE CREATION ERA
(Genesis 1—11)

 Far from the land of everyday, out in the distant curves of the universe, lay strange and fantastic realms, unlike anything in our wildest dreams. Hidden by the barriers of time and space, they have lived forever beyond the reach of man, unknown and unexplored.

But now, just now, the cosmic veils have begun to lift a little. Man has had his first glimpses of these once-secret domains, and their bizarre ways have left him stunned. They challenge his very notions of matter and energy. Along with Alice in Wonderland, he says, "One can't believe impossible things."

And impossible, indeed, they seem to be. In those far reaches of the universe, in those bewildering worlds, are far places . . .

where a teaspoon of matter weighs as much as two hundred million elephants . . .

where a tiny whirling star winks on and off thirty times a second . . .

where a small, mysterious object shines with the brilliance of ten trillion suns . . .

where matter and light are continually sucked up by devouring black holes, never to be seen again.

Small wonder that the late British scientist J. B. S. Haldane could say, "The universe is not only queerer than we suppose, but queerer than we can suppose."

We used to think that the universe was simply our Milky Way Galaxy. Today we know that galaxies are as common as blades of grass in a meadow. They number perhaps a hundred billion.

33

How does one comprehend the incredible size of this galaxy-filled universe? For such awesome distances, scientists and astronomers think in terms of time, and they use the telescope as a time machine. They measure space by a unit called the light-year, the distance light travels in one year at the rate of 186,282 miles per second—about six trillion miles. (From *National Geographic*, May 1974.)

If you could shoot a gun whose bullet would travel around the world at the speed of light, the bullet would go around the world and pass through you seven times in one second!

Perhaps more than anything else, the mystery and the enormity of our universe capture our imagination and incite in us a fascination about the subject of Creation. There are countless unknowns and just as many "unbelievables." As we begin to explore the Creation Era, we will adopt a pattern that will be followed throughout the remainder of this section:

   I. You will review the main era, central figure, and main location you learned in the last chapter.

  II. You will read a brief story-line summary of the events of that era, built around the central figure, with a three-word theme of each summary appearing in italics. Then you will be asked to review those three words to fill in the blanks.

 III. You will read an expansion of the summary of the events of that era.

I.   Review: Fill in the blanks for this era.

Story of the Old Testament

ERA	FIGURE	LOCATION	STORY-LINE SUMMARY
_____	_____	_____	To be completed in this chapter.

II.   Story-Line Summary: Adam is created by God, but he *sins* and *destroys* God's original *plan* for man.

ERA	SUMMARY
Creation:	Adam is created by God, but he _____ and _____ God's original _____ for man.

III. Expansion: There are four major events within the Creation Era. They are the accounts of:

1. Creation
2. Fall
3. Flood
4. Tower of Babel

1. Creation: Man created in the image of God (Genesis 1—2)

After a dramatic display of power in creating the heavens and the earth, God creates man. Adam and Eve are created in the image of God, in perfect fellowship and harmony with Him. Living in an idyllic setting in the Garden of Eden, they are individuals of beauty and high intelligence. The "image" is not a physical likeness, but a personal and spiritual likeness. Man has intellect, emotion, and will. He has a moral sense of right and wrong. He is a creative being. These are some characteristics of God that are shared by man, and in this sense, *man is created in the image of God.*

2. Fall: Sin entered the world (Genesis 3)

Satan, appearing in the form of a serpent, lures Adam and Eve into rebelling against God and violating the one prohibition God had given them: not to eat from the tree of the knowledge of good and evil. They are driven out of the Garden of Eden, and a curse is placed on the earth. When Adam and Eve rebel, *sin enters the world.* All the pain, all the evil, all the suffering endured by mankind for all time can be traced to that one act, which is, therefore, appropriately called the "fall" of man.

3. Flood: Judgment for sin (Genesis 6—10)

Over the next several hundred years, as man multiplies in numbers, so his tendency to sin multiplies, until a time comes when God can find only eight people who are willing to live in a righteous relationship with Him: Noah, his wife, his three sons, and their wives. So, in *judgment for sin,* God performs surgery on the human race, cutting out the cancerous tissue, as it were, and leaving behind the healthy tissue to restore itself. He does this by sending a worldwide flood which destroys mankind, except for Noah and his family, who are saved in Noah's ark.

4.   Tower: Beginning of the nations (Genesis 11).

God's post-flood mandate to man was to spread out, populate, and subdue the whole earth. In direct disobedience to that command, man stays in one place and begins building a monument to himself, the Tower of Babel. God causes this large congregation of people to begin speaking different languages. Lack of communication prevents them from further progress on the tower, and the people of each tongue disperse to the four corners of the earth and form the *beginning of the nations* of the world as we know them today.

Self-Test

A.   The Four Main Events of the Creation Era

(Write in the correct event from the options at left.)

OPTIONS:	EVENT:	DESCRIPTION:
Creation	_____	Judgment for sin
Fall	_____	Beginning of the nations
Flood	_____	Sin entered the world
Tower	_____	Man in the image of God

B.   Story-Line Summary

(Fill in the blanks from memory.)

ERA	SUMMARY
Creation:	Adam is created by God, but he _____ and _____ God's original _____ for man.

C. Arc of Bible History

(Fill in the name of the era. To check your answer, see the Appendix.)

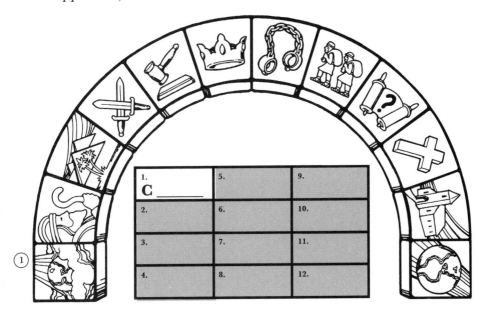

1. C _____	5.	9.
2.	6.	10.
3.	7.	11.
4.	8.	12.

D. The Geography of the Creation Era

(Circle the dot indicating the possible location of Eden.)

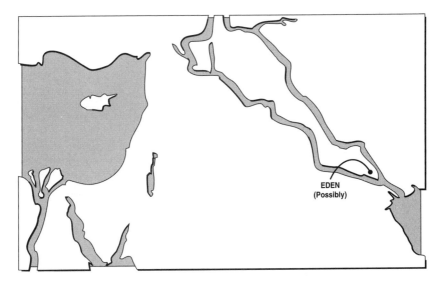

EDEN
(Possibly)

E. Story of the Old Testament

(Fill in the blanks.)

ERA	SUMMARY
Creation:	Adam is created by God, but he _____ and _____ God's original _____ for man.

THE PATRIARCH ERA
(*Genesis 12—50*)

Any parent will admit that controlling children is a difficult and uncertain task.

Psychologist Henry Brandt tells the story of the time he and his wife invited the president of the college he was attending to their house for dinner. They were nervous and had spent considerable time preparing the house and meal for a good impression. When the president arrived, they stumbled over themselves to make him comfortable. They sat him next to their two-year-old daughter for the meal. That was a mistake. During the meal, this little tot said to the president in her bird-like voice: "Please pass the salt." No one paid attention; they were listening to the president. So she tried again: "Will you please pass the salt?" Her small voice was easy to ignore as the adults strained for the president's every word. Finally, she hammered the distinguished guest on the arm and yelled, "Pass the salt, or I'll knock your block off!"

Even a president of the United States was perplexed by the antics of his child. Alice Roosevelt, daughter of Theodore Roosevelt, was an unruly girl whose antics scandalized the staid Washington "society" during her father's tenure at the White House. When a visitor objected to the girl's wandering in and out of the president's office while he was conducting important business with her father, Roosevelt said, "I can be president of the United States, or I can control Alice. I cannot possibly do both."

The Patriarch Era was a time of godly men presiding over a growing family. Abraham, Isaac, Jacob, and Joseph, successive generations of the same family, ruled over the Hebrew people in the earliest days of their existence.

On more than one occasion, Abraham must have felt a little like Brandt and Roosevelt. His descendants did not behave the way he wanted them to. Passion for God and what He wanted to do in and through the Hebrew people burned like a flame in Abraham's heart. But the flame dimmed in successive generations. However, the time of slavery in Egypt sharpened the spiritual hunger of the Hebrew people, and a great family, which became a great nation, emerged.

I.   Review: Fill in the blanks to bring the chart up-to-date with this era.

Story of the Old Testament

ERA	FIGURE	LOCATION	STORY-LINE SUMMARY
_____	_____	_____	Adam is created by God, but he _____ and _____ God's original _____ for man.
_____	_____	_____	To be completed in this chapter.

II.   Story-Line Summary: *Abraham* is *chosen* by God to "father" a *people* to *represent* God to the world.

ERA	SUMMARY
Patriarch:	*Abraham* is _____ by God to "father" a _____ to _____ God to the world.

III. Expansion: There are four major men in the Patriarch Era:

    1. Abraham
    2. Isaac
    3. Jacob
    4. Joseph

1. Abraham: Father of the Hebrew people (Genesis 12—23)

Because of Adam's sin and the fall of man, God's attention is now focused on a plan of redemption for mankind. God wants a people through whom He can work to produce a reflection of Himself, and through whom He can spread the message of redemption to the world. He chooses Abraham, who becomes the *father of the Hebrew people*, and promises him a country (land), countless descendants (seed), and a worldwide and timeless impact (blessing). Abraham is living in Ur, near the convergence of the Tigris and Euphrates Rivers, at the time. God leads him to the land of Canaan, where Abraham settles and has two sons, Ishmael and Isaac.

2. Isaac: Second father of promise (Genesis 24—26)

Isaac becomes the *second father of promise* as the fulfillment of Abraham's promises are passed down to him. He witnesses several major miracles during his life. He lives in the land of Abraham, becomes prosperous, and dies at an old age after having fathered two sons, Esau and Jacob.

3. Jacob: Father of the nation of Israel (Genesis 27—35)

The promises given to Abraham are passed through Isaac to Jacob, Isaac's younger son. Jacob begins life as a conniving scoundrel. However, through a series of miracles and other encounters with God, he mends his ways. Jacob has twelve sons, and the promises of Abraham are passed down to them all as a family. While Abraham is the father of the Hebrew people, Jacob is the *father of the nation of Israel*, as from his twelve sons emerge the twelve tribes of the nation of Israel.

4. Joseph: Leader in Egypt (Genesis 37—50)

Jacob's sons, for the most part, have very little commitment to God's call on them as a nation. They sell their brother Joseph as a slave, and he is taken to Egypt. Because of Joseph's righteousness, he rises to become a great *leader in Egypt*. During a severe famine, his family comes to Egypt for food, is reunited with Joseph, and as a result, enjoys peace and comfort. After Joseph dies, however, his people are enslaved for the next four hundred years. This time of trial sharpens the spiritual hunger of the Hebrew people, and they cry out to God for deliverance.

Self-Test

A. Major Men of the Patriarch Era

(Write in the correct name from the options at left.)

OPTIONS:	NAME:	DESCRIPTION:
Abraham	_____	Father of nation of Israel
Isaac	_____	Leader in Egypt
Jacob	_____	Father of Hebrew people
Joseph	_____	Second father of promise

B. Story-Line Summary

(Fill in the blanks from memory.)

ERA	SUMMARY
Patriarch:	*Abraham* is _____ by God to "father" a _____ to _____ God to the world.

C. Arc of Bible History

(Fill in the names of the eras. To check your answers see the Appendix.)

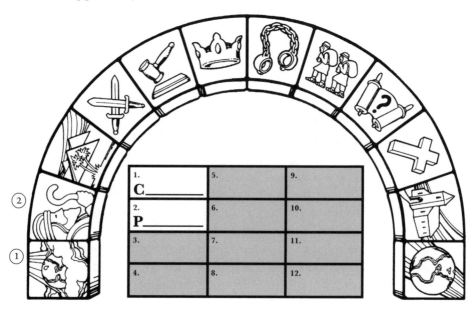

1. **C**_____	5.	9.
2. **P**_____	6.	10.
3.	7.	11.
4.	8.	12.

D. The Geography of the Patriarch Era

(Draw an arrow from Ur, where Abraham lived, to Canaan, and from Canaan to Egypt, to represent the geographical movements of the Patriarch Era.)

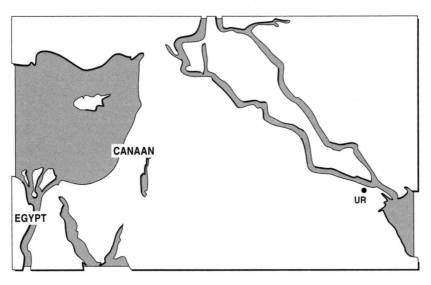

E. Story of the Old Testament

(Fill in the blanks.)

ERA	FIGURE	LOCATION	STORY-LINE SUMMARY
_____	_____	_____	Adam is created by God, but he _____ and _____ God's original _____ for man.
_____	_____	_____	Abraham is _____ by God to "father" a _____ to _____ God to the world.

SIX

THE EXODUS ERA
(Exodus–Deuteronomy)

 The Exodus was the mass movement of the Israelites out of slavery in Egypt back to the Promised Land in Canaan. It was not an easy movement. The Pharaoh of Egypt did not want them to go, and he threatened them with military retaliation. The miracles God performed during this time are among the most spectacular recorded in the Bible—the Nile River turned to blood, shepherds' rods turned into snakes, the firstborn of every Egyptian household died, and the Red Sea parted to allow the Israelites to cross over on dry land, escaping the Egyptian army.

Movies have sometimes portrayed this event as a little band of nomads roaming about the desert, camping under palm trees and singing Hebrew folk songs around a small campfire. This picture could hardly be further from the truth. The book of Numbers tells us that when the Israelites left Egypt, there were six hundred thousand fighting men. It is reasonable to assume that if there were six hundred thousand fighting men, there were also six hundred thousand fighting women. That's 1,200,000. Each of those families may have had at least two children. That's another 1,200,000. In addition there were the men who were too old to fight, and their wives. There was the priestly tribe, the Levites, who didn't fight, and their wives and their children. There were, conservatively speaking, between two and a half to three million people who left Egypt during this "exodus."

This was not a little tribe of nomads roaming about the desert. This was a nation on the move. Look at the state of Texas on a map and imagine the city of Dallas beginning to move across the map, and you get an idea of the magnitude of the Exodus. When you add all the animals they took with them for food and milk, as well as for sacrifices, this qualified as a horde! Instead of looking for a flat spot under a palm tree to camp, they had to look for a valley ten miles square. When they lined up to cross the Red Sea, it was more than a little aisle that was required. If they crossed the Red Sea one hundred abreast, counting the animals, the column would have stretched perhaps as far as fifty miles back into the desert.

Personal beliefs aside, this ranks as one of the greatest historical events of the ancient world, and this was an event over which Moses presided. To get a better look at the specifics of the Exodus, we will now review our previous chapters and then look at the four main events of the Exodus Era.

I. **Review:** Fill in the blanks to bring the chart up-to-date with this era. To check your answers see the Appendix.

Story of the Old Testament

ERA	FIGURE	LOCATION	STORY-LINE SUMMARY
_____	_____	_____	Adam is created by God, but he _____ and _____ God's original _____ for man.
_____	_____	_____	Abraham is _____ by God to "father" a _____ to _____ God to the world.
_____	_____	_____	To be completed in this chapter.

II.   Story-Line Summary: Through Moses God *delivers* the Hebrew people from *slavery* in Egypt and then gives them the *Law*.

ERA	SUMMARY
Exodus:	Through Moses God _____ the Hebrew people from _____ in Egypt and then gives them the _____.

III.   Expansion: There are four major events in the Exodus Era:

1. Deliverance
2. The Law
3. Kadesh Barnea
4. Forty Years of Wandering

1.   Deliverance: Freedom from slavery in Egypt
(Exodus 1—18)

The Hebrews have languished under slavery in Egypt for four hundred years when they cry out to God for deliverance. God raises up Moses as His spokesman to Pharaoh, the ruler of Egypt, asking for spiritual freedom for the Hebrew people. Pharaoh refuses, and a series of ten plagues is levied on Egypt to prompt Pharaoh to let the people go. The plagues start out bad and they get worse—from frogs, to gnats, to water turned to blood, to the death of the firstborn in every household of Egypt. Finally, Pharaoh consents to let the Hebrews leave Egypt. After they have gone, he changes his mind and attempts to recapture them. They are as far as the Red Sea when God parts the Red Sea and the Hebrew people cross over to the other side. The waters come together again, protecting them from the Egyptian army, and *freeing them from slavery in Egypt.* God, of course, has only one destination for them: the Promised Land of Canaan . . . the land "flowing with milk and honey." The land that their father Abraham had first settled is again to be their home.

2. The Law: God's commandments at Mount Sinai
(Exodus 19—40)

The Hebrew people now begin to take on a national identity as Israel. From the Red Sea, the Israelites travel south to the bottom of the Sinai Peninsula and camp at Mount Sinai. They receive *God's commandments at Mount Sinai*. Moses meets with God alone at the top of Mount Sinai, where he receives the Ten Commandments written in tablets of stone by the finger of God. Moses also receives a full revelation of the Law that is to govern Israel's national life as well as her relationship to God. God promises to bless her abundantly for obedience and curse her soundly for disobedience.

3. Kadesh Barnea: Place of rebellion against God
(Numbers 10—14)

Israel leaves Mount Sinai and migrates north to an oasis, Kadesh Barnea, which is the southern gateway into the Promised Land. From this vantage point, twelve spies are sent into the Promised Land, one spy from each of the twelve tribes of Israel. The land is inhabited by the Canaanites, who would not take kindly to an Israelite horde coming back into the land. When the spies return, they have some good news and some bad news. The good news is that the land *is* beautiful and bountiful: "flowing with milk and honey." The bad news is that there are giants and hostile armies throughout the land. Ten spies report that the land is indomitable (in spite of the fact that God has promised to give them victory over any opposing forces). Two spies, Joshua and Caleb, exhort the people to believe God and go into the land. The people believe the majority report and refuse to follow Moses into the land. Thus, this becomes known as *a place of rebellion against God*.

4. Forty Years of Wandering: Consequences of rebelling against God (Numbers 20—36)

As a *consequence of rebelling against God* at Kadesh Barnea, the "Exodus" generation is condemned to wander in the wilderness until everyone who was twenty-one years old or older at the time dies. In the ensuing forty years, a new generation comes to leadership; it is willing to follow their leaders into the land. Moses leads them to the north of the Dead Sea near Jericho, the eastern gateway to the Promised Land. Moses encourages the people, gives them additional instruction found in the Book of Deuteronomy, and then dies.

Self-Test

A.   Four Major Events in the Exodus Era

(Write in the correct name from the options at left.)

OPTIONS:	EVENT:	DESCRIPTION:
Deliverance	_____	God's commandments at Mount Sinai
The Law		
Kadesh Barnea	_____	Place of rebellion against God
Forty Years of Wandering		
	_____	Consequences of rebelling against God
	_____	Freedom from slavery in Egypt

B.   Story-Line Summary: Through Moses God *delivers* the Hebrew people from *slavery* in Egypt and then gives them the *Law*.

ERA	SUMMARY
Exodus:	Through Moses God _____ the Hebrew people from _____ in Egypt and then gives them the _____.

C.   Arc of Bible History

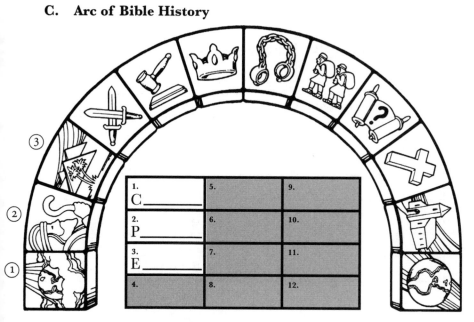

1. C_____	5.	9.
2. P_____	6.	10.
3. E_____	7.	11.
4.	8.	12.

(Fill in the names of the eras.)

D.   The Geography of the Exodus Era

(Draw an arrow from Egypt through the Red Sea to Mount Sinai to Kadesh Barnea, and then to the top of the Dead

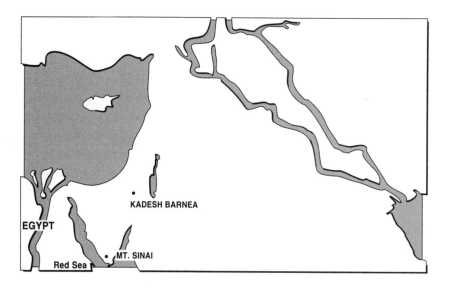

Sea on the east side of the Jordan River. This represents the geographical movement of the Exodus Era.)

E. Story of the Old Testament
   (Fill in the blanks. To check your answers, see the Appendix.)

ERA	FIGURE	LOCATION	STORY-LINE SUMMARY
_____	_____	_____	Adam is created by God, but he _____ and _____ God's original _____ for man.
_____	_____	_____	Abraham is _____ by God to "father" a _____ to _____ God to the world.
_____	_____	_____	Through Moses God _____ the Hebrew people from _____ in Egypt and then gives them the _____.

THE CONQUEST ERA
(Joshua)

 The days were dark indeed for Great Britain in 1940. The British people were at war with Germany and were being pressed hard on every side by the Nazi military machine. Supplies and morale were low. Their national destiny hung in the balance. Then a new prime minister came on the scene: Winston Churchill. He was a man of intense conviction, deep resolve, and unquenchable optimism. His speeches in the first months of his term burst upon the world with sudden and magnificent power. From them we read:

> To form an administration of this scale and complexity is a serious undertaking in itself, but it must be remembered that we are in the preliminary stage of one of the greatest battles in history, that we are in action at many points in Norway and in Holland, that we have to be prepared in the Mediterranean, that the air battle is continuous, and that many preparations have to be made here at home. I would say to the House, as I said to those who have joined this Government: I have nothing to offer but blood, toil, tears, and sweat.
>
> You ask what is our policy? I will say: It is to wage war by sea, land, and air with all our might and with all the strength that God can give us: to wage war against a monstrous tyranny, never surpassed in the dark, lamentable catalogue of human crime. That is our policy. You ask, what is our aim? I can answer in a word: Victory—victory at all costs, victory in spite of all the terror, victory however long and hard the road may be; for without victory, there is no survival.

I have, myself, full confidence that if all do their duty, if nothing is neglected, and if the best arrangements are made, as they are being made, we shall prove ourselves once again able to defend our island home . . . to ride out the storm of war, and to outlive the menace of tyranny. Even though large tracts of Europe and many old and famous states have fallen or may fall into the grip of the Gestapo and all the odious apparatus of Nazi rule, we shall not flag or fail. We shall go on to the end, we shall fight in France, we shall fight on the seas and oceans, we shall fight with growing confidence and growing strength in the air, we shall defend our island, whatever the cost may be, we shall fight on the beaches, we shall fight on the landing grounds, we shall fight in the fields and in the streets, we shall fight in the hills; we shall never surrender.

After the Exodus, the circumstances were also perilous for the Israelites. They had wandered in the wilderness for forty years because of rebellion and unbelief at Kadesh Barnea. Now they were at Jericho, and the test was the same. Would they resolve to forge ahead, or would they shrink from the circumstances as their fathers had done?

The task of rallying and leading the people fell to Joshua. Moses, the great leader of the last forty years, was dead. Would the people galvanize behind Joshua? Or would they refuse his leadership? Just as England faced a crossroads when Churchill became its leader, so also the Israelites faced a critical fork in the road.

I.   Review: Fill in the blanks to bring the chart up-to-date with this era.

Story of the Old Testament

ERA	FIGURE	LOCATION	STORY-LINE SUMMARY
_____	_____	_____	Adam is created by God, but he _____ and _____ God's original _____ for man.
_____	_____	_____	Abraham is _____ by God to "father" a _____ to _____ God to the world.

ERA	FIGURE	LOCATION	STORY-LINE SUMMARY
_____	_____	_____	Through Moses God _____ the Hebrew people from _____ in Egypt and then gives them the _____.
_____	_____	_____	To be completed in this chapter.

II. Story-Line Summary: *Joshua* leads the *conquest* of the *Promised Land.*

ERA	SUMMARY
Conquest:	*Joshua* leads the _____ of the _____ _____.

III. Expansion: There are four main events in the Conquest Era:

1. Jordan
2. Jericho
3. Conquest
4. Dominion

1. Jordan: A miraculous parting of water (Joshua 1—5)

Moses dies, and God hand-picks Joshua to succeed him. Joshua's first challenge is to cross the Jordan River at flood stage. God commands him to prepare the nation for a ceremonial procession and to begin walking, priests first, toward the Jordan River. When the priests touched water, God would part the water for them. (This is the second *miraculous "parting of water"* that God performed for Israel. The first was the parting of the Red Sea.) The people respond, and God parts the Jordan River for a distance of about twenty miles. They cross without incident, and the water begins flowing again.

2.   Jericho: A miraculous conquest of a city (Joshua 6)

The city of Jericho, a small oasis on the west side of the Jordan River near the Dead Sea, is not only the eastern gateway to the Promised Land, but it is also a fortified city and poses a threat to the welfare of Israel. Joshua is a brilliant military strategist, so much so that his campaigns in the Bible are still studied in the Army War College today. As he stands overlooking the city, contemplating how to conquer it, the angel of the Lord appears to him and instructs him to march around the city once a day for seven days. On the seventh day, he is to march around it seven times and the people are to shout. The city wall will fall down. They did, and it did . . . *a miraculous conquest of a city!*

3.   Conquest: The defeat of Canaan (Joshua 7—12)

The Canaanites are united in their hatred of the Israelites, but not in their military opposition to them. Primarily, the region is characterized by individual kings, each with his own city and surrounding country. Joshua cuts through the mid-section toward the Mediterranean Sea. Having divided the land, he then begins to conquer, from South to North. In about seven years the initial *defeat of Canaan* is complete.

4.   Dominion: Finalizing dominion (Joshua 13—20)

Each of the twelve tribes of Israel is given a land area by lottery and is responsible for *finalizing dominion* over that area. All twelve tribes inhabit their area and take up a relationship of loose federation with the other tribes.

Self-Test

A.   Four Major Events in the Conquest Era

(Write in the correct event from the options at left.)

OPTIONS:	EVENT:	DESCRIPTION:
Jordan	_____	The defeat of Canaan
Jericho	_____	A miraculous parting of water
Conquest	_____	Finalizing dominion
Dominion	_____	A miraculous conquest of a city

B.   Story-Line Summary (Fill in the blanks from memory.)

ERA	SUMMARY
Conquest:	*Joshua* leads the _____ of the _____ _____.

C.   Arc of Bible History (Fill in the names of the eras. To check your answers, see the Appendix.)

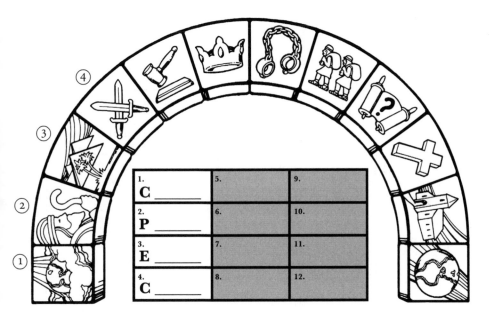

1. **C** _____	5.	9.
2. **P** _____	6.	10.
3. **E** _____	7.	11.
4. **C** _____	8.	12.

D.   The Geography of the Conquest Era

(Draw an arrow from Jericho across to the Mediterranean Sea. Then draw an arrow into the southern half of the land. Now draw an arrow into the northern half of the land. This represents the geographical movement of the Conquest Era.) (*See top of next page.*)

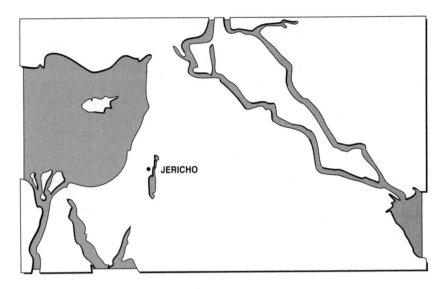

E.   Story of the Old Testament (Fill in the blanks.)

ERA	FIGURE	LOCATION	STORY-LINE SUMMARY
_____	_____	_____	Adam is created by God, but he _____ and _____ God's original _____ for man.
_____	_____	_____	Abraham is _____ by God to "father" a _____ to _____ God to the world.
_____	_____	_____	Through Moses God _____ the Hebrew people from _____ in Egypt and then gives them the _____.
_____	_____	_____	Joshua leads the _____ of the _____ _____.

E I G H T

THE JUDGES ERA

(Judges–Ruth)

WOMAN IN RAGS, GARBAGE, REVEALED AS HEIRESS

So read the headline in the *San Francisco Chronicle* concerning a lady known as "Garbage Mary" who was picked up in a shopping mall in Delray Beach, Florida. She appeared to be just another derelict whose mind had faded. Neighbors told stories of her scrounging through garbage cans for food, which she hoarded in her car and her two-room apartment. There were mounds of garbage in the small apartment, stuffed in the refrigerator, the stove, the sink, the cabinets, and the bathtub. There were paths between the garbage. Other than in the kitchen, there were no chairs to sit in because they were piled with trash.

Police finally identified her as the daughter of a well-to-do lawyer and bank director from Illinois who had died several years earlier. In addition to the garbage, police found Mobil Oil stock worth more than four hundred thousand dollars, documents indicating ownership of oil fields in Kansas, stock certificates from firms such as U.S. Steel, Uniroyal, and Squibb, and passbooks for eight large bank accounts.

Garbage Mary was a millionaire who was living like a derelict. Untold wealth was at her disposal, and yet she scrounged through garbage rather than claim the resources that were rightly hers.

The parallel between Garbage Mary and Israel during the time of the judges is striking. This was a dark period, indeed, in the history of the Jewish people. They had lost their spiritual moorings and, as is recorded in the final verse of the Book of Judges, "everyone did what was right in his own eyes." The result was a morally degraded, socially perverted, and spiritually bankrupt time of almost four hundred years. Israel had all the wealth of the promises of God at their disposal. Yet they scavenged through the garbage of life, eking out a pitiful existence. They could have been kings but lived like paupers.

I. **Review:** Fill in the blanks to bring the chart up-to-date with this era.

Story of the Old Testament

ERA	FIGURE	LOCATION	STORY-LINE SUMMARY
_____	_____	_____	Adam is created by God, but he _____ and _____ God's original _____ for man.
_____	_____	_____	Abraham is _____ by God to "father" a _____ to _____ God to the world.
_____	_____	_____	Through Moses God _____ the Hebrew people from _____ in Egypt and then gives them the _____.
_____	_____	_____	Joshua leads the _____ of the _____ _____.
_____	_____	_____	To be completed in this chapter.

II. Story-Line Summary: *Samson* and others were chosen as *judges* to *govern* the people for *four hundred* rebellious years.

ERA	SUMMARY
Judges:	*Samson* and others were chosen as _____ to _____ the people for _____ rebellious years.

III. Expansion: There are four main subjects in the Judges Era:

1. Judges
2. Rebellion
3. Cycles
4. Ruth

1. Judges: The leaders of Israel (Judges)

As seen in the Book of Judges, these judges are not men who wear long, flowing black robes, sit on high benches, and make legal decisions. Rather, they are political-military *leaders of Israel* who exercise nearly absolute power because of their office and abilities. The four major judges are:

- Deborah, a woman judge early in the Judges Era
- Gideon, who defeats an army of thousands with only three hundred men
- Samson, the most famous judge, whose fabulous strength has captured our imagination for thousands of years
- Samuel, a transitional character held in very high regard in Scripture, who is both the last judge and the first prophet

2. Rebellion: The breaking of God's Law (Judges)

The Book of Judges records the darkest period in Israel's history, following one of the brightest eras: the Conquest Era under Joshua. Just before Moses dies, he instructs Israel (in Deuteronomy 7:1–5) to do three things:

1. Destroy all the inhabitants of Canaan.
2. Avoid intermarriage with the Canaanites.
3. Shun worship of the Canaanite gods.

Israel fails on all three accounts. *The breaking of God's Law* and the record of Israel's subsequent moral degradation are sad indeed.

3. Cycles: Repetition of Israel's misfortunes (Judges)

Much of the Era of Judges involves a series of seven cycles that are recorded in the Book of Judges. Each cycle has five component parts: (1) Israel "sins," (2) God disciplines them through military "conquest" by a neighboring country, (3) Israel "repents" and cries out to God for deliverance, (4) God raises up a judge who "delivers" them from bondage, and (5) God "frees" the land from military oppression for the remainder of that judge's life. That is one cycle: sin, conquest, repentance, deliverance, and freedom. Then, when a judge dies, the *repetition of Israel's misfortunes* begins again. The Israelites fall into sin again, followed by conquest, followed by repentance, etc. Seven such cycles are recorded in the Book of Judges.

4. Ruth: A model woman (Ruth)

Standing out in refreshing contrast to the general background of the Judges Era is Ruth, described in the book that bears her name. This *model woman* who lives during the Era of Judges is an example of moral and spiritual strength. Her story is one of love, purity, and commitment. She is a living illustration of blessings that God showers on those who live in faithful obedience to Him. One example of God's blessings toward Ruth is that she, a non-Hebrew, is listed in the lineage from Abraham to Jesus.

Self-Test

A. Four Major Subjects in the Judges Era

(Write in the correct subject from the options at left.)

OPTIONS:	SUBJECT:	DESCRIPTION:
Judges	_____	A model woman
Rebellion	_____	The leaders of Israel
Cycles	_____	The breaking of God's Law
Ruth	_____	Repetition of Israel's misfortunes

B. Story-Line Summary

(Fill in the blanks from memory.)

ERA	SUMMARY
Judges:	*Samson* and others were chosen as _____ to _____ the people for _____ rebellious years.

C. Arc of Bible History

(Fill in the names of the eras. To check your answers, see the Appendix.)

1. C_____	5. J_____	9.
2. P_____	6.	10.
3. E_____	7.	11.
4. C_____	8.	12.

D. The Geography of the Judges Era

(Match the numbers below with the blanks on the map to see the countries conquering Israel in the Judges Era.)

1. Philistia	3. Mesopotamia	5. Ammon
2. Moab	4. Canaan	6. Midian

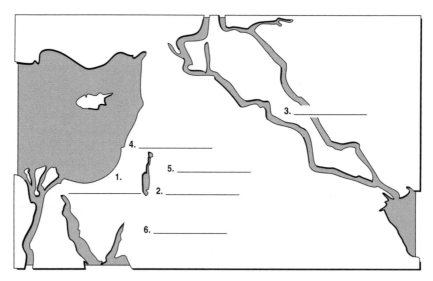

E.   Story of the Old Testament

(Fill in the blanks.)

ERA	FIGURE	LOCATION	STORY-LINE SUMMARY
			Adam is created by God, but he _____ and _____ God's original _____ for man.
			Abraham is _____ by God to "father" a _____ to _____ God to the world.
			Through Moses God _____ the Hebrew people from _____ in Egypt and then gives them the _____.
			Joshua leads the _____ of the_____.
			Samson and others were chosen as _____ to _____ the people for _____ rebellious years.

THE KINGDOM ERA
(1 Samuel–2 Chronicles)

If you would be free to sail the seven seas, you must make yourself a slave to the compass. By nature, man desires something he cannot have: total freedom. There are certain freedoms we can have, but they have corresponding bondages. And there are certain bondages we can have that afford us corresponding freedoms. For example, you can be free from the toothbrush and in bondage to cavities, or you can make yourself a slave to the toothbrush and be free from cavities. You cannot be free from the toothbrush *and* free from cavities. That kind of freedom, total freedom, does not exist.

Throughout life, we are constantly making choices, and for those choices, we pay certain inescapable consequences. Freedom comes with a price.

The kings of Israel wanted total freedom. They wanted the freedom to ignore the directives God had given them on how to rule and wage war. But at the same time, they wanted the freedom to have economic and military prosperity. This was not possible. As a result, the Kingdom Era was a very turbulent time with many ups and downs. When a righteous king ruled, the nation would prosper. When an unrighteous king gained the throne, the nation would falter.

The barnacles of unrighteousness began to affix themselves to the Israeli ship of state, and before the books of history were completed, the nation had collapsed and suffered at the hands of warring neighbors.

I. **Review:** Fill in the blanks to bring the chart up-to-date with this
    era. To check your answers, see the Appendix.

Story of the Old Testament

ERA	FIGURE	LOCATION	STORY-LINE SUMMARY
			Adam is created by God, but he _____ and _____ God's original _____ for man.
			Abraham is _____ by God to "father" a _____ to _____ God to the world.
			Through Moses God _____ the Hebrew people from _____ in Egypt and then gives them the _____.
			Joshua leads the _____ of the _____ _____.
			Samson and others were chosen as _____ to _____ the people for _____ rebellious years.
			To be completed in this chapter.

II. **Story-Line Summary:** *David,* the greatest king in the new
    monarchy, is followed by a succession of mostly *unrighteous* kings,
    and God eventually *judges* Israel for her sin, sending her into exile.

ERA	SUMMARY
Kingdom:	*David,* the greatest king in the new _____, is followed by a succession of mostly _____ kings, and God eventually _____ Israel for her sin, sending her into exile.

III. Expansion: There are four main periods in the Kingdom Era:

1. United Kingdom
2. Division of the Kingdom
3. Northern Kingdom
4. Southern Kingdom

1. United Kingdom: A new monarchy (1 and 2 Samuel)

The twelve tribes of Israel, jealous of other nations around them, are united in their demand to God for a king. God allows Samuel, the last judge, to anoint Saul to be the first king, beginning *a new monarchy.* Because Saul is not a righteous king, God does not honor his reign or establish his family on the throne of Israel. His successor, David, though having shortcomings, is a righteous king, and Israel prospers under him. David's son Solomon becomes king upon David's death. Solomon rules righteously at first, then drifts from the Lord.

2. Divided Kingdom: A civil war (1 Kings)

As a result of Solomon's spiritual drifting, *a civil war* erupts upon his death, and the kingdom is divided. There is now a northern kingdom, consisting of ten tribes, and a southern kingdom, consisting of the tribes of Judah and Benjamin. The northern ten tribes retain the name "Israel," and the southern two tribes adopt the name "Judah," after the name of the larger tribe.

3. Northern Kingdom: The unrighteous kingdom (2 Kings)

In the civil war that splits the kingdom, Jeroboam commands the northern kingdom of Israel. He is unrighteous, and every other king (nineteen total) who succeeds him during the two-hundred-fifty-year life of the northern kingdom is also unrighteous. Because of this unrighteousness, God raises up Assyria to conquer the northern kingdom and scatter His people to the four winds. *The unrighteous kingdom* is never restored.

4.   Southern Kingdom: The inconsistent kingdom (2 Kings)

Rehoboam, Solomon's son, commands the southern kingdom of Judah. He is also unrighteous. The southern kingdom fares somewhat better than the northern. Lasting for four hundred years, its life is prolonged by eight righteous kings out of a total of twenty. Judah's sins finally catch up to her, however, and God brings judgment on *the inconsistent kingdom* by raising up Babylonia (which had conquered Assyria) to conquer Judah. Babylonia gathers all the leaders, artisans, musicians, and promising children, and takes them away to captivity in Babylonia.

Self-Test

A.   Four Major Subjects in the Kingdom Era

(Write in the correct subject from the options at left.)

OPTIONS:	SUBJECT:	DESCRIPTION:
United Kingdom	_____	The unrighteous kingdom
Divided Kingdom	_____	A new monarchy
Northern Kingdom		
	_____	The inconsistent kingdom
Southern Kingdom		
	_____	A civil war

B.   Story-Line Summary (Fill in the blanks from memory.)

ERA	SUMMARY
Kingdom:	*David,* the greatest king in the new _____, is followed by a succession of mostly _____ kings, and God eventually _____ Israel for her sin, sending her into exile.

C. Arc of Bible History

(Fill in the names of the eras. To check your answers, see the Appendix.)

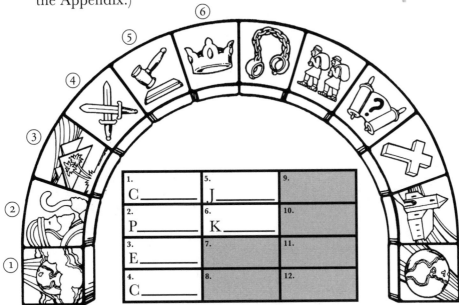

1. C_____	5. J_____	9.
2. P_____	6. K_____	10.
3. E_____	7.	11.
4. C_____	8.	12.

D. The Geography of the Kingdom Era

(Draw an arrow from Israel to Assyria. Draw another arrow from Judah to Babylonia. This represents the geographical movement of the Kingdom Era.)

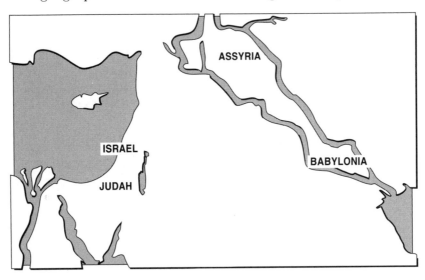

E. Story of the Old Testament

(Fill in the blanks.)

ERA	FIGURE	LOCATION	STORY-LINE SUMMARY
_____	_____	_____	Adam is created by God, but he _____ and _____ God's original _____ for man.
_____	_____	_____	Abraham is _____ by God to "father" a _____ to _____ God to the world.
_____	_____	_____	Through Moses God _____ the Hebrew people from _____ in Egypt and then gives them the _____.
_____	_____	_____	Joshua leads the _____ of the _____ _____.
_____	_____	_____	Samson and others were chosen as _____ to _____ the people for _____ rebellious years.
_____	_____	_____	David, the greatest king in the new _____, is followed by a succession of mostly _____ kings, and God eventually _____ Israel for her sin, sending her into exile.

TEN

THE EXILE ERA
(Ezekiel–Daniel)

It is one of the basic laws of physics that things tend to run down or deteriorate. Deterioration in relationships can be illustrated in something as mundane as the common cold. An old edition of *The Saturday Evening Post* included this description of "The Seven Stages of the Married Cold":

Stage 1: Sugar dumpling, I'm really worried about my baby girl. That's a bad sniffle and there's no telling about these things with all the "strep" that's going around. I'm going to put you in the hospital for a general check-up and good rest. I know the food's terrible, but I'm going to bring you dinner every night from "Rosini's." I've got it all arranged with the floor supervisor.

Stage 2: Listen, darling, I don't like the sound of that cough. I'm going to call Doc Miller to rush over here. Now you go to bed like a good girl just for papa.

Stage 3: Maybe you'd better lie down, honey. Nothing like a little rest when you feel lousy. I'll bring you something. Have you got any canned soup?

Stage 4: Now look, dear, be sensible. After you've fed the kids and gotten the dishes done and the floor mopped, you'd better lie down.

Stage 5: Why don't you take a couple of aspirin?

Stage 6: If you'd just gargle something instead of sitting around barking like a seal all evening. . . .

Stage 7: Would you stop coughing on me?! Are you trying to give me pneumonia?!

We must recognize also that our actions have certain repercussions in our relationships.

A troubled man was standing at the top of the World Trade Center in New York and finally he decided to jump off, ending his own life. After he had fallen awhile and was only one hundred stories off the ground, he realized he had made a mistake. It was wrong to commit suicide, and he knew it. He said, "O God, if you hear me . . . I'm sorry for the foolish mistake I made in jumping off this building. I repent, and I would like to know if you would forgive me." A voice came back. "Of course I forgive you. Don't think a thing about it. I will never bring it up again. And by the way, I'll see you in just a minute."

Sin is a fact of human existence. And God will forgive whoever comes to Him in repentance. But that doesn't change the fact that sin has consequences. God forgives the man for jumping off the building, but the man will still fall to the ground.

Israel tasted this bitter reality. Their relationship with the Lord deteriorated. They lived in roller-coaster rebellion against Him for four hundred years during the Kingdom Era, continually paying the price. Finally, the debt became so great that judgment came in the form of military conquest. During the time of the Exile, there were some great spiritual leaders, and there was repentance on the part of a segment of the Jewish people. However, this did not remove the penalty for the years of rebellion, and the full price of the Exile was exacted.

I.　**Review:** Fill in the blanks to bring the chart up-to-date with this era.

Story of the Old Testament

ERA	FIGURE	LOCATION	STORY-LINE SUMMARY
____	____	____	Adam is created by God, but he _____ and _____ God's original _____ for man.
____	____	____	Abraham is _____ by God to "father" a _____ to _____ God to the world.

ERA	FIGURE	LOCATION	STORY LINE SUMMARY
_____	_____	_____	Through Moses God _____ the Hebrew people from _____ in Egypt and then gives them the _____.
			Joshua leads the _____ of the _____ _____.
			Samson and others were chosen as _____ to _____ the people for _____ rebellious years.
			David, the greatest king in the new _____, is followed by a succession of mostly _____ kings, and God eventually _____ Israel for her sin, sending her into exile.
			To be completed in this chapter.

II. **Story-Line Summary:** *Daniel* gives *leadership* and encourages *faithfulness* among the *exiles* for the next seventy years.

ERA	SUMMARY
Exile:	*Daniel* gives _____ and encourages _____ among the _____ for the next seventy years.

III. Expansion: As mentioned before in chapter 1 of this book, some history is contained in books that are primarily Prophetical Books, and that is the case in the Exile Era. You will note that the biblical references for the four main divisions of this era will include some Prophetical Books. There are four main divisions in the Exile Era:

1. Prophecy
2. Prophets
3. Exiles
4. Power Change

1. Prophecy: Warning of impending captivity (Jeremiah)

The northern kingdom, Israel, has been conquered by Assyria and is dispersed in 722 B.C. During the time of the events described in 2 Kings, the southern kingdom, Judah, receives a *warning of impending captivity* through Jeremiah (called the "Weeping Prophet"), who prophesies that the nation will be taken into captivity at the hands of the Babylonians. This happens in 586 B.C. He also accurately prophesies that the captivity will last seventy years.

2. Prophets: Encouraging faithfulness of exiles
(Ezekiel and Daniel)

There are two prophets who write books of the Bible during the exile: Ezekiel and Daniel. Not a great deal is known about the prophet Ezekiel since his book is mostly prophetic and not autobiographical. He foretells of national restoration and *encourages faithfulness among the exiles.* Daniel's book, while a book of prophecy, is more biographical. He is a prominent governmental leader, much like Joseph in Egypt. While Daniel's personal life is an example to his people, his prophecies tend to concern the future destruction of the world.

3. Exiles: Assimilated into the culture (Daniel)

The Book of Daniel also gives us a glimpse of life among the exiles. Apparently, the Jews are *assimilated into the culture* in which they are exiled. They experience discrimination, which has always been true of displaced Jews. Yet, in spite of this, they seem fairly well integrated into society, and some of them achieve positions of prominence.

4. Power Change: Persian empire expands (Daniel)

While the Jews are in exile in Babylonia, Persia rises to become the dominant military power of that region. Persia conquers Babylonia (which had conquered Assyria), so now Persia rules not only her own land, but the land once dominated by Assyria and Babylonia. The *Persian empire expands* from the Tigris River to the Mediterranean Sea.

Self-Test

A. Four Major Subjects in the Exile Era

(Write in the correct subject from the options at left.)

OPTIONS:	SUBJECT:	DESCRIPTION
Prophecy	_____	Persian empire expands
Prophets	_____	Assimilated into the culture
Exiles		
Power Change	_____	Warning of impending captivity
	_____	Encouraging faithfulness of exile

B. Story-Line Summary

(Fill in the blanks from memory.)

ERA	SUMMARY
Exile:	*Daniel* gives _____ and encourages _____ among the _____ for the next seventy years.

C. Arc of Bible History
(Fill in the names of the eras.)

1. C_____	5. J_____	9.
2. P_____	6. K_____	10.
3. E_____	7. E_____	11.
4. C_____	8.	12.

D. The Geography of the Exile Era

(Draw a line from Babylonia toward Assyria and circle Assyria. Draw another line from Persia toward Babylonia, encircling both Babylonia and Assyria. This represents the shift in power during the Exile Era. Assyria had conquered Israel. Then Babylonia conquered Assyria and Judah. Finally, Persia conquered Babylonia and ended up ruling everyone.)

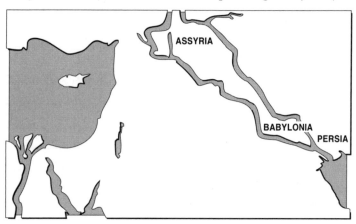

E. Story of the Old Testament

(Fill in the blanks. To check your answer, see the Appendix.)

ERA	FIGURE	LOCATION	STORY-LINE SUMMARY
___	___	___	Adam is created by God, but he _____ and _____ God's original _____ for man.
___	___	___	Abraham is _____ by God to "father" a _____ to _____ God to the world.
___	___	___	Through Moses God _____ the Hebrew people from _____ in Egypt and then gives them the _____.
___	___	___	Joshua leads the _____ of the _____ _____.
___	___	___	Samson and others were chosen as _____ to _____ the people for _____ rebellious years.
___	___	___	David, the greatest king in the new _____, is followed by a succession of mostly _____ kings, and God eventually _____ Israel for her sin, sending her into exile.
___	___	___	Daniel gives _____ and encourages _____ among the _____ for the next seventy years.

THE RETURN ERA

(Ezra–Esther)

In the middle 1970s, newspapers and magazines were awash with the story of Peter Jenkins, who walked across America. He was consumed with the disillusionment of his generation, and he set out to find his country and himself.

His amazing story is one of long hours, days, and weeks of solitude and drudgery punctuated with occasional life-threatening surprises. He faced danger from weather, accidents, wild animals, and people. He almost died in a snow storm, was attacked by animals, and hunted by cruel men who might have killed him if they had caught him.

Many times he wanted to quit his search. Each time, he was befriended by people who restored his body, his soul, and his faith in America. He lost his dog but gained a wife, a new world view, and a deep appreciation for the grandeur of his country and its people.

Finally, after more than five long and grueling years of walking, he stepped into the Pacific Ocean. His journey was done. When Peter Jenkins walked into the Oregon waters, he was quite a different person from the one who left his home in Alfred, New York. The trials, the time, the solitude, the people, and the physical and mental challenge had transformed him. On his departure, he was little more than a confused boy. On his return, he was a man.

The return of the nation of Israel from seventy years of captivity in Babylonia in many ways parallels the story of Peter Jenkins. The Israelites went into exile a drifting and confused people. They spent agonizing years in solitude, and in physical and mental torment. They were ministered to unexpectedly by people sent from God. They returned to Israel a sobered people. They were home, refocused in their purpose as a nation, ready to begin again the worship of Jehovah: the God of creation, and the God of Israel.

I.   **Review:** Fill in the blanks to bring the chart up-to-date with this era.

Story of the Old Testament

ERA	FIGURE	LOCATION	STORY-LINE SUMMARY
_____	_____	_____	Adam is created by God, but he _____ and _____ God's original _____ for man.
_____	_____	_____	Abraham is _____ by God to "father" a _____ to _____ God to the world.
_____	_____	_____	Through Moses God _____ the Hebrew people from _____ in Egypt and then gives them the _____.
_____	_____	_____	Joshua leads the _____ of the _____ _____.
_____	_____	_____	Samson and others were chosen as _____ to _____ the people for _____ rebellious years.
_____	_____	_____	David, the greatest king in the new _____, is followed by a succession of mostly _____ kings, and God eventually _____ Israel for her sin, sending her into exile.

ERA	FIGURE	LOCATION	STORY-LINE SUMMARY
————	————	————	Daniel gives _____ and encourages _____ among the _____ for the next seventy years.
————	————	————	To be completed in this chapter.

II. Story-Line Summary: *Ezra leads* the people back from *exile* to rebuild *Jerusalem.*

ERA	SUMMARY
Return:	*Ezra* _____ the people back from _____ to rebuild _____.

III. Expansion: There are four major subjects in the Return Era:

1. Disrepair
2. Temple
3. People
4. Walls

1. Disrepair: Destruction from war and neglect
(Nehemiah 1:1–3)

During the seventy years of captivity, the leadership of Judah has been taken into exile, and the city of Jerusalem falls into disrepair. Not only has the city suffered the ravages of the military campaign during the initial conquest, but it has also fallen victim to the erosion of neglect. The *destruction from war and neglect* leaves Jerusalem in a state of abject ruin.

2. Temple: Rebuilding the temple (Ezra 1—6)

God prompts Cyrus, king of Persia, to initiate the financing and rebuilding of the Jewish temple in Jerusalem. Under the direction of Zerubbabel, a notable Jewish figure in Persia, the *rebuilding of the temple* is begun. Considerable opposition from

Gentiles around Jerusalem is encountered. At the urging of Haggai and Zechariah, two Jewish prophets living in Jerusalem, the restoration of the temple is completed.

3. People: Spiritual rebuilding (Ezra 7—10)

Rebuilding the temple is a direct parallel to the *spiritual rebuilding* of the Jewish people. Temple worship has been discontinued for seventy years. Most of the Jews have never seen or heard the Law of Moses. They have to be instructed in a national reeducation program. Ezra sets his heart to study the Law of the Lord, to practice it, and to teach God's statutes and ordinances in Israel to rebuild the people as they return from exile.

4. Walls: Restoration complete (Nehemiah)

Even though not all Jews returned when they could have (see the Book of Esther, whose events take place during this Era) many Jews are now back home in Jerusalem. The temple stands restored as the dominant structure in the city, but the walls of the city are still broken down. This is a security threat as well as a source of national humiliation. Nehemiah, another Jewish notable serving Artaxerxes, king of Persia, is burdened to rebuild the walls. He is given permission and financing by the king of Persia to do so. A short time later, the walls frame the noble city of Jerusalem, home of the temple of God. *Restoration is complete* as the temple is rebuilt, the people are rebuilt, and the walls are rebuilt.

Self-Test

A. Four Major Subjects in the Return Era

(Write in the correct subject from the options at left.)

OPTIONS:	SUBJECT:	DESCRIPTION:
	_____	Spiritual rebuilding
Disrepair	_____	Rebuilding the temple
Temple		
People	_____	Destruction from war and neglect
Walls		
	_____	Restoration complete

B.   Story-Line Summary

(Fill in the blanks from memory.)

ERA	SUMMARY
Return:	*Ezra* _____ the people back from _____ to rebuild _____.

C.   Arc of Bible History

(Fill in the names of the eras.)

1. C_____	5. J_____	9.
2. P_____	6. K_____	10.
3. E_____	7. E_____	11.
4. C_____	8. R_____	12.

D.   The Geography of the Return Era

(Draw an arrow from Persia to Jerusalem on the map at the top of the next page to represent geographical movements during the Return Era.)

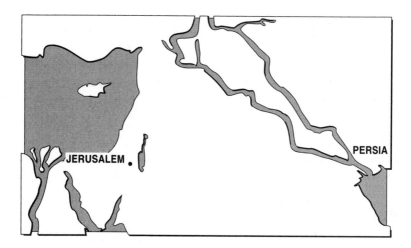

E. Story of the Old Testament

(Fill in the blanks. To check your answers, see the Appendix.)

ERA	FIGURE	LOCATION	STORY-LINE SUMMARY
_____	_____	_____	Adam is created by God, but he _____ and _____ God's original _____ for man.
_____	_____	_____	Abraham is _____ by God to "father" a _____ to _____ God to the world.
_____	_____	_____	Through Moses God _____ the Hebrew people from _____ in Egypt and then gives them the _____.
_____	_____	_____	Joshua leads the _____ of the _____ _____.
_____	_____	_____	Samson and others were chosen as _____ to _____ the people for _____ rebellious years.

ERA	FIGURE	LOCATION	STORY-LINE SUMMARY
————	————	————	David, the greatest king in the new _____, is followed by a succession of mostly _____ kings, and God eventually _____ Israel for her sin, sending her into exile.
————	————	————	Daniel gives _____ and encourages _____ among the _____ for the next seventy years.
————	————	————	Ezra _____ the people back from _____ to rebuild _____.

TWELVE

THE SILENCE ERA

(Between the Old and New Testaments)

 A lion who was caught up with his mastery of the jungle decided to make sure all the other animals knew he was king of the jungle. He was so confident that he bypassed the smaller animals and went straight to the bear. "Who is king of the jungle?" the lion demanded. The bear replied, "Why, you are, of course." The lion gave a mighty roar of approval.

Next, he went to the tiger. "Who is the king of the jungle?" he roared. The tiger quickly responded, "Everyone knows that you are, O mighty lion." The lion swelled with pride.

Next on the list was the elephant. The lion faced the elephant and leveled his question. "Who is king of the jungle?" he challenged. The elephant grabbed the lion with his trunk, whirled him around in the air five or six times, and slammed him against a tree. Then he pounded him on the ground several times, sat on him once, dipped him in the lake, and dumped him out on the shore.

The lion, battered and bruised, struggled to his feet, peered at the elephant through his good eye, and said, "Look, just because you don't know the answer is no reason to get mean about it."

The religious leaders of the Silence Era were very much like the lion. They pretended to have power, and they became self-absorbed. It has been said that some people drink at the fountain of knowledge while others only gargle. All this pride caused a pattern of religious hypocrisy that was leading to self-destruction and made this period one of the more disappointing in the nation's history.

I. Review: Fill in the blanks to bring the chart up-to-date with this era.

Story of the Old Testament

ERA	FIGURE	LOCATION	STORY-LINE SUMMARY
_____	_____	_____	Adam is created by God, but he _____ and _____ God's original _____ for man.
_____	_____	_____	Abraham is _____ by God to "father" a _____ to _____ God to the world.
_____	_____	_____	Through Moses God _____ the Hebrew people from _____ in Egypt and then gives them the _____.
_____	_____	_____	Joshua leads the _____ of the _____ _____.
_____	_____	_____	Samson and others were chosen as _____ to _____ the people for _____ rebellious years.
_____	_____	_____	David, the greatest king in the new _____, is followed by a succession of mostly _____ kings, and God eventually _____ Israel for her sin, sending her into exile.
_____	_____	_____	Daniel gives _____ and encourages _____ among the _____ for the next seventy years.

ERA	FIGURE	LOCATION	STORY-LINE SUMMARY
____	____	____	Ezra _____ the people back from _____ to rebuild _____.
			To be completed in this chapter.

II. Story-Line Summary: *Pharisees* and others *entomb* the *Israelites* in *legalism* for the next *four hundred* years.

ERA	SUMMARY
Silence:	*Pharisees* and others _____ the _____ in _____ for the next _____ years.

III. Expansion: There are four major subjects in the Silence Era:

    1. The Changing Guard
    2. Political Sects
    3. Religious Sects
    4. Messianic Hope

1. The Changing Guard: The march of nations

At the close of the Old Testament, Jerusalem is ruled by Persia. Alexander the Great defeats the Persians in 333 B.C. and establishes Greek culture and the Greek language as a unifying force for that part of the world. When Alexander dies, his kingdom is quartered, but Hellenistic (Greek) culture is still advanced and remains the dominant influence. When Rome conquers that part of the world, Roman influences are introduced but for now the Greek influence is still strong. *The march of nations* passes from Persia to Greece to Rome.

2.   Political Sects: The Maccabeans and Zealots

Throughout the four hundred Silent Years, there are militant Jews who attempt to revolt against foreign rule and make Jerusalem and the surrounding area of Judea an independent country. These include the *Maccabeans* and the *Zealots*.

3.   Religious Sects: Pharisees and Sadducees

There are two primary religious "parties" in Jerusalem during this time. Unfortunately, neither offers much guidance in true spirituality, as they are caught up in promoting a religious "legalism" of external adherence to rules while overlooking inner motivations and attitudes. The Pharisees are orthodox and conservative, and they foster separation between themselves and "secular" society. The Sadducees are more liberal. They are the party of the Jerusalem aristocracy, and they use their wealth and influence to keep the political waters calm. A ruling board, called the Sanhedrin, is made up of representatives from both the *Pharisees* and *Sadducees*, but the two groups have little in common except their desire for religious freedom and, later, their antagonism for Jesus of Nazareth.

4.   Messianic Hope: Expectation of a savior

The "Messiah," or "Savior," is one who is prophesied throughout the Old Testament to come save the Jews. Some feel they need spiritual salvation, and others are looking only for political salvation. For both reasons, the expectation and hope for the coming of the Messiah is strong during the four hundred Silent Years. Events of the Silence Era seem to especially prepare the world for the coming of the Messiah:

(1) This part of the world has a common language and a common culture, which facilitates the spread of a Messianic message.

(2) The Roman Empire has brought this region military peace, an extensive system of roads and sea travel, and a common government so that people can travel extensively without interference.

(3) The Jews are suffering such religious persecution and political humiliation that widespread hope and *expectation of a savior* exists.

These facts make the coming of Jesus of Nazareth, claiming to be the Messiah, an event that captures the attention of the entire Jewish world.

Self-Test

A. Four Major Subjects in the Silence Era

(Write in the correct subject from the options at left.)

OPTIONS:	SUBJECT:	DESCRIPTION:
The Changing Guard	_____	Pharisees and Sadducees
	_____	The march of nations
Political Sects		
Religious Sects	_____	Expectation of a savior
Messianic Hope	_____	Maccabeans and Zealots

B. Story-Line Summary

(Fill in the blanks from memory.)

ERA	SUMMARY
Silence:	*Pharisees* and others _____ the _____ in _____ for the next _____ years.

C. Arc of Bible History

(Fill in the names of the eras. To check your answers, see the Appendix.)

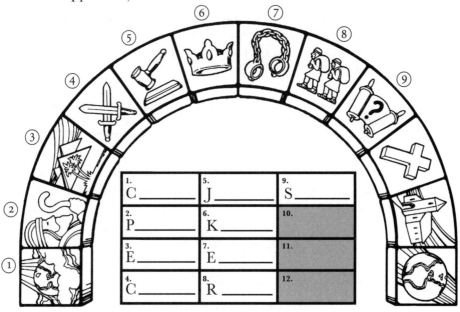

1. C_____	**5.** J_____	**9.** S_____
2. P_____	**6.** K_____	**10.**
3. E_____	**7.** E_____	**11.**
4. C_____	**8.** R_____	**12.**

D. The Geography of the Silence Era

(Put a 1 next to Persia, a 2 next to Greece, and a 3 next to Rome. Then draw an arrow from Persia to Greece to Rome, to represent the geographical movement of the Silence Era.)

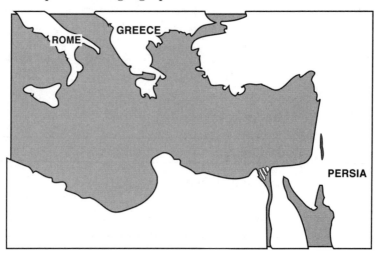

E. Story of the Old Testament

(Fill in the blanks.)

ERA	FIGURE	LOCATION	STORY-LINE SUMMARY
___	___	___	Adam is created by God, but he _____ and _____ God's original _____ for man.
___	___	___	Abraham is _____ by God to "father" a _____ to _____ God to the world.
___	___	___	Through Moses God _____ the Hebrew people from _____ in Egypt and then gives them the _____.
___	___	___	Joshua leads the _____ of the _____ _____.
___	___	___	Samson and others were chosen as _____ to _____ the people for _____ rebellious years.
___	___	___	David, the greatest king in the new _____, is followed by a succession of mostly _____ kings, and God eventually _____ Israel for her sin, sending her into exile.
___	___	___	Daniel gives _____ and encourages _____ among the _____ for the next seventy years.

ERA	FIGURE	LOCATION	STORY-LINE SUMMARY
————	————	————	Ezra _____ the people back from _____ to rebuild _____.
————	————	————	Pharisees and others _____ the Israelites in _____ for the next _____ years.

Congratulations! You have just passed another milestone! You have completed the overview of the Historical Books of the Old Testament, the ones that tell the story of the Old Testament. Now we will take a look at the Poetical Books and the Prophetical Books in the next two chapters.

THE POETICAL BOOKS

(Job–Song of Solomon)

It is no secret that, historically speaking, poets have "marched to the beat of a different drummer," and not everyone has appreciated their poetry. Charles Babbage, a British mathematician, objected to Alfred Lord Tennyson's line from "The Vision of Sin": "Every moment dies a man, / Every moment one is born," saying that if that were true, "the population of the world would be at a standstill." In the interest of accuracy, he wrote to Tennyson, the lines should be amended to read, "Every moment dies a man, / Every moment one and one-sixteenth is born."

Those who do not dislike poetry either think they can write it or wish they could. It is much more difficult to write enduring poetry than one imagines, however, and amateur attempts are rarely widely appreciated. Euripides once confessed that it had taken him three days to write three verses. His astonished friend, a poet of lesser abilities, exclaimed, "I could have written a hundred in that time!" "I believe it," replied Euripides, "but they would have lived only three days."

King Louis XIV showed Nicolas Beaulieu, a French poet of the day, some poems he had written, and asked his opinion of them. The great poet was also an accomplished diplomat: "Sire, nothing is impossible for Your Majesty. Your Majesty has set out to write bad verses and has succeeded."

Poetry is a song of the soul. Wherever great civilizations have existed, poetry has been written, and the poetry of Israel is among the finest. The psalms of David and the proverbs of Solomon stand up well when compared with any body of poetry ever written.

I.   **Review:** We remind ourselves that there are three kinds of books in the Old Testament: Historical, Poetical, and Prophetical. There are five Poetical Books that follow the first seventeen Historical Books, as seen below.

The Three Kinds of Books in the Old Testament

Historical	*Poetical*	*Prophetical*
Genesis	Job	Isaiah
Exodus	Psalms	Jeremiah
Leviticus	Proverbs	Lamentations
Numbers	Ecclesiastes	Ezekiel
Deuteronomy	Song of Solomon	Daniel
Joshua		Hosea
Judges		Joel
Ruth		Amos
1 Samuel		Obadiah
2 Samuel		Jonah
1 Kings		Micah
2 Kings		Nahum
1 Chronicles		Habakkuk
2 Chronicles		Zephaniah
Ezra		Haggai
Nehemiah		Zechariah
Esther		Malachi

To review, history has now come to an end. The Historical Books are completed, and the books of poetry of the people of Israel begin. The Poetical Books, the middle five books of the Old Testament, can be located in the time line constructed by the Historical Books. Job was written during the time of the events of the Book of Genesis; Psalms, during the life of David in 2 Samuel; and Proverbs, Ecclesiastes, and Song of Solomon were written during the lifetime of Solomon in the time covered in 1 Kings. See the following figure for a visual representation.

Poetical Books

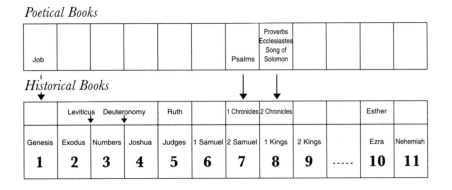

						Proverbs Ecclesiastes Song of Solomon				
Job					Psalms					

Historical Books

	Leviticus	Deuteronomy		Ruth		1 Chronicles	2 Chronicles		Esther	
Genesis	Exodus	Numbers	Joshua	Judges	1 Samuel	2 Samuel	1 Kings	2 Kings	Ezra	Nehemiah
1	**2**	**3**	**4**	**5**	**6**	**7**	**8**	**9**	-----	**10**	**11**

II. **Overview Summary:** *The Poetical Books* fall into three major *types* of poetry within which the poets used a number of different literary *techniques* to communicate God's message.

REVIEW:

The Poetical Books fall into three major _____ of poetry within which the poets used a number of different literary _____ to communicate God's message.

The three major types of Hebrew poetry are:

1. *Lyric poetry*—to be *accompanied by music*, like a song.

2. *Instructional poetry*—to *teach principles of living* through pithy maxims.

3. *Dramatic poetry*—a narrative that *tells a story* in poetic form.

REVIEW OF THE THREE MAJOR TYPES OF HEBREW POETRY:

1. *Lyric poetry*—to be *accompanied by music*, like a song.

2. *Instructional poetry*—to *teach principles of living* through pithy maxims.

3. *Dramatic poetry*—a narrative that *tells a story* in poetic form.

The two main literary techniques are

    1. *Parallelism*

    2. *Figures of speech*

1.   Parallelism: The matching of ideas

Summary Definition: Rather than matching sounds, a Hebrew poet was more concerned with *matching ideas,* a technique called "parallelism."

REVIEW:

Rather than matching sounds, a Hebrew poet was more concerned with _____ _____, a technique called "parallelism."

Six of the most common forms of parallelism are:

    1. *Synonymous parallelism:* The ideas presented are similar.

        Make me know Thy ways, O LORD;
        Teach me Thy paths. (Psalm 25:4)

    2. *Synthetic parallelism:* The second thought completes the first thought.

        The LORD is my shepherd,
        I shall not want. (Psalm 23:1)

    3. *Antithetic parallelism:* The second thought contrasts with the first.

        For the LORD knows the way of the righteous,
        But the way of the wicked shall perish. (Psalm 1:6)

    4. *Emblematic parallelism:* The first line uses a figure of speech to illustrate the idea stated in the second line.

        As the deer pants for the water brooks,
        So my soul pants for Thee, O God. (Psalm 42:1)

    5. *Climactic parallelism:* The second line repeats the first with the exception of the last word or words.

        It is not for kings, O Lemuel,
        It is not for kings to drink wine. (Proverbs 31:4)

6. *Formal parallelism:* Both lines of poetry must exist for a complete thought.

> But as for Me, I have installed My King
> Upon Zion, My holy mountain. (Psalm 2:6)

Review

(Fill in the blanks from the options listed.)

1. In synonymous parallelism, the ideas are _____.
   a. ridiculous.
   b. similar.
   c. spelled the same.

2. In synthetic parallelism, _____.
   a. the second thought is made of nylon.
   b. the second thought completes the first.
   c. the second thought doesn't exist.

3. In antithetic parallelism, _____.
   a. the second thought is written backward.
   b. the second thought contrasts with the first.
   c. the first thought has no counterpart in the universe.

4. In emblematic parallelism, _____.
   a. a small metallic emblem is affixed to the first line.
   b. a figure of speech in the first line illustrates the idea in the second line.
   c. the ideas are drawn in primitive art form.

5. In climactic parallelism, _____.
   a. the second thought is very cold.
   b. the second line repeats the first with the exception of the last word or words.
   c. the thought is completed in the third act.

6. In formal parallelism, _____.
   a. the first line appears in a black tie.
   b. both lines of poetry must exist for a complete thought.
   c. the second line doesn't slurp its soup.

(The answer to all the above questions is the first letter in the word basketball.*)*

2. Figures of Speech: Creating visual images

Summary Definition: Since the Hebrew poets wanted mental pictures to pop into the reader's mind, a prime consideration was *creating visual images,* which they accomplished with vivid "figures of speech."

REVIEW:

Since the Hebrew poets wanted mental pictures to pop into the reader's mind, a prime consideration was _____ _____ _____, which they accomplished with vivid "figures of speech."

Five of the most common figures of speech are:

1. *Simile:* a comparison between two unlike things.

    Keep me as the apple of the eye. (Psalm 17:8)

2. *Metaphor:* a comparison in which one thing is said to be another.

    The LORD is my shepherd. (Psalm 23:1)

3. *Hyperbole:* deliberate overstatement for the sake of emphasis.

    Every night I make my bed swim,
    I dissolve my couch with my tears. (Psalm 6:6)

4. *Rhetorical question:* asking a question for the purpose of making a statement.

    Who can speak of the mighty deeds of the LORD,
    Or can show forth all His praise? (Psalm 106:2)

5. *Personification:* assigning the characteristics of a human to lifeless objects.

    The sun knows the place of its setting. (Psalm 104:19)

While there are other figures of speech, these are the most notable. The ones listed here, in particular, express the visual imagery to which the Hebrew poets were committed in order to cause mental pictures to pop into our minds.

If you can get away from the need to hear rhyme and rhythm, you can gain an appreciation for Hebrew poetry. These men were "wordsmiths" and "thoughtsmiths" who played with words and ideas, contrasting them, comparing them, completing them in ways that lifted them above mere prose.

III. Expansion: The Five Poetical Books

1. Job
2. Psalms
3. Proverbs
4. Ecclesiastes
5. Song of Solomon

1. Job: Suffering and God's sovereignty

Job is a very wealthy, godly man whose life fortunes are suddenly and dramatically reversed. He loses his health, his wealth, and his family and is plunged into profound suffering. The book presents, in "dramatic poetry," the internal struggles of Job, and a series of debates with three friends trying to gain a proper perspective on *suffering and God's sovereignty*. In the end, God reveals His majesty and power. Though Job's questions are never answered, he willingly submits to the sovereignty of God, and his fortunes are restored and doubled.

2. Psalms: Praise in public worship

Psalm means "book of praises." The Book of Psalms is a collection of 150 psalms that are divided into five smaller "books." The Psalms are used as a book of prayer and *praise in public worship* in the tabernacle, temple, and synagogues. There are three primary types of psalms: praise, thanksgiving, and lament. King David writes almost half of them, while several different authors complete the rest.

3. Proverbs: Wisdom, skill for living

The purpose of proverbs is to impart *wisdom,* or *"skill for living."* More specifically, they highlight practical wisdom, discernment, self-discipline, and moral courage. This "instructional poetry" is written in short, pithy maxims focusing on one's relationship to

God and others—money, morals, speech, industry, honesty, etc. The message is that a life of wisdom and righteousness should preempt a life of foolishness and unrighteousness.

4. Ecclesiastes: Futility of temporal pursuits

Solomon, with his unlimited resources and opportunity, tries to find meaning in life through industry, pleasure, wealth, wisdom, and power, and finds them all unsatisfying. After he reviews these efforts and the *futility of temporal pursuits*, he concludes in this "instructional poetry" that there is only one thing that can satisfy man: to "fear God and keep His commandments" (12:13).

5. Song of Solomon: God's marriage manual

The Song of Solomon is *God's marriage manual*. This "dramatic poetry" pictures the intimate love relationship between Solomon and his Shulammite bride. In doing so, it presents God's perspective on married love.

Self-Test

The Five Poetical Books

(Write in the correct book from the options at left.)

OPTIONS:	BOOK:	DESCRIPTION:
Job	_____	Futility of temporal pursuits
Psalms	_____	Suffering and God's sovereignty
Proverbs		
Ecclesiastes	_____	God's marriage manual
Song of Solomon	_____	Praise in public worship
	_____	Wisdom; skill for living

THE PROPHETICAL BOOKS
(Isaiah–Malachi)

 Prophecy gets a grip on us like nothing else. We are mesmerized and spellbound by it. What does the future hold? That question grabs us by the collar, throws us up against the wall, sinks its thumbs into our jugular, and holds us there for an answer. Some look into crystal balls, read tea leaves, study astrological charts, and consult prophets for a glimpse into the unknown. From "When will the world end?" to "What should I wear tomorrow?" they hunger to probe into the depths of that which has not yet happened.

There is an intuitive sense that a veil hangs between the human and the divine, and that prophets will help us peer beyond the veil. Outside of the Bible, however, prophets have had an uneven track record. Croesus lived in the sixth century B.C. and was king of Lydia in Asia Minor. Deliberating whether to attack the Persian Empire, he asked the oracle at Delphi if the undertaking would prosper. The oracle replied that if he went to war, he would destroy a great empire. Encouraged, Croesus invaded the Persian realms. He was decisively beaten, and the Persians then invaded Lydia, captured its capital, and threw Croesus himself into chains. Croesus again sent an emissary to Delphi, this time with the question, "Why did you deceive me?" The priestess of the oracle replied that she had not deceived him—Croesus had indeed destroyed a great empire.

Girolamo Cardano, an Italian mathematician of the sixteenth century, was known throughout Europe as an astrologer, even visiting England to cast the horoscope of the young king,

Edward VI. A steadfast believer in the accuracy of his so-called science, Cardano constructed a horoscope predicting the hour of his own death. When the day dawned, it found him in good health and safe from harm. Rather than have his prediction fail, Cardano killed himself.

Biblical prophets find themselves in a different league, however, from the run-of-the-mill prophets. If a man was a true prophet from God, no prediction of his would ever fail. If a prophet ever voiced a prophecy that failed, he was to be stoned to death. This discouraged the impostors and made the biblical prophets highly reliable. There were many true prophets in the Old Testament, but not all of them committed their messages to writings that were preserved. In the Bible, we have sixteen men who wrote down their messages. These writings are called the Prophetical Books, and they comprise the final seventeen books of the Old Testament, as seen in the review below.

I. Review:

Structure of the Old Testament

Historical	*Poetical*	*Prophetical*
Genesis	Job	Isaiah
Exodus	Psalms	Jeremiah
Leviticus	Proverbs	Lamentations
Numbers	Ecclesiastes	Ezekiel
Deuteronomy	Song of Solomon	Daniel
Joshua		Hosea
Judges		Joel
Ruth		Amos
1 Samuel		Obadiah
2 Samuel		Jonah
1 Kings		Micah
2 Kings		Nahum
1 Chronicles		Habakkuk
2 Chronicles		Zephaniah
Ezra		Haggai
Nehemiah		Zechariah
Esther		Malachi

Our history is completed. From Genesis, the first Historical Book, to Nehemiah, the last Historical Book, we stretched out a time line that told the story of ancient Israel. Then we dropped the Poetical Books in their proper place. Now we do the same with the Prophetical Books, as seen below.

Historical Books

	Leviticus	Deuteronomy		Ruth		1 Chronicles	2 Chronicles			Esther	
Genesis	Exodus	Numbers	Joshua	Judges	1 Samuel	2 Samuel	1 Kings	2 Kings	-----	Ezra	Nehemiah
1	**2**	**3**	**4**	**5**	**6**	**7**	**8**	**9**		**10**	**11**

Prophetical Books

							To Israel: Hosea Amos To Judah: Habakkuk Isaiah Jeremiah Joel Micah Zephaniah Lamentations To Assyria: Jonah Nahum To Edom: Obadiah	Ezekiel Daniel	Haggai Zechariah	Malachi

Twelve of the Prophetical Books were written during the time covered in the book of 2 Kings, which records the decline of the nation. This is because the primary message of the prophets was to the nation to stop sinning and return to the Lord. The prophets predicted what would happen to the nation if the people did not heed the warning. Of the remaining books, two prophets (Ezekiel and Daniel) ministered during the exile, and three (Haggai, Zechariah, and Malachi) during the return.

II. **Overview Summary:** *Prophecy is proclaiming the Word of God, both for the future and in the present.*

REVIEW:

Prophecy is _____ the Word of God, both for the _____ and in the _____.

III. Expansion: There are four main features of the Prophetical writings:

1. Designation
2. Time Period
3. Foretelling
4. Forthtelling

1. Designation: Major and minor prophets

In recent history, the Prophetical Books have had two designations: *major prophets* and *minor prophets*. The major prophets are the first five Prophetical Books: Isaiah, Jeremiah, Lamentations, Ezekiel, and Daniel. The minor prophets are the remaining twelve. The major prophets are called "major" because they are longer books, while the others are called "minor" because they are shorter writings than the major prophets.

2. Time Period: Pre-exile, exile, or post-exile

The Prophetical Books are divided into three chronological periods: *pre-exile, exile,* and *post-exile*. Most of the prophetical ministries and books occur before the exile. Three prophets, Haggai, Zechariah, and Malachi, prophesy during the return. Of those who prophesy before the exile, two prophesy primarily to Israel (the northern kingdom), seven primarily to Judah (the southern kingdom), and three to other countries, as seen in the following lists.

Structure of the Prophetical Books

Pre-Exile

TO ISRAEL:	TO JUDAH:	TO ASSYRIA:	TO EDOM:
Hosea	Habakkuk	Jonah	Obadiah
Amos	Isaiah	Nahum	
	Jeremiah		
	Joel		
	Micah		
	Zephaniah		
	Lamentations		

Exile	*Post-Exile*
FROM BABYLONIA:	TO JERUSALEM:
Ezekiel	Haggai
Daniel	Zechariah
	Malachi

3. Foretelling: Predicting the future

The most famous characteristic of a prophet is that he can occasionally *predict the future*. This is not an ability inherent within himself. Rather, this information is given to him by God. In Israel, the test of a true prophet is that he must be 100 percent accurate. If a prophet ever says anything that does not come true, he is not a prophet of God. And the penalty for giving a prophecy that does not come true is death by stoning. This keeps the ranks of the prophets pure.

4. Forthtelling: Proclaiming the teachings of God

While the ministry of "foretelling" (telling the future) is more dramatic, the ministry of "forthtelling" is vastly more common in the life of a prophet. Forthtelling means simply *proclaiming the teachings of God* to the people. Primarily it relates to righteous living. There are three characteristics of this part of a prophet's ministry.

1. Exposing sin and calling people to a higher moral lifestyle.
2. Warning of judgment if the people don't reform.
3. Proclaiming the coming Messiah.

The prophets usually warned about judgments related to the nation of Israel or Judah being militarily conquered and taken out of the land.

Self-Test

A. Four Main Features of the Prophetical Books

(Write in the correct feature from the options at left.)

OPTIONS:	FEATURE:	DESCRIPTION:
Designation	_____	Predicting the future
Time Period	_____	Proclaiming the teachings of God
Foretelling	_____	Pre-exile, exile, post-exile
Forthtelling	_____	Major and minor prophets

B. The Geography of the Prophetical Books

The primary locations in which prophets ministered are found on the map below. Match the country with the location by filling in the blanks according to the numbers.

1. Israel   4. Assyria
2. Judah   5. Babylonia
3. Edom   6. Jerusalem

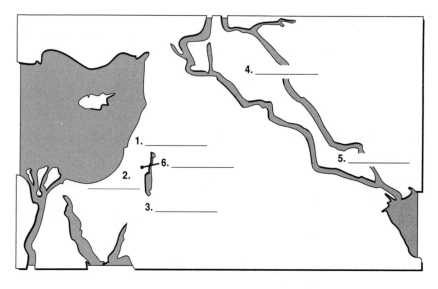

Wonderful! You have now completed Section 1, the Story of the Old Testament. This is a major milestone in understanding the Bible. The remaining three sections have been structured so that they are challenging, but not overwhelming. If you completed the Old Testament, you can complete the entire book, and you're almost halfway through!

Now, having just overviewed the Poetical and Prophetical Books of the Old Testament and having seen where they fit into the Story of the Bible, we are ready to continue that story as we begin Section 2, the Story of the New Testament.

THE
STORY
OF THE
NEW
TESTAMENT

FIFTEEN

THE GEOGRAPHY AND STRUCTURE OF THE NEW TESTAMENT

 Hiding among the giant Andes Mountains in the South American country of Peru lies a flat valley about forty miles long, isolated from the rest of the world. Roads and paths lie all over the floor of this vast valley, strewn like long, thin trees that have fallen at random. For years, archaeologists have guessed that they were a forgotten network of roads, left by an ancient civilization.

Perspective was changed radically, however, when someone chanced to study the valley from the air. From this vantage point, what seemed to be haphazard and random now became quite clear. They were not roads and paths at all, but a monumental desert mural picturing objects that were many miles in height. What the murals are, what they mean, how they were built, for whom they were built, and by whom they were built are all lost to the mist of time.

The monumental mural has a symbolic message for us all, however. Often, the whole picture of something cannot be seen if we are too close to it. We must get back away from the details of what we are studying to see the overview.

This is certainly true of the geography of the New Testament. When in the Gospels you read of going from the cities of Jericho to Jerusalem to Cana, those are just words on a page with no meaning until you have overviewed the geography. You have no realization that someone has just walked seventy-five miles,

107

as the crow flies, the distance from Baltimore to Philadelphia, or that it also included walking up thirteen hundred feet in altitude and then down another one thousand.

In fact, gaining perspective on the geography of the New Testament is in itself a fascinating study. Israel is a tiny country compared to the United States. Draw a line fifty miles wide from New York to Boston, or stand Massachusetts on end, or shrink New Hampshire by 10 percent, and you have the approximate land area of Israel.

Yet it is a remarkably varied land. From low desert to high mountain, with lush valleys and rolling hills in between, the gamut is run in topography. Any body of water that you cannot swim across is a "sea," and every hill higher than your head is a "mountain." The Sea of Galilee is seven miles by fourteen miles, almost a mud puddle compared to the Great Lakes. The Dead Sea is ten miles by fifty miles, smaller than some virtually nameless reservoirs in the U.S. The "mighty" Jordan is little more than a strong-running creek compared to the truly mighty rivers of the world like the Amazon or Mississippi. Perhaps because it is such a small country, everything is exaggerated.

To be able to create mental pictures as you read the events in the New Testament is to help the narrative come alive. So, as we begin looking at the New Testament, we begin with the geography.

The Geography of the Gospels

The difference between the geography of the Gospels and the geography of the Book of Acts is significant enough to warrant separate treatment.

Bodies of Water

Once you have mastered the geography of the Old Testament, the geography of the New Testament is fairly simple. The bodies of water are among those of the Old Testament studied in chapter 2. (To review, go to the map that follows and write in the name of the bodies of water by matching the numbers.)

1. Mediterranean Sea
2. Sea of Galilee
3. Jordan River
4. Dead Sea

Bodies of Water in the Gospels

(Fill in the appropriate blanks on the following map. The names and numbers should match those on the preceding list.)

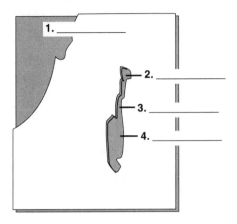

Provinces and Cities

The primary geographical area in the Gospels is the same as that which was ruled by the nation of Israel in the Old Testament. However, the land, now known as Palestine, is ruled by Rome and has been divided into sections, or provinces. (*As you read these descriptions, write the location on the map that follows by matching the letters.*)

A. The Province of Galilee

Located between the Mediterranean Sea and the sea that shares its name, Galilee, is the province Jesus considered His home province. Both Nazareth, His early home, and Capernaum, His later home, are in Galilee. Hence, the phrase "the man from Galilee."

B. The Province of Samaria

Located between the Mediterranean Sea and the Jordan River, Samaria is home to Samaritans. Part Jewish, part Gentile people, they live in constant animosity with the Jews.

C. The Province of Judea

Located between the Mediterranean Sea and the Dead Sea, Judea is approximately the same area as the southern tribe of

Judah in the Old Testament. Encompassing the city of Jerusalem, it is home to most of the Jews in the New Testament.

D.   The Province of Perea

A long, narrow province on the east bank of the Jordan
River, Jesus spent some concentrated time there with His disciples toward the end of His ministry.

E.   The City of Nazareth

Located in Galilee just west of the Sea of Galilee, it is the
town where Mary and Joseph lived, and in which Jesus grew up.

F.   The City of Capernaum

Located on the very top of the Sea of Galilee, it is where
Jesus called home during His ministry years.

G.   The City of Jerusalem

Located in Judea, just off the top of the Dead Sea, it is the
home of the temple, the holy city, and the center of activity for Jews.

H.   The City of Bethlehem

The birthplace of Jesus, it is five miles southwest of Jerusalem.

Provinces and Cities of the Gospels

(Fill in the appropriate blanks below. The letters and names
should match those from the list above.)

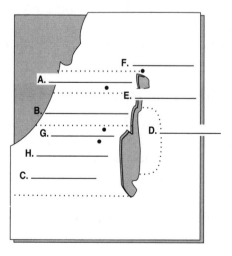

The Geography of Acts

Bodies of water

The bodies of water are the same as for the Gospels, only more of the Mediterranean is involved. Therefore, you already know them.

Countries and Cities

As we move out of the Gospels and into Acts, our geography expands from Palestine further into the Roman Empire. (*As you read the descriptions, write the location on the map that follows.*)

1. The Country of Galatia

Located in modern-day Turkey, it was the destination of the apostle Paul's first missionary journey to take the gospel message to Gentiles.

2. The Country of Greece

Located in modern Greece, it was the destination for Paul's second missionary journey.

3. The Country of Asia

Located on the western coast of modern Turkey, it was the destination of Paul's third missionary journey.

4. The Country of Italy

Located in modern Italy, it was the country of Paul's final imprisonment and death.

5. The City of Jerusalem

Located in modern Jerusalem, it is the location of the beginning of the early Christian Church.

6. The City of Damascus

Located in modern Damascus, in the modern country of Syria, it was Paul's destination when he was temporarily blinded by Jesus and converted to Christianity.

7. The City of Caesarea

Located on the Mediterranean coast just south of the Sea of Galilee, it was the site of Paul's trials.

8. The City of Antioch

On the Mediterranean coast north of Israel, near modern Turkey, it was the beginning point for all three of Paul's missionary journeys.

9. The City of Rome

Located in modern Rome, it was the political and cultural heart of the Roman Empire.

The Geography of Acts

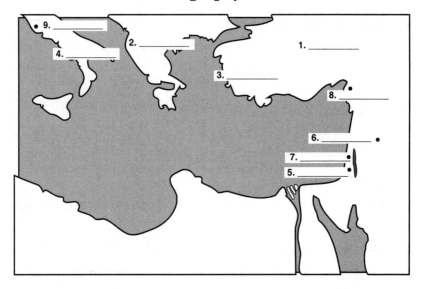

Self-Test

The Geography of the Gospels

(Now, from the options listed, fill in the bodies of water, provinces, and cities on the map that follows.)

Numbers = bodies of water	*Letters = cities and provinces*
Dead Sea	Bethlehem
Jordan River	Capernaum
Mediterranean Sea	Galilee
Sea of Galilee	Jerusalem
	Judea
	Nazareth
	Perea
	Samaria

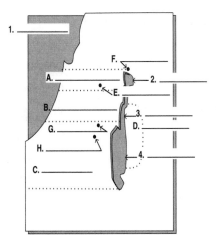

The Geography of Acts

(From the options listed, fill in the countries and cities on the following map.)

Countries:

Asia
Galatia
Greece
Italy

Cities:

Antioch
Caesarea
Damascus
Jerusalem
Rome

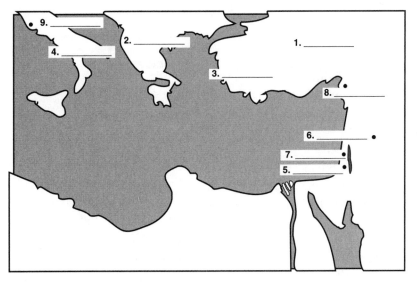

The Historical Books of the New Testament

Having mastered the geography of the New Testament, we are now ready to continue the story of the Bible with the three main eras that remain. You will recall that the twenty-seven books of the New Testament can be divided into three different kinds of books: five Historical Books, thirteen Pauline Epistles, and nine General Epistles.

As we did with the Historical Books in the Old Testament, first we will overview the events of the Historical Books of the New Testament, the Gospels and the Acts. Then, in the following chapters, we will expand the story line.

The Three Main Eras of the New Testament

1.   Gospels

The life of Jesus of Nazareth as told in the *Gospels.*

2.   Church

The formation of the Christian *Church.*

3.   Missions

The expansion of the Church into the Roman Empire through *missions.*

Review

Write in the correct era on the proper line matching the description.

OPTIONS:	ERA:	DESCRIPTION:
Missions	_____	The life of Jesus of Nazareth, as told in the *Gospels*
Gospels		
Church	_____	The formation of the Christian *Church*
	_____	The expansion of the Church into the Roman Empire through *missions*

We are now able to add this new information to our story-line chart from the Old Testament, as seen on the following page.

Story of the Bible

ERA	FIGURE	LOCATION	STORY-LINE SUMMARY
Creation	*Adam*	*Eden*	Adam is created by God, but he *sins* and *destroys* God's original *plan* for man.
Patriarch	*Abraham*	*Canaan*	Abraham is *chosen* by God to "father" a *people* to *represent* God to the world.
Exodus	*Moses*	*Egypt*	Through Moses God *delivers* the Hebrew people from *slavery* in Egypt and then gives them the *Law*.
Conquest	*Joshua*	*Canaan*	Joshua leads the *conquest* of the *Promised Land*.
Judges	*Samson*	*Canaan*	Samson and others were chosen as *judges* to *govern* the people for *four hundred* rebellious years.
Kingdom	*David*	*Israel*	David, the greatest king in the new *monarchy*, is followed by a succession of mostly *unrighteous* kings, and God eventually *judges* Israel for her sin, sending her into exile.
Exile	*Daniel*	*Babylonia*	Daniel gives *leadership* and encourages *faithfulness* among the *exiles* for the next seventy years.
Return	*Ezra*	*Jerusalem*	Ezra *leads* the people back from *exile* to rebuild *Jerusalem*.
Silence	*Pharisees*	*Jerusalem*	Pharisees and others *entomb* the *Israelites* in *legalism* for the next *four hundred* years.

ERA	FIGURE	LOCATION	STORY-LINE SUMMARY
Gospels	To be supplied later.	To be supplied later.	To be supplied later.
Church	To be supplied later.	To be supplied later.	To be supplied later.
Missions	To be supplied later.	To be supplied later.	To be supplied later.

The Three Central Figures of the New Testament

ERA:	FIGURE:	DESCRIPTION:
Gospels	Jesus	The predicted *Messiah*
Church	Peter	The *leader* of the early Church
Missions	Paul	The first Christian *missionary*

Review

Fill in the blanks.

ERA:	FIGURE:	DESCRIPTION:
Gospels	Jesus	The predicted_____
Church	Peter	The _____ of the early Church
Missions	Paul	The first Christian _____

We are now able to add the central figures from the New Testament to our story-line chart, as seen on the following page, which shows just the New Testament Eras.

ERA	FIGURE	LOCATION	STORY-LINE SUMMARY
Gospels	*Jesus*	To be supplied later.	To be supplied later.
Church	*Peter*	To be supplied later.	To be supplied later.
Missions	*Paul*	To be supplied later.	To be supplied later.

Our final task is to identify the general or primary geographic location of the events of the three main eras of the New Testament. As an exercise in memory, write in each main era and central historical figure as you read the description of the geographical location.

The Three Main Locations of the New Testament

ERA:	FIGURE:	LOCATION:	DESCRIPTION:
G_____	J_____	Palestine	The general land area that was known as Canaan and Israel in the Old Testament is commonly known as Palestine in the New. It includes the Roman provinces of Galilee, Samaria, and Judea.
C_____	P_____	Jerusalem	The ancient city of Jerusalem has been in the same location throughout most of biblical history after the Kingdom Era. It is the city that gave birth to the early Church.

ERA:	FIGURE:	LOCATION:	DESCRIPTION:
M _____	P _____	Roman Empire	As Paul spread the message of Christianity he took it to the heart of the Roman Empire. From Palestine, north into what is modern Turkey, and west through modern Greece, to Italy.

Review

(Now, from the options listed at right, write in the location to match the era and figure.)

ERA:	FIGURE:	LOCATION:	OPTIONS:
Gospels	*Jesus*	_____	Roman Empire
Church	*Peter*	_____	Palestine
Missions	*Paul*	_____	Jerusalem

We are now able to add the main locations from the New Testament to our story-line chart, as seen in the following.

ERA	FIGURE	LOCATION	STORY-LINE SUMMARY
Gospels	*Jesus*	*Palestine*	To be supplied later.
Church	*Peter*	*Jerusalem*	To be supplied later.
Missions	*Paul*	*Roman Empire*	To be supplied later.

Arc of Bible History

(Fill in the names of the eras. To check your answers, see the Appendix.)

1. C_____	5. J_____	9. S_____
2. P_____	6. K_____	10. G_____
3. E_____	7. E_____	11. C_____
4. C_____	8. R_____	12. M_____

From memory fill in the New Testament story-line chart.

ERA	FIGURE	LOCATION	STORY-LINE SUMMARY
_____	_____	_____	To be supplied later.
_____	_____	_____	To be supplied later.
_____	_____	_____	To be supplied later.

Congratulations! You have just taken a big step toward mastering an overview of the New Testament. From now on, we will get more specific, but you have the basic structure well in hand.

SIXTEEN

THE GOSPEL ERA

(Matthew–John)

 Dr. Richard Selzer is a brilliant surgeon who wrote a penetrating book entitled *Mortal Lessons: Notes on the Art of Surgery.* In it he writes:

> I stand by the bed where a young woman lies, her face postoperative, her mouth twisted in a palsy, clownish. A tiny twig of a facial nerve, the one to the muscles of her mouth, has been severed. She will be thus from now on. The surgeon had followed with religious fervor the curve of her flesh; I promise you that. Nevertheless to remove the tumor in her cheek, I had to cut the little nerve.
>
> Her husband is in the room. He stands on the opposite side of the bed, and together, they seem to dwell in the evening lamplight. Isolated from me, private. Who are they, I ask myself, he and this wry-mouth I have made, who gaze at each other, and touch each other generously, greedily?
>
> The young woman speaks. "Will I always be like this?" she asks. "Yes," I say. "It is because the nerve was cut." She nods and is silent. But the young man smiles. "I like it," he says. "It's kind of cute."
>
> All at once I know who he is. I understand, and I lower my gaze. One is not bold in an encounter with a god. Unmindful, he bends to kiss her crooked mouth, and I am so close I can see how he twists his own lips to accommodate hers, to show that their kiss still works. I remember that the gods appeared in ancient Greece as mortals, and I hold my breath and let the wonder in.

That is the spirit of Jesus. Man's link with God had been severed through sin. And He twisted Himself to accommodate

120

us, and gave us the kiss of eternal life. But not without giving His own life on our behalf. Jesus. At the same time, so tender and powerful. The most remarkable figure ever to have lived. And why not? He was God incarnate.

The birth of Jesus split history like a thunderbolt on a hot July evening. Everything before His birth we call B.C., before Christ. Everything after, we call A.D., anno Domini, in the year of our Lord. His story, predicted throughout the Old Testament, is told in the four Gospels: Matthew, Mark, Luke, and John. While the Gospels are biographical, they are actually thematic portraits of Christ's life that place very little emphasis on His early life and great emphasis on the last week of His life. The Gospels tend to follow the chronology of His life, but not slavishly. Not all the Gospels cover the same events in His life. When all four Gospels are put together and "harmonized," only about fifty days of Jesus' active ministry are dealt with.

I.   **Review:** Fill in the blanks to begin the chart for this era.

Story of the New Testament

ERA	FIGURE	LOCATION	STORY-LINE SUMMARY
___	___	___	To be supplied later.

II.   **Story-Line Summary:** *Jesus* comes in fulfillment of the Old Testament *prophecies* of a savior and offers *salvation* and the true kingdom of God. While some accept Him, most *reject* Him, and He is crucified, buried, and resurrected.

ERA	SUMMARY
Gospels:	*Jesus* comes in fulfillment of the Old Testament _____ of a savior and offers _____ and the true kingdom of God. While some accept Him, most _____ Him, and He is crucified, buried, and resurrected.

III. Expansion: There are four main divisions in the Gospel Era:

1. Early Life
2. Early Ministry
3. Later Ministry
4. Death and Resurrection

1. Early Life: Childhood to baptism

Through a miraculous conception by the Holy Spirit, Jesus is born of the Virgin Mary in Bethlehem of Judea. After a brief excursion into Egypt to save Him from Herod's attempt on His life, Jesus travels with Mary and her husband Joseph to live in Nazareth. There He learns the trade of a carpenter and apparently lives a fairly normal life from *childhood to the time of His baptism,* when He is thirty years old. His cousin, John the Baptist, is ministering and baptizing people in the Jordan River near the Dead Sea. After Jesus is baptized by John, a remarkable event takes place. God the Father is heard speaking from heaven, saying, "This is My beloved Son, in whom I am well pleased," and the Holy Spirit, in the visible form of a dove, descends on Him. Then He is led by the Holy Spirit into the wilderness of Judea, where He is tempted by Satan for forty days. Satan makes every attempt to get Jesus to follow him rather than God. Satan offers Jesus everything God the Father offers Him, but on a different time table and with different requirements. Jesus remains sinless and validates His readiness to begin making Himself known as the Messiah.

2. Early Ministry: Initial acceptance

It is not until after Jesus' baptism and temptation that He begins His public ministry. His message has a two-fold focus: first, that He is the predicted Messiah or, as the word is translated in the New Testament, the Christ, and people should believe in Him, and second, to challenge the people to live a life of genuine righteousness, not the external hypocrisy of the religious leaders. He validates His message by performing astounding miracles, and the signs of *initial acceptance* by the crowds are encouraging. Much of this early activity takes place around Jerusalem.

3. Later Ministry: Growing rejection

Jesus' initial popularity does not last. The religious leaders are profoundly jealous of Him and begin stirring up animosity toward Him. This *growing rejection* results in a progression in Jesus' ministry pattern. He begins to focus more attention on the mounting opposition from the religious leaders, warning them of the seriousness of their attitude. At the same time, He begins setting aside more and more time for the twelve disciples whom He has chosen, preparing them to carry on without Him. Also, He begins challenging the multitude to count the cost of following Him. Though Jesus travels quite a bit during this time, His home base is Capernaum, on the north bank of the Sea of Galilee.

4. Death and Resurrection: Final rejection

The Jews become more and more polarized about Jesus, either following Him enthusiastically or resenting Him deeply. In the volatile atmosphere of the festival time of the Passover when Jesus and many other Jews are in Jerusalem, the religious leaders are finally able to stir up enthusiasm for Jesus' crucifixion. They subject Him to a series of mock trials on false charges. Then Jesus is crucified on Friday, buried that night, and rises again from the dead on Sunday, after being in the tomb three days.

Self-Test

A. Four Main Divisions in the Gospel Era

(Write in the correct division from the options at left.)

OPTIONS:	DIVISION:	DESCRIPTION:
Early Life	_____	Initial acceptance
Early Ministry		
Later Ministry	_____	Final rejection
Death and Resurrection	_____	Childhood to baptism
	_____	Growing rejection

B.   Story-Line Summary

(Fill in the blanks from memory.)

ERA	SUMMARY
Gospels:	*Jesus* comes in fulfillment of the Old Testament _____ of a savior and offers _____ and the true kingdom of God. While some accept Him, most _____ Him, and He is crucified, buried, and resurrected.

C.   Arc of Bible History

(Fill in the names of the eras.)

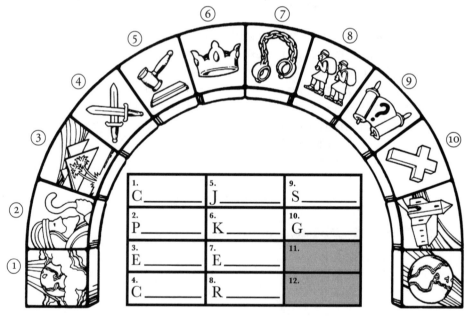

1. C_____	5. J_____	9. S_____
2. P_____	6. K_____	10. G_____
3. E_____	7. E_____	11.
4. C_____	8. R_____	12.

D.   The Geography of the Gospel Era

(Draw an arrow from Bethlehem to Egypt to Nazareth to represent the geographical movement in Jesus' early life, and label it 1. Draw an arrow from Nazareth to Jerusalem to represent His initial acceptance, and label it 2. Draw an arrow from Jerusalem to Capernaum to represent the growing rejection, and label it 3. Draw an arrow from Capernaum to Jerusalem to represent His final rejection, and label it 4.)

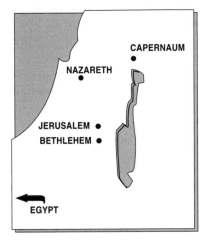

E. Story of the Bible

(Fill in the blanks. To check your answers, see the Appendix.)

ERA	FIGURE	LOCATION	STORY-LINE SUMMARY
____	____	____	Adam is created by God, but he _____ and _____ God's original _____ for man.
____	____	____	Abraham is _____ by God to "father" a _____ to _____ God to the world.
____	____	____	Through Moses God _____ the Hebrew people from _____ in Egypt and then gives them the _____.
____	____	____	Joshua leads the _____ of the _____ _____.

ERA	FIGURE	LOCATION	STORY-LINE SUMMARY
————	————	————	Samson and others were chosen as _____ to _____ the people for _____ rebellious years.
————	————	————	David, the greatest king in the new _____, is followed by a succession of mostly _____ kings, and God eventually _____ Israel for her sin, sending her into exile.
————	————	————	Daniel gives _____ and encourages _____ among the _____ for the next seventy years.
————	————	————	Ezra _____ the people back from _____ to rebuild _____.
————	————	————	Pharisees and others ____ the Israelites in _____ for the next _____ years.
————	————	————	Jesus comes in fulfillment of the Old Testament _____ of a savior and offers _____ and the true kingdom of God. While some accept Him, most _____ Him, and He is crucified, buried, and resurrected.

THE CHURCH ERA
(Acts 1—12)

A lot of potshots have been taken at the Church over the years. One skalleywag wrote:

> To live above with saints we love,
> O, that will be glory.
> To live below with saints we know,
> Well, that's another story.

Another one wrote about hymns we really sing:

> When morning guilds the skies
> My heart awakening cries
> Oh no! Another day!

> Amazing grace, how sweet the sound
> That saved a wretch like you.

> Jesus, I am resting, resting,
> Resting, resting, resting, resting.

> The strife is o'er, the battle done,
> The church has split, and our side won.

William Blake wrote in the "Everlasting Gospel":

> Both read the Bible day and night,
> But Thou read'st black where I read white.

In spite of its obvious imperfections, the Church is the means that has been chosen to carry the message of the gospel to the world. One wonders why a better system could not have been devised. Then one realizes that any system that has people in it is going to be imperfect.

Alexander Solzhenitsyn wrote in the *Gulag Archipelago* that it was in prison where he learned that the line separating good and evil passes not through states, not through classes, not through political parties, either, but right through every human heart and through all human hearts.

When we give ourselves serious evaluation, we find things hiding in our hearts that, if we could choose, we would remove. Our hearts have been described as "a zoo of lusts, a bedlam of ambitions, a nursery of fears, a harem of fondled hatreds." Yet the Church, by its very nature, must be made up of the likes of us.

However, we are not left to ourselves. God is at work in the lives of all willing people, changing and transforming them into something more than they were.

"Imagine yourself a living house," wrote C.S. Lewis. "God comes in to rebuild that house. At first, perhaps, you can understand what He is doing. He is getting the drains right and stopping the leaks in the roof and so on. But presently He starts knocking the house about in a way that hurts abominably and does not seem to make any sense. What on earth is He up to? The explanation is that He is building quite a different house from the one you thought of—throwing out a new wing here, putting on an extra floor there, running up towers, making courtyards. You thought you were going to be made into a decent little cottage; but He is building a palace."

And thus is the message of the Church. The gospel is carried *to* imperfect people *by* imperfect people. Then those imperfect people are to band together to help one another grow to spiritual maturity. Salvation in Christ, and growth to Christian maturity—warts and all.

I. Review: Fill in the blanks to bring the chart up-to-date with this era.

Story of the New Testament

ERA	FIGURE	LOCATION	STORY-LINE SUMMARY
_____	_____	_____	*Jesus* comes in fulfillment of the Old Testament _____ of a savior and offers _____ and the true kingdom of God. While some accept Him, most _____ Him, and He is crucified, buried, and resurrected.

ERA	FIGURE	LOCATION	STORY-LINE SUMMARY
____	____	____	To be supplied later.

II. **Story-Line Summary:** *Peter,* shortly after the *ascension* of Jesus, is used by God to *establish* the *Church,* God's next major plan for man.

ERA	SUMMARY
Church:	*Peter,* shortly after the _____ of Jesus, is used by God to _____ the _____, God's next major plan for man.

III. **Expansion:** There are four major subjects in the Church Era:

1. Creation
2. Growth
3. Persecution
4. Transition

1. **Creation: Birth of the Church** (Acts 1—5)

The birthplace of the Church is Jerusalem. After His death, burial, and resurrection, Jesus instructs His disciples to wait in Jerusalem until they receive the power of the Holy Spirit and then to be witnesses to Him in Jerusalem (their city), Judea and Samaria (the surrounding provinces), and the remotest part of the earth (the rest of the world). Then Jesus ascends into heaven right before their eyes. Shortly after that, on the Jewish feast day of Pentecost, the Holy Spirit comes upon Jesus' disciples. While they are gathered in a house, a sound like a violent rushing wind fills the place and flames of fire rest on each disciple, and they are filled with the Holy Spirit. They begin speaking in different foreign languages, with the result that many of the Jews from different parts of the world hear them speak in their own language. This and other notable miracles associated with the *birth of the Church* take place in the early days as the number of converts to Christianity increases rapidly in Jerusalem.

2.   Growth: Organization of the Church (Acts 6)

As the number of converts increases, some measures are taken for the *organization of the Church*, giving structure to their activities and responsibilities. Peter organizes a relief effort for needy Christians. Those who have possessions can sell them and give money to the apostles, who distribute it according to the needs. Then deacons are chosen to look after the material needs of the Church while the apostles attend to the spiritual needs.

3.   Persecution: The first Christian martyr (Acts 7)

Stephen, one of the early preachers, is arrested by the Jewish leaders for preaching about Jesus. When he does not recant his message but presses it further, the Jews stone him to death on the spot, making Stephen *the first Christian martyr.* This incident kicks off a round of persecution against new Christians that is so severe many of them have to flee Jerusalem for their very lives. As they do, they take the message of the gospel with them to the surrounding provinces of Judea and Samaria.

4.   Transition: A missionary to the Gentiles (Acts 8—12)

A zealous Pharisee, Saul of Tarsus, looks after the cloaks of those who stone Stephen. Shortly afterward, he is journeying to Damascus to find and persecute other Christians when Jesus appears to him from heaven, and Saul is converted to Christianity. Jesus changes Saul's name to Paul, and he becomes known as the apostle Paul. Jesus expressly tells Paul that he will become *a missionary to the Gentiles.* Shortly after that, the apostle Peter has a vision in which the Lord tells him that the message of the gospel is to be taken to the Gentiles also. This marks a transition in the nature of the Church because, up to this time, the message has been circulated exclusively to Jews.

Self-Test

A. Four Major Subjects of the Church Era

(Write in the correct subject from the options at left.)

OPTIONS:	SUBJECT:	DESCRIPTION:
Creation	_____	Organization of the Church
Growth	_____	A missionary to the Gentiles
Persecution	_____	Birth of the Church
Transition	_____	The first Christian martyr

B. Story-Line Summary

(Fill in the blanks from memory.)

ERA	SUMMARY
Church:	*Peter,* shortly after the _____ of Jesus, is used by God to _____ the _____, God's next major plan for man.

C. Arc of Bible History (Fill in the names of the eras.)

1. C_____	5. J_____	9. S_____
2. P_____	6. K_____	10. G_____
3. E_____	7. E_____	11. C_____
4. C_____	8. R_____	12.

D. The Geography of the Church Era

(Draw an arrow from Jerusalem into Samaria, and one from Jerusalem into Judea to represent the geographical movement of the Church Era.)

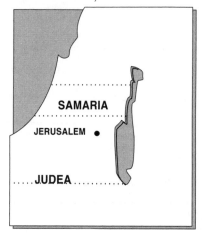

E. Story of the Bible

(Fill in the blanks. To check your answers, see the Appendix.)

ERA	FIGURE	LOCATION	STORY-LINE SUMMARY
_____	_____	_____	Adam is created by God, but he _____ and _____ God's original _____ for man.
_____	_____	_____	Abraham is _____ by God to "father" a _____ to _____ God to the world.
_____	_____	_____	Throut Moses God_____ the Hebrew people from _____ in Egypt and then gives them the _____.
_____	_____	_____	Joshua leads the _____ of the _____ _____.

ERA	FIGURE	LOCATION	STORY-LINE SUMMARY
_____	_____	_____	Samson and others were chosen as _____ to _____ the people for _____ rebellious years.
_____	_____	_____	David, the greatest king in the new _____, is followed by a succession of mostly _____ kings, and God eventually _____ Israel for her sin, sending her into exile.
_____	_____	_____	Daniel gives _____ and encourages _____ among the _____ for the next seventy years.
_____	_____	_____	Ezra _____ the people back from _____ to rebuild _____.
_____	_____	_____	Pharisees and others ____ the Israelites in _____ for the next _____ years.
_____	_____	_____	Jesus comes in fulfillment of the Old Testament _____ of a savior and offers _____ and the true kingdom of God. While some accept Him, most _____ Him, and He is crucified, buried, and resurrected.
_____	_____	_____	Peter, shortly after the _____ of Jesus, is used by God to _____ the _____, God's next major plan for man.

THE MISSIONS ERA
(Acts 13—28)

A missionary ministering in the South Sea Islands was teaching his people about Christmas. "The giving of gifts is a spontaneous act of celebration over an extremely joyous event. And that," he explained, "is why many people give gifts to others at Christmas time. It is an act of celebration over the joyous occasion of the birth of Christ."

Following this teaching, one of the young men wanted to give the missionary a gift for Christmas, but since it was a very poor island, presents were not readily available.

On Christmas morning, a knock came at the hut of the missionary. At the door, he found the young man, who then gave him an extremely rare and particularly beautiful seashell that was found only at the distant end of the island.

The missionary thanked the young man for giving him such a rare and beautiful gift from such a distance, to which the young man replied, "Long walk part of gift."

What a beautiful sentiment. "Long walk part of gift." Such was also true of the apostle Paul, who gave up a life of comfort and safety and took upon himself the arduous life of a missionary to take the message of the gospel to the Gentile people in the surrounding nations.

I. **Review:** Fill in the blanks to bring the chart up-to-date with this era.

Story of the New Testament

ERA	FIGURE	LOCATION	STORY-LINE SUMMARY
_____	_____	_____	Jesus comes in fulfillment of the Old Testament _____ of a savior and offers _____ and the true kingdom of God. While some accept Him, most _____ Him, and He is crucified, buried, and resurrected.
_____	_____	_____	Peter, shortly after the _____ of Jesus, is used by God to _____ the _____, God's next major plan for man.
_____	_____	_____	To be supplied later.

II. **Story-Line Summary:** *Paul expands* the Church into the *Roman* Empire during the next two *decades*.

ERA	SUMMARY
Missions:	*Paul* _____ the Church into the _____ Empire during the next two _____.

III. **Expansion:** There are four major subjects in the Missions Era:

1. First Missionary Journey
2. Second Missionary Journey
3. Third Missionary Journey
4. Trials and Imprisonment

1.   First Missionary Journey: Galatia for two years
(Acts 13—14)

In Paul's first missionary journey, he and Barnabas are selected by the Holy Spirit to travel to Galatia and take the gospel
to Gentiles living there. They depart from Antioch, the point of
departure for all three missionary journeys, and are in *Galatia
for two years*, experiencing encouraging results. After they return
to Jerusalem, a council is held amid much controversy, which
determines that the Gentiles do not have to become Jewish in
addition to becoming Christians.

2.   Second Missionary Journey: Greece for three years
(Acts 15—17)

Paul leaves from Antioch to visit the believers from his first
journey. However, he receives a vision of a man in Macedonia
(Greece) and changes his plans, going to Greece with the gospel
message for the Gentiles there. He travels in *Greece for three years.*

3.   Third Missionary Journey: Asia for four years
(Acts 18—21).

Again, Paul leaves to encourage the believers from his first
two trips and to spread the message of the gospel into Asia. He
has great success and great opposition. In Ephesus, the whole city
breaks out in riot over his visit. Though Paul is warned that he
will be imprisoned upon his return to Jerusalem, he returns anyway,
after being in *Asia for four years*, and is immediately arrested.

4.   Trials and Imprisonment: Roman prison for two years
(Acts 22—28)

Jewish leaders in Jerusalem have Paul arrested on false
charges. Since his life is threatened there, even under guard, he
is moved to Caesarea, the Roman capital in the area. There, he
is tried under three men: Felix, Festus, and Agrippa. In order to
thwart a miscarriage of justice in the process, Paul exercises his
right as a Roman citizen to take his case before Caesar in Rome.
He is taken to Rome, but his case never comes to trial. After being
in a *Roman prison for two years*, it is said he was beheaded (the established means of execution for a Roman citizen).

Self-Test

A. Four Major Subjects of the Missions Era

(Match the missionary journey with its location, choosing from the options at left.)

OPTIONS:	JOURNEY:	LOCATIONS:
First Missionary Journey	_____	Roman prison for two years
Second Missionary Journey	_____	Galatia for two years
Third Missionary Journey	_____	Asia for four years
Trials and Imprisonment	_____	Greece for three years

B. Story-Line Summary (Fill in the blanks from memory.)

ERA	SUMMARY
Missions:	Paul _____ the Church into the _____ Empire during the next two _____.

C. Arc of Bible History (Fill in the names of the eras.)

1. C_____	5. J_____	9. S_____
2. P_____	6. K_____	10. G_____
3. E_____	7. E_____	11. C_____
4. C_____	8. R_____	12. M_____

D. The Geography of the Missions Era

(Draw an arrow from Antioch to Galatia and put a 1 next to it. Draw an arrow from Antioch to Greece and put a 2 next to it. Draw an arrow from Antioch to Asia and put a 3 next to it. This represents the geographical movement of Paul's missionary journeys. Now, draw an arrow from Caesarea to Rome and put a 4 next to it to represent Paul's trials and imprisonment during the Missions Era.)

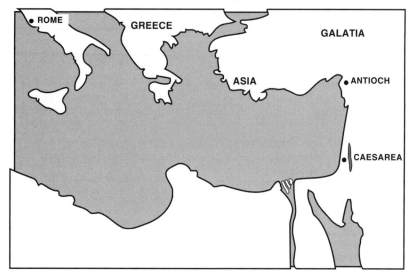

E. Story of the Bible

(Fill in the blanks.)

ERA	FIGURE	LOCATION	STORY-LINE SUMMARY
_____	_____	_____	Adam is created by God, but he _____ and _____ God's original _____ for man.
_____	_____	_____	Abraham is _____ by God to "father" a ____ to _____ God to the world.
_____	_____	_____	Through Moses God _____ the Hebrew people from _____ in Egypt and then gives them the _____.

ERA	FIGURE	LOCATION	STORY-LINE SUMMARY
_____	_____	_____	Joshua leads the _____ of the _____ _____.
_____	_____	_____	Samson and others were chosen as _____ to _____ the people for _____ rebellious years.
_____	_____	_____	David, the greatest king in the new _____, is followed by a succession of mostly _____ kings, and God eventually _____ Israel for her sin, sending her into exile.
_____	_____	_____	Daniel gives _____ and encourages _____ among the _____ for the next seventy years.
_____	_____	_____	Ezra _____ the people back from _____ to rebuild _____.
_____	_____	_____	Pharisees and others ____ the Israelites in _____ for the next _____ years.
_____	_____	_____	Jesus comes in fulfillment of the Old Testament _____ of a savior and offers _____ and the true kingdom of God. While some accept Him, most _____ Him, and He is crucified, buried, and resurrected.

ERA	FIGURE	LOCATION	STORY-LINE SUMMARY
_____	_____	_____	Peter, shortly after the _____ of Jesus, is used by God to _____ the _____, God's next major plan for man.
_____	_____	_____	Paul _____ the Church into the _____ Empire during the next two _____.

NINETEEN

THE EPISTLES

(Romans–Revelation)

In a *Reader's Digest* article entitled "Send Someone a Smile," a captivating story is told:

One day shortly after my third child was born I received a note from another young mother, a friend of mine who lived just three blocks from me. We hadn't seen each other all winter.

"Hi, friend," she wrote. "I think of you often. Someday we'll have time to spend together like in the old days. Keep plugging. I know you're a super mother. See you soon, I hope." It was signed: "Your friend on hold, Sue Ann."

The few words lifted my spirits and added a soothing ointment of love to a hectic day. I remember thinking, *Thanks, Sue Ann. I needed that.*

When I went out to mail a note, I noticed a neighbor checking his mailbox. Mr. Williams' head drooped and his pace seemed slower as he shuffled back to his house empty-handed. I hurried back into my own house because I could hear my baby crying, but I couldn't get Mr. Williams off my mind. It wasn't a check he was waiting for; he was quite well-to-do. He was probably looking for some love in his mailbox. While Meagan drew a picture of a mailbox with a smile in it and Tami drew a rainbow, I wrote a little note. "We are your secret admirers," it began. We added a favorite story and a poem. "Expect to hear from us often," I wrote on the envelope.

The next day my children and I watched Mr. Williams take out his mail and open the envelope right in the driveway. Even at a distance, we could see he was smiling.

My mind began reeling when I thought of all the people who could use smiles in their mailboxes. What about the 15-year-old

Down's-syndrome girl near my parents whose birthday was coming up? The people in the rest home near our house? The invalid woman in our old neighborhood? The endless people I didn't even know who still believed in courtesy and in doing a good job in stores and offices and restaurants? Even on busy days I could find the time to write at least one note.

Notes can be short, and should be anonymous. At first, I wanted credit for the notes. But now, writing them in secret adds a sense of adventure. It's more fun. I once overheard talk of the Phantom Note Lady. They were discussing me, but they didn't know, and I wasn't telling.

Paul and other writers of the Bible had similar concerns for people they loved. They wrote letters both to church congregations and to individuals to encourage them and to instruct them. In the providence of God, these letters were saved and eventually compiled in the "Epistles" section of the Bible. The Epistles were simply letters.

You will recall that thirteen of the Epistles were written by the apostle Paul while the remaining nine had a number of different authors. The chart in the review section below shows the distinction between the Pauline Epistles and the General Epistles.

I.   Review:

Structure of the New Testament

Historical	*Pauline*	*General*
Matthew	TO CHURCHES:	Hebrews
Mark	Romans	James
Luke	1 Corinthians	1 Peter
John	2 Corinthians	2 Peter
Acts	Galatians	1 John
	Ephesians	2 John
	Philippians	3 John
	Colossians	Jude
	1 Thessalonians	Revelation
	2 Thessalonians	
	TO INDIVIDUALS:	
	1 Timothy	
	2 Timothy	
	Titus	
	Philemon	

Our history study is now completed. From Matthew through Acts, we stretched out a time line for the history of the New Testament. Some of the Epistles were written during this time line, and some of them were written after the time line ends at the close of the Book of Acts. This makes it a little confusing, and somewhat frustrating, because we wish that the Historical Books told all the history during the time the Epistles were being written. They don't, however, and we are left to piece together what history we can from references in the Epistles.

The following chart shows when the Epistles were written in relationship to the time recorded in the Historical Books. The numbers are the years after Christ's birth. The Gospels cover the time from Christ's birth to His death at approximately age thirty. Acts starts almost immediately after, and records events until about A.D. 60. We see then that Galatians was written during the time of the Book of Acts, A.D. 48 specifically. First and Second Thessalonians were written about A.D. 50, etc. Books in the second section are Pauline Epistles, and the books in the last section are the General Epistles.

Time Line of the New Testament

Historical Books

Gospel–Acts						post–Acts		
A.D. **0**	A.D. **30**	A.D. **48**	A.D. **50**	A.D. **53**	A.D. **60**	A.D. **62**	A.D. **67**	A.D. **95**

Pauline Epistles

| | | Galatians | 1 Thessalonians 2 Thessalonians | 1 Corinthians 2 Corinthians Romans | Ephesians Colossians Philemon Philippians | 1 Timothy Titus | 2 Timothy | |

General Epistles

| | | James | | | | 1 Peter 2 Peter | Hebrews Jude | 1 John 2 John 3 John Revelation |

II.   Overview Summary: The *Epistles* are letters to churches and to individuals to *encourage* them and *instruct* them in the Christian faith.

REVIEW:

The *Epistles* are letters to churches and to individuals to _____ them and _____ them in the Christian faith.

III.   Expansion: There are four main topics to be dealt with in studying the Epistles:

1.   The Nature of the Epistles
2.   Pauline Epistles to Churches
3.   Pauline Epistles to Individuals
4.   General Epistles

1.   The Nature of the Epistles: Doctrine, then duty

Epistles are letters written to churches, individuals, or in some cases, general letters to the Christian public at large. They deal with specific problems and issues of the day but do so in a way that the information is universal and timeless. The typical pattern is to write a section of doctrinal truth and follow up with the practical implications of that truth. *Doctrine, then duty.* Principle, then practice.

2.   Pauline Epistles to Churches: Letters to local churches

Thirteen of the twenty-two Epistles of the New Testament are written by the apostle Paul. Nine of these are *letters to local churches* and are named according to which church they are written.

(As you read the description of the book, notice the words in *italics*. Immediately following the description of each book, the description is repeated with a blank space in place of the *italic* word. Fill in the blank space.)

Romans: heavily doctrinal, with the most complete doctrine of *salvation* by grace through faith in all the Bible.

Romans: heavily doctrinal, with the most complete doctrine of _____ by grace through faith in all the Bible.

1 and 2 Corinthians: heavily practical, dealing with a series of specific *problems* in the Corinthian church.

1 and 2 Corinthians: heavily practical, dealing with a series of specific _____ in the Corinthian church.

Galatians: written to some of Paul's first converts, refuting *legalism*.

Galatians: written to some of Paul's first converts, refuting _____.

Ephesians: deals with the believer's *position* in Christ and its practical implications.

Ephesians: deals with the believer's _____ in Christ and its practical implications.

Philippians: a warm letter of *joy* despite trials.

Philippians: a warm letter of _____ despite trials.

Colossians: the *preeminence* of Christ is its major theme.

Colossians: the _____ of Christ is its major theme.

1 and 2 Thessalonians: very personal letters dealing with specific issues in the Thessalonian church, including *prophecy* and *practical* living.

1 and 2 Thessalonians: very personal letters dealing with specific issues in the Thessalonian church, including _____ and _____ living.

3. **Pauline Epistles to Individuals: Letters to individuals and pastors.**

Four of Paul's letters are written *to individuals and pastors,* named according to whom they were written.

1 and 2 Timothy: two letters to a young pastor in Ephesus. The first letter *counsels* him on local church issues, and the second *encourages* him to remain strong in the faith in the midst of trials.

1 and 2 Timothy: two letters to a young pastor in Ephesus. The first letter _____ him on local church issues, and the second _____ him to remain strong in the faith in the midst of trials.

Titus: written to the pastor of the church on the island of Crete, it deals largely with local church issues, including the *qualifications* for church leaders.

Titus: written to the pastor of the church on the island of Crete, it deals largely with local church issues, including the _____ for church leaders.

Philemon: written to a slave owner, it urges lenient treatment of a runaway *slave* who has become a Christian and is returning to his Christian master.

Philemon: written to a slave owner, it urges lenient treatment of a runaway _____ who has become a Christian and is returning to his Christian master.

4. General Epistles: Letters to the Christian public

Written by various authors, the nine General Epistles are *letters to the Christian public* at large (with the exception of 2 and 3 John). They are usually named according to their authorship.

Hebrews: heavily *doctrinal,* this book draws largely on Old Testament truth in teaching New Testament truth to a Jewish audience.

Hebrews: heavily _____, this book draws largely on Old Testament truth in teaching New Testament truth to a Jewish audience.

James: an incisive and practical treatment of the proper outworking of Christian *faith* in everyday life.

James: an incisive and practical treatment of the proper outworking of Christian _____ in everyday life.

1 and 2 Peter: written to believers scattered throughout Asia and Galatia, it deals with the proper response to *suffering* and opposition.

1 and 2 Peter: written to believers scattered throughout Asia and Galatia, it deals with the proper response to _____ and opposition.

1, 2, and 3 John: letters from the apostle John dealing with the *love* of God and its outworking in Christians' lives.

1, 2, and 3 John: letters from the apostle John dealing with the _____ of God and its outworking in Christians' lives.

Jude: a brief but powerful book *warning* against ungodly living.

Jude: a brief but powerful book _____ against ungodly living.

Revelation: a giant of a book, heavily prophetical, dealing with the nature and chronology of the *end times.*

Revelation: a giant of a book, heavily prophetical, dealing with the nature and chronology of the _____ .

Review

(On the following pages match the correct book with its description.)

1. Pauline Epistles to Churches:

a. Colossians

b. Ephesians

c. Galatians

d. 1–2 Corinthians

e. Romans

f. 1–2 Thessalonians

g. Philippians

_____ heavily doctrinal, with the most complete doctrine of *salvation* by grace through faith in all the Bible

_____ heavily practical, dealing with a series of specific *problems* in the Corinthian church

_____ written to some of Paul's first converts, refuting *legalism*

_____ deals with the believer's *position* in Christ and its practical implications

_____ a warm letter of *joy* despite trials

_____ the *preeminence* of Christ is its major theme

_____ very personal letters dealing with specific issues in the Thessalonian church, including *prophecy* and *practical* living

2. Pauline Epistles to Individuals:

a. Philemon

b. 1–2 Timothy

c. Titus

_____ two letters to a young pastor in Ephesus. The first letter *counsels* him on local church issues, and the second *encourages* him to remain strong in the faith in the midst of trials

_____ written to the pastor of the church on the island of Crete, it deals largely with local church issues, including the *qualifications* for church leaders

_____ written to a slave owner, it urges lenient treatment of a runaway *slave* who has become a Christian and is returning to his Christian master

3. General Epistles:

a. Revelation

b. 1–2–3 John

c. Hebrews

d. 1–2 Peter

e. James

f. Jude

_____ heavily *doctrinal*, this book draws largely on Old Testament truth in teaching New Testament truth to a Jewish audience

_____ an incisive and practical treatment of the proper outworking of Christian *faith* in everyday life

_____ written to believers scattered throughout Asia and Galatia, it deals with the proper response to *suffering* and opposition

_____ letters from the apostle John dealing with the *love* of God and its outworking in Christians' lives

_____ a brief but powerful book *warning* against ungodly living

_____a giant of a book, heavily prophetical, dealing with the nature and chronology of the *end times*

Self-Test

Four Main Distinctions to Consider in Studying the Epistles

(Write in the correct epistles from the options at right.)

OPTIONS:	EPISTLES:	DESCRIPTION:
The Nature of the Epistles	_____	Letters to individuals and pastors
Pauline Epistles to Churches	_____	Letters to local churches
Pauline Epistles to Individuals	_____	Letters to the Christian public
General Epistles	_____	Doctrine, then duty

Congratulations! You have just completed a basic overview of the Story of the Bible, all sixty-six books! From the Historical Books of the Old and New Testaments, you have learned: all the main eras, all the central figures, and the main locations of geography, all tied together with a Story-Line Summary of the chronological Story of the Bible. You have also learned where the other books, the Poetical and Prophetical books of the Old Testament and the Epistles of the New Testament, fit into that chronological Story of the Bible.

You are now ready for the next section, which will give you a general overview of the entire Bible.

SECTION THREE

GENERAL
OVERVIEW
OF THE
BIBLE

A COMPARISON OF
THE FOUR GOSPELS

As I was writing this chapter, a friend of mine told me how confused he used to be about the fact that there were *four* Gospels. He was in the army in Vietnam, in a safe area, and bored to death, so he began to read the Book of Matthew in a New Testament that had been issued to him. He was mesmerized by it. He had never read the Bible before. When he finished Matthew, he immediately began reading Mark. He was surprised that it was largely the same story. In fact, almost all of Mark is contained within Matthew. But, still strongly interested, he kept reading. When he finished Mark he started Luke and, lo and behold! It was the same story. At that point, he made the assumption that all the books of the New Testament contained the same story, the story of the life of Christ, so it was no surprise to him when he finished Luke and started John that it was the same story once again. But John, he realized, was a little different from the first three Gospels.

With all this reading, he fell under the conviction of the Holy Spirit and yielded his life to Christ while reading the Gospel of John. When he finished John, as a new Christian, he eagerly started the Book of Acts, expecting it to be yet another account of the life of Christ. Imagine his surprise when it wasn't! His whole concept of the New Testament was shattered, though he admitted it was a welcome surprise. He remained confused for some time, however, as to why there were four Gospels.

The greater the person, the more books written about him after he dies. You find a great many books written about leaders such as Thomas Jefferson, Abraham Lincoln, and Winston Churchill. The reason is that different authors have different perspectives and different pieces of information about great persons. We are all aware of the political exploits of Thomas Jefferson, who wrote the Declaration of Independence and was our third president. But we are perhaps less aware of his abilities as an astronomer or as a musician or as a farmer. I have a book in my library entitled *The Domestic Life of Thomas Jefferson* that focuses on his home, his family, and his daily habits at Monticello, the plants he cultivated, the foods he preferred, the manner in which he entertained his friends, and so on. It hardly touches on his political life. I was very enriched by reading it, and I am glad that someone chose to write about his life from a perspective other than his political accomplishments.

That, in essence, is why there are four Gospels in the New Testament. These four men all had personal knowledge about Jesus. Some had spent years with Him. They all had different perspectives from which they observed His life. They were writing for different audiences. Matthew was a Jew and a tax collector. Luke was a Gentile and a physician. Mark had worked with Peter, Paul, and Barnabas. John waited longer to write his account. By having books written by all four of them, we have a more complete picture.

The New Testament opens with the four books called Gospels because they present the "good news" (the literal meaning of *gospel*) that God has come to die for man so that man can live with God. The four Gospels are targeted at different audiences, and each emphasizes a distinctive aspect of Jesus' identity and mission. Together these complementary accounts provide a rich and clear picture of Jesus. Matthew, Mark, and Luke are called the Synoptic (literally, "seen together") Gospels because, in contrast to John, they view Christ's life from much the same viewpoint and share many common details. John is different from the Synoptic Gospels and stands alone as a unique picture of the life of Christ.

1. Matthew

a. Overview

Matthew is the Gospel best suited to serve as the bridge between the Old Testament and the New. Matthew presents

Jesus as Israel's promised messianic king. It was written by a Jew
to convince a Jewish audience, and thus it has a strong Jewish
flavor. The book begins with a genealogy that goes back to
Abraham, the father of all Jews, to show Jesus' legal right to the
throne of David. Matthew makes a special effort to demonstrate
that all the significant events in the life of Jesus—His birth, birthplace, home, ministry, and death—directly fulfilled Old
Testament prophecy, and he quotes from the Old Testament
more than any other Gospel writer does.

b. Authorship

Each of the four Gospels is anonymous in the sense that
none specifically identifies the author, as many other New
Testament books do (for example, Rom. 1:1–4). The oldest
Greek manuscripts we possess title the first Gospel, "According to Matthew."

Matthew, also known as Levi (Mark 2:14; Luke 5:27), was
a publican, a Jewish tax collector who collected taxes for
the occupying Roman government. The tax collectors were
despised because of both their collaboration with the Romans, something no "good" Jew would do, and their greed
(they were allowed to keep as profit any money they could
collect above what they had promised the Romans). As a
tax collector, Matthew was (humanly speaking) one of the
least likely people in Israel to be chosen to serve as an
apostle (9:9–13; Mark 2:14; Luke 5:27) or to write one of
the four Gospels. However, evidence supports Matthew's
authorship of the first Gospel.

From the earliest times the ancient Church clearly and
unanimously identified Matthew as the author. A number
of internal indications also support authorship by this tax
collector. For example, the first Gospel has more references
to money than do any of the other three Gospels. Three
terms used in Matthew to describe money are found nowhere else in the New Testament: "the two-drachma tax"
(17:24), "a four-drachma coin" (17:27), and "talents"
(18:24). Matthew shows his Christian humility by continually referring to himself as "Matthew the tax collector."

c. Date

A date before A.D. 70 is probable since: (1) the destruction
of Jerusalem is predicted in Matthew 24, (2) the Gospel does

not indicate that Jerusalem had fallen, and (3) references to Jerusalem as the "Holy City" (4:5; 27:53) imply its continued existence.

d. Occasion and Purpose

First, Matthew wanted to convince unbelieving Jews that Jesus is the Messiah. Second, Matthew wrote to encourage Jewish believers by explaining God's plan for His kingdom. If the Jews had indeed crucified their Messiah and King, what would become of them? Matthew explains that although God would judge that generation of Israelites, the promised Davidic kingdom would be established at a later time. In the interim, believers are responsible to proclaim a message of faith in the Messiah while making disciples among all nations as the kingdom takes a different form.

Summary: The Gospel of Matthew was written by a Jew to an audience of Jews to convince them that Jesus was the Messiah, the *King* of the Jews.

REVIEW:

The Gospel of Matthew was written by a Jew to an audience of Jews to convince them that Jesus was the Messiah, the _____ of the Jews.

---

2. Mark

a. Overview

Mark's Gospel presents Jesus as the Servant who came "to serve, and to give His life a ransom for many" (10:45). Although Jesus starts by serving the multitudes, the second half of Mark focuses on His teaching and ministering to His disciples. Mark devotes 36 percent of his book to the events of Christ's final week, the eight days from His entry into Jerusalem (11:1–11) to His resurrection (16:1–8). This shortest of the Gospels is direct and to the point, emphasizing action rather than detailed teaching. The word *immediately* is found again and again throughout the book.

b. Authorship

The early church fathers unanimously agreed that: (1) the second Gospel was written by Mark, and (2) the source of information for this Gospel is the preaching of Peter.

We assume that the "Mark" referred to is the same person as the "John [Hebrew name], also called Mark [Latin name]" (Acts 12:12, 25; 15:37) mentioned ten times in the New Testament (see also Acts 13:5, 13; 15:39; Col. 4:10; 2 Tim. 4:11; Philem. 24; 1 Pet. 5:13).

John Mark was a Jewish Christian, the son of Mary, whose house was an early Christian meeting place (Acts 12:12). He may have become a Christian under the influence of Peter (note 1 Peter 5:13, where Peter referred to him as "my son"). After a falling out with the apostle Paul during a missionary trip, the rift was apparently healed, because Paul sent for Mark later on, writing "he is helpful to me in my ministry" (2 Tim. 4:11).

c. Date

The account in Mark centering around Jesus' prediction of the destruction of the temple in Jerusalem suggests a date before A.D. 70, which is when the temple was destroyed by the Roman army. Many scholars believe that Matthew and Luke used Mark's Gospel as a source for their own Gospels. If so, the book was probably written between A.D. 55 and 63.

d. Occasion and Purpose

The overwhelming testimony of the early church is that the second Gospel was written in Rome primarily for Gentile Roman Christians, and many features of the book support that conclusion. For example, Mark doesn't quote from the Old Testament much; he wouldn't be expected to do so for people who would be largely unacquainted with it. He explains Jewish customs, which he wouldn't have to do if he were writing to Jews (7:3–4). He uses the Roman method of measuring time (6:8), etc.

Mark's Gospel presents Jesus as the Servant who came "to serve, and to give His life as a ransom for many" (10:45); his purpose was primarily pastoral. The Greek word for *disciple* ("learner") occurs some forty times, always in the plural and always referring to more than the twelve apostles. One of the more striking aspects of Mark's presentation of the disciples is how often they misunderstand God's ways and Jesus' identity, and even deny Him (for example, 4:13, 40; 6:52; 7:17–19; 8:17–21; 14:21, 27). Mark apparently wanted his readers to understand that discipleship and failure are not mutually exclusive; biblical realism would help keep the Roman Christians from giving up in disillusionment when they faced hardship and stumbled.

Summary: Mark is a Jewish Christian, writing to Roman Christians, presenting Jesus as a perfect *Servant.*

REVIEW:

Mark is a Jewish Christian, writing to Roman Christians, presenting Jesus as a perfect _____.

---

3. Luke

a. Overview

Luke's Gospel presents Jesus as the perfect "Son of Man" who "came to seek and to save what was lost" (19:10). Luke emphasizes the perfect humanity and redemptive mission of Jesus. Christ's human qualities would be of particular interest to the Gospel's intended audience, first a government official known as Theophilus (1:3) and then others of an idealistic, Greek mind-set. Luke emphasizes the universal message of the gospel more than the other Gospel writers, writing often about the faith of women and children, outcasts from Jewish society, Gentiles, and Samaritans.

b. Authorship

No one in the early church questioned that the third Gospel was written by Luke, the "beloved physician" (Col. 4:14) and fellow missionary with Paul. The prologues to both Luke's Gospel (1:1–4) and Acts (1:1–5) indicate that both books are written to a man named Theophilus as a two-part story.

Luke was apparently a Gentile because in Col. 4:10–14 Paul notes that three other people were his only Jewish co-workers, but lists Luke with two Gentiles. The Greek language found in Luke and Acts is generally considered to be the finest among the New Testament writings. Luke's skillful use of Greek and his attitudes suggest that he was himself Greek. Tradition says he was from Antioch in Syria.

c. Date

Most scholars believe that Luke's Gospel was written subsequent to Mark's, which it used as a source. Luke clearly wrote the third Gospel before Acts, where it is referred to as "my former book" (Acts 1:1). Acts was most likely written before the time of Nero's persecution (A.D. 64), because Acts closes with Paul still alive and still in prison. Therefore, a time in the late fifties or early sixties seems to fit.

d. Occasion

Luke's Gospel is dedicated to "most excellent Theophilus" (1:3), a name meaning "dear to God" or "friend of God." The title "most excellent" or "most noble" indicates high social standing (compare with Acts 23:26; 24:3; and 26:25, where it is used to describe government officials). Theophilus may have been Luke's literary patron who would see that the book reached a wider audience. In any event, it is probable that Theophilus was a Gentile because of the book's special subject matter and the emphasis throughout the book that the proper response for *all* people is to follow Jesus.

Luke had two purposes in writing his Gospel. The first was to authenticate the faith of Theophilus by demonstrating that what he had been taught was firmly grounded in history (1:3–4). However, Luke's second purpose was to present Jesus as the Son of Man who has brought the salvation of God's kingdom to all who follow Him, Gentiles as well as Jews. As noted in the overview to this discussion, the theme of this Gospel is that Jesus is the perfect "Son of Man" who "came to seek and to save what was lost" (19:10).

Summary: Luke is a Greek who writes to a Greek audience to convince them that Jesus was the perfect Son of *Man*.

REVIEW:

Luke is a Greek who writes to a Greek audience to convince them that Jesus was the perfect Son of _____.

---

4. John

a. Overview

John writes to convince a universal audience that Jesus is the Son of God so that they might have eternal life through belief in Him (20:30–31). To this end John tells us that he is building his Gospel around seven miraculous signs that

Jesus did. In addition to the seven signs, John records seven great sayings of Christ that begin with the words "I am."

b. Authorship

Strictly speaking, the fourth Gospel, like the other three, is anonymous. The author is identified only as the disciple "whom Jesus loved" (13:23; 20:2; 21:7; and compare with 19:26). Evidence from the early church fathers favors an identification with John the elder of Ephesus, who was probably the apostle John. A process of elimination leaves the apostle John as the most likely candidate.

John and his brother James were sons of Zebedee; Jesus nicknamed them "Sons of Thunder" (Mark 3:17). Both were Galilean fishermen prior to their call by Jesus (John 1:19–51). A comparison of several texts suggests that they were also first cousins to Jesus. (This would help explain Jesus' command from the cross for John to take care of His mother Mary; see 19:27.) Both James and John were selected as apostles (Mark 3:16–19) and, with Peter, served as the inner circle of that group (for example, see Mark 5:37; 9:32; 14:33). Most scholars believe that John was "the disciple whom Jesus loved," or the apostle to whom Christ was closest.

John became one of the leaders in the early church at Jerusalem along with Peter and James (the half-brother of Christ, not the brother of John who became an early martyr) (Gal. 2:9). There is a strong tradition that John later spent many years laboring in the church at Ephesus that Paul had founded. John is believed to have died in exile on Patmos, an island off the coast of Asia Minor (compare with Rev. 1:9–11).

c. Date

The probable range for this work, which, according to tradition, was written in Ephesus, is A.D. 70–90.

d. Occasion and Purpose

This Gospel clearly states its purpose: "these [miraculous signs] are written that you may believe that Jesus is the Christ, the Son of God, and that by believing you may have life in his name" (20:31 NIV). John wrote his Gospel to supplement the already-written three Synoptic Gospels. He indicated that he was selective in his choice of material (20:30). He picked certain signs to prove that Jesus was worthy of faith. Whereas Matthew clearly wrote for a Jewish audience and Mark and Luke seem to have had the Gentile world (Roman and Greek) in mind, John's Gospel appears to be directed toward a universal audience. John wanted to convince his Jewish readers that Jesus is the Messiah and his Gentile readers that Jesus is the Son of God. He wrote not so much to present new information as to confront his readers with the necessity of making a choice so that they might gain eternal life.

Summary: John wrote to a universal audience to convince them that Jesus was the Son of *God*.

REVIEW:

John wrote to a universal audience to convince them that Jesus was the Son of _____.

Review

1. Overview:

   a. The four Gospels record the life of Jesus, each from a different *perspective*.

   b. Three Gospels are called synoptic (literally, "seen together") because they present the life of Christ from basically the same *historical* point of view. They are Matthew, Mark, and Luke.

   c. John presents the life of Christ from a *thematic* viewpoint, highlighting seven miracles and seven "sayings" of Christ.

2. Gospels:

   a. Matthew was a Jew, writing to an audience of Jews to convince them that Jesus was the Messiah, the *King* of the Jews.

   b. Mark was a Jewish Christian, writing to Roman Christians, presenting Jesus as a perfect *Servant*.

c. Luke wrote to a Greek audience to convince them that Jesus was the perfect Son of *Man*.

d. John wrote to a universal audience to convince them that Jesus was the Son of *God*.

Self-Test

1. Overview:

a. The four Gospels record the life of Jesus, each from a different _____.

b. Three Gospels are called synoptic (literally, "seen together") because they present the life of Christ from basically the same _____ point of view. They are Matthew, Mark, and Luke.

c. John presents the life of Christ from a _____ viewpoint, highlighting seven miracles and seven "sayings" of Christ.

2. Gospels:

a. Matthew was a Jew, writing to an audience of Jews to convince them that Jesus was the Messiah, the _____ of the Jews.

b. Mark was a Jewish Christian, writing to Roman Christians, presenting Jesus as a perfect _____.

c. Luke wrote to a Greek audience to convince them that Jesus was the perfect Son of _____.

d. John wrote to a universal audience to convince them that Jesus was the Son of _____.

TWENTY-ONE

THE PARABLES OF JESUS

 We all love a good story, so we all love a good storyteller. A person who can tell a good story will never lack an audience. All comedians are, essentially, just good storytellers. The most popular speakers are often good storytellers. Presidents John Kennedy and Ronald Reagan were both great storytellers. Their humor, candor, and ability to poke fun at themselves were winsome characteristics that endeared them to the American public.

Kennedy was especially clever with quips. During World War II, Kennedy held a commission in the U.S. Navy and served in the Pacific. In August 1943 in Blackout Strait in the Solomon Islands, a Japanese destroyer rammed his ship. Kennedy, with some others, reached a nearby island but found it was held by the Japanese. He and another officer then swam to another island, where they persuaded the inhabitants to send a message to other U.S. forces, who rescued them. After his election as president, Kennedy's comment on his reputation as a hero was, "It was involuntary. They sank my boat."

Ronald Reagan was great with quips and stories. In his autobiography (*Ronald Reagan, An American Life*, p. 700), he tells of the time when he was negotiating a reduction in nuclear arms with Mikhail Gorbachev, then general secretary of the Soviet Union. Reagan felt that a story would loosen both of them up a bit.

> I told him I'd been collecting stories about the Russians; although there were quite a few I'd heard that I *couldn't* tell him, I told him one about an American and a Russian who

were arguing over the respective merits of their countries. The American said, "Look, in my country I can walk into the oval office and I can pound on the president's desk and say, 'Mr. President, I don't like the way you are running the country,'" to which the Russian said, "I can do that, too." The American said, "You can?" and his friend said: "Sure, I can go into the Kremlin and pound on the general secretary's desk and say, 'Mr. General Secretary, I don't like the way President Reagan is running his country.'"

The interpreter translated the joke, and when he got to the punch line, Gorbachev howled.

Then I told him about an order that had gone out to traffic policemen in Moscow stating that, in the future, anyone caught speeding would be given a traffic ticket, no matter how important he might be. One day, I said, the general secretary was leaving his home in the country and, discovering he was late for a meeting in the Kremlin, he told his driver: "Here, you get in the back seat and I'll drive."

Down the road, they passed two motorcycle policemen and one of them took after the car. A few minutes later, he rejoined the other policeman, who asked him, "Did you give him a ticket?"

"No," the traffic cop said.

"Why not? We were told that no matter who it was, we were to give him a ticket."

"No, this guy was too important," his friend said.

"Who was it?"

His friend said: "I don't know. I couldn't recognize him, but his driver was Gorbachev."

He howled again.

Jesus was a great storyteller. Not in the same way that Reagan and Kennedy were. Reagan and Kennedy's stories were often funny. Jesus' stories were told to impart spiritual information and wisdom. His stories were called *parables*. Approximately one-third of Jesus Christ's teaching as recorded in the Gospels is in this distinctive literary form. Indeed, Jesus used parables so often that Matthew wrote that "he did not say anything to them without using a parable" (13:34 NIV). What are parables? Why did Jesus employ them so frequently? How are parables to be interpreted? What are some of the key truths Christ sought to communicate through this form? These are the questions we will answer in this chapter.

1. The Nature of Parables

One typical definition of a parable is "a saying or story that seeks to drive home a point the speaker wishes to emphasize by illustrating it from a familiar situation of common life" (F. F. Bruce, *Zondervan Pictorial Encyclopedia of the Bible,* vol. 4, p. 590). As J. Dwight Pentecost points out in his book, *The Parables of Jesus,* the word *parable* is used to describe a number of different figures of speech. For example, a parable may take the form of a *simile,* a stated likeness using the words *like* or *as.* Jesus said, "I am sending you out *like* sheep among wolves. Therefore be *as* shrewd *as* snakes and *as* innocent *as* doves."

A second form a parable may take is that of a *metaphor,* an implied likeness. For example, Jesus urged His disciples, "Do not be afraid, little flock, for your Father has been pleased to give you the kingdom" (Luke 12:32 NIV).

A parable may take the form of a *similitude* in which the truth being taught is based on what people generally do rather than on what a certain individual actually did. One example is when Christ stated, "The kingdom of heaven is like yeast that a woman took and mixed into a large amount of flour until it worked all through the dough" (Matt. 13:33 NIV). Anyone familiar with the bread-making process can learn the truth through this reference to a common procedure.

The form of the parable Jesus used most frequently to teach His hearers was the *story.* The story-parable teaches truth by relating a specific incident and calling attention to what one individual did. Consequently, Christ introduced story-parables with words such as, "There was a man who had two sons" (Luke 15:11 NIV) and, "In a certain town there was a judge" (Luke 18:2 NIV). The story-parable is what most people think of when they think of parables.

The common denominator among these and less-common forms of the parable is that all teach truth based upon transference from reality. The content is familiar and possible.

> **Summary**: A parable is a story intended to communicate a *spiritual* truth, illustrating it with a familiar situation of common life.

REVIEW:

A parable is a story intended to communicate a _____
truth, illustrating it with a familiar situation of common life.

---

2. The Purpose of Parables

Why did Jesus Christ use parables so extensively? He Himself explained why He employed parables in response to His disciples' question, "Why do you speak to the people in parables?" (Matt. 13:10 NIV). They raised the question immediately after He related the parable of the sower, the seed, and the soils (Matt. 13:3–9). The timing of the disciples' question is interesting. Christ had employed other parable forms before, but this was the first time He had used the extended story-parable form. Jesus explained His use of story-parables this way:

> The knowledge of the secrets of the kingdom of heaven has been given to you, but not to them. Whoever has will be given more, and he will have an abundance. Whoever does not have, even what he has will be taken from him. This is why I speak to them in parables: Though seeing, they do not see; / though hearing, they do not hear or understand./In them is fulfilled the prophecy of Isaiah: "You will be hearing but never understanding; / you will be ever seeing but never perceiving." (Matt. 13:11–14 NIV)

In other words, Jesus' parables had two basic purposes. The first purpose was to reveal truth to believers. Parables can communicate truth more vividly and more powerfully than ordinary dialogue. For example, Christ could have simply instructed His hearers to be persistent in prayer, an exhortation they might have shrugged off and forgotten. Instead, He told them the story of a widow whose continued begging for help finally persuaded an unjust judge to grant her petitions so that she would no longer bother him (Luke 18:1–8). The lesson: If an unjust and uncaring judge will respond to continued pleas, how much more will persistent prayer be answered by a loving heavenly Father?

The second basic purpose of parables is to hide truth from those who have already hardened their hearts against it. Christ taught a mixed audience, some of whom had placed their faith in His person and message while others had already decided to reject Him. He wished to teach believers, but not to increase the responsibility (and guilt) of those who would not believe, by revealing additional truth to them (see Luke 12:47–48). Resistance to known spiritual truth hardens the heart and makes one less and less able to understand and respond in faith.

> **Summary**: Jesus taught in parables to *reveal* truth to the believers and to *conceal* truth from the unbelievers.

REVIEW:

Jesus taught in parables to _____ truth to the believers and to _____ truth from the unbelievers.

---

3. The Interpretation of Parables

Christ expected believers to understand the parables He related and to perceive the truth He sought to communicate through them. After the Jewish leaders rejected Him as Messiah, Jesus interpreted only two parables: the parable of the sower, the seeds, and the soils, and the parable of the weeds. Christ offered these two interpretations to serve as a model for how to understand this new teaching form. Proper interpretation of the parables demands the correct application of certain principles.

The parables were not spoken in a vacuum. Each parable addresses a particular situation, problem, or question. For example, the parable of the laborers in the vineyard (Matt. 20:1–16) should be understood in terms of the immediate context. Just prior to this parable Jesus, realizing that what hindered the rich young ruler from fully following God was his wealth, had instructed the man to give away his riches and become a disciple. The young man went away sad because he was unwilling to part with his wealth.

Peter then asked Christ, "We have left everything to follow you! What then will there be for us?" (Matt. 19:27 NIV). After promising that His disciples would be well rewarded for their service, Jesus told the parable of the laborers. The parable was a gentle rebuke to Peter's self-righteous attitude that said (in effect), "See how much I have done. Unlike the rich young ruler,

I have left all to follow You. How will You reward my great sacrifice?" Peter's attitude was one of self-interest and concern for personal benefit rather than recognizing that service in God's kingdom is to be motivated by love.

Once you have found a limit to the interpretation of the parable from the context, you must study the parable itself to determine the point at issue. An important principle of interpretation is that each parable is designed to communicate one central idea; details are only significant to the degree that they relate to that idea. For example, the parable of the persistent widow (Luke 18:1–8) focuses not on the character of the judge but on the persistence of the widow as an illustration of how we should persist in prayer. If we give undue attention to the detail of the judge's character, we might (falsely) conclude that God is an unrighteous and uncaring person who will only answer our prayers if we weary Him with our requests.

Summary: Parables must be interpreted in light of the *context* in which they are found.

REVIEW:

Parables must be interpreted in light of the _____ in which they are found.

---

4.   The Historical Setting of Parables

You cannot understand the parable of the sower unless you understand the process of sowing seeds. You cannot understand the parable about putting new wine into old wineskins unless you understand thoroughly the process of winemaking in Jesus' day. We need to understand the details from the perspective of Christ's original hearers. Tools such as a biblical encyclopedia and a book on biblical customs can help you understand the culture, customs, and daily life of those to whom Christ was communicating.

Summary: Parables must be interpreted in light of the *historical* setting in which they occur.

REVIEW:

Parables must be interpreted in light of the _____ setting in which they occur.

Review

1. A parable is a story intended to communicate a *spiritual* truth, illustrating it with a familiar situation of common life.

2. Jesus taught in parables to *reveal* truth to the believers and to *conceal* truth from the unbelievers.

3. Parables must be interpreted in light of the *context* in which they are found.

4. Parables must be interpreted in light of the *historical* setting in which they occur.

Self-Test

1. A parable is a story intended to communicate a _____ truth, illustrating it with a familiar situation of common life.

2. Jesus taught in parables to _____ truth to the believers and to _____ truth from the unbelievers.

3. Parables must be interpreted in light of the _____ in which they are found.

4. Parables must be interpreted in light of the _____ setting in which they occur.

MIRACLES IN THE BIBLE

 A man once asked a pastor, in a rather cynical tone, what a miracle was. The pastor gave the man a full and complete explanation. All during the explanation, the man was fidgeting, his body language betraying that he didn't think much of the answer he was getting. "Now won't you give me an example of a miracle?" he demanded when the pastor finally finished.

"Well," said the pastor, "step over here in front of me, bend over, and I will see what I can do." As the man did the pastor gave him a terrific kick in the seat of the pants.

"Did you feel that?" the pastor asked.

"I sure did feel it!" the startled man replied.

"Well," said the pastor, "it would have been a miracle if you hadn't."

Miracles are often misunderstood. People have the wrong expectations of God and the wrong understanding of the purpose of miracles, and they can fall into discouragement or disappointment with God or with Christianity as a result. Other people doubt the possibility of miracles altogether.

The figures vary from one survey to the next, but from 75 percent to 95 percent of the people in America, as of this writing, claim to believe in God. Yet some of those people don't believe in miracles. That seems ridiculous to me. If you are going to have a God, what good is He if He can't do a miracle? If God could not perform miracles He, by definition, is no longer God.

Christianity, unlike other religions, rests upon God's *doing* miracles. The claims of Christianity stand or fall depending upon these miracles, especially the Resurrection. As Paul recognized, if Jesus Christ has not been raised from the dead then our faith is futile, we are still in our sins, and we are more to be pitied than all men (1 Cor. 15:17–19).

But it is important to understand why and when God does miracles. So in this chapter we will look at miracles in the Bible and see if we can gain a clearer understanding and a greater appreciation of them.

1. The Possibility and Nature of Miracles

What is the biblical concept of miracles? A miracle is an event that runs contrary to the observed processes of nature— that is, to *what is known* of nature. Different words are used in the Bible to refer to miracles. Those terms highlight different aspects of the nature of miracles. The word *wonder* reveals that such events are amazing, while the term *power* implies the need for more than human capability. The word *sign* indicates that they must be visible events, for this is essential to their purpose.

Some people have argued on philosophic or scientific grounds that miracles such as those described in the Bible are impossible. But one can only deny the possibility of miracles if one denies the existence of God. If God is a living, personal being, "miracles are not only possible, they are appropriate; and whether or not one has occurred is not a question for secular science, but is a matter of testimony by divinely appointed witnesses" (Christian philosopher Gordon Clark in *Zondervan Pictorial Encyclopedia of the Bible,* vol. 4, p. 249).

> **Summary**: Miracles are events that run contrary to what we know of nature and are *possible* if God exists.

REVIEW:

Miracles are events that run contrary to what we know of nature and are _____ if God exists.

---

2. The Purpose of Biblical Miracles

What is the purpose of miracles? Scripture states their aim in various places. For example, in Exodus 4:5 God instructed

Moses to perform miracles "that they may believe that the LORD, the God of their fathers, . . . has appeared to you." Miracles attested to Moses' divine mission. Likewise, miracles supported the claims of Jesus and demonstrated, as they did for Moses (Deut. 18:15), that He was the promised prophet. That was the basis for the request by some of the Pharisees and teachers of the law, "Teacher, we want to see a miraculous sign from You" (Matt. 12:38). Nicodemus recognized that Jesus was a teacher from God because of the miraculous signs He was performing (John 3:2). So miracles served to validate the authority and message of a divine messenger.

> **Summary**: Miracles *validate* the authority and message of the divine messenger.

REVIEW:

Miracles _____ the authority and message of the divine messenger.

---

3. The Periods of Biblical Miracles

Contrary to the impression of many, miracles were *not* God's typical way of working with His people in Scripture. Most biblical miracles revolve around the giving of new revelation in three brief periods of history: the two-generation eras of Moses and Joshua, Elijah and Elisha, and Jesus and the apostles. Comparatively few miracles are recorded during the intervening centuries. Let's look at each of these periods.

a. Moses and Joshua (1441–1370 B.C.)

God was delivering the Israelites out of bondage in Egypt and into the Promised Land of Canaan. New revelation was being given through the Law, the first five books of the Bible. God used miracles to authenticate: (1) Moses and his message, (2) Joshua and his authority, and (3) His own identity as the true God (see Ex. 10:1–2).

In Exodus 10:1–2 God revealed to Moses that part of His motivation in performing the "signs" of judgment known as the ten plagues was to demonstrate that He was the Lord. The Bible reveals that God judged the many gods of Egypt and demonstrated His superiority over them through the ten plagues (Ex. 12:12; 18:11; Num. 33:4). Each of the plagues showed God's superiority over one or more of the Egyptian gods. For example, the first plague was turning the Nile River into blood (Ex. 7:14–25). This river was seen as the source of Egypt's prosperity and life. The recognition of their dependence upon the river led the Egyptians to deify it under the figure of the bull god Hapi (also called Apis). The Nile was also associated with other gods such as the goddess Isis, who protected children, and Khnum, ram god and guardian of the Nile. The annual rebirth of the god of the earth and vegetation, Osiris, was symbolized by the Nile's yearly flooding of its banks. The transformation of the Nile resulted in fish dying, the water becoming undrinkable due to its stench, and Egyptian agriculture being threatened (7:21). The river seen as the source of life for Egypt became tainted with death.

During the life of Moses and Joshua, many stupendous miracles were performed, but they always were for the purpose of bolstering the faith of the people to believe in God and to trust in Him for their lives.

b. Elijah and Elisha (870–785 B.C.)

Worship of the false god Baal had become a serious threat to Israel's existence as a nation under God. It seems incredible, but even the Israelites were worshiping the false god. Therefore, God raised up Elijah and Elisha as prophets to promote revival and call the people to repentance. Miracles were used to prove that these men came from God, and that God was superior to Baal. One noteworthy example is found in 1 Kings 18:20–40, where there is a great contest, if you will, between God and Baal. God wins. The miracles ceased after these prophets delivered their unique message.

c. Christ and the apostles (c. 30–70 A.D.)

Proof was needed to demonstrate that Jesus was both God and man. John tells us that Jesus did many miraculous signs that John did not record, but that the signs he did include were written "that you may believe that Jesus is the Christ, the Son of God; and that believing you may have life in His name" (John 20:31). The purpose of the miracles is illustrated and confirmed by Jesus' statement that He had completed the work the Father had given Him (John 17:4), though there were doubtless still sick people, for example.

Now imagine that you were a sincere Jew. You want to be open to whatever God is doing in the world. Particularly, you don't want to miss the Messiah; that is all you have been waiting for all your life! So here comes a man who claims to be the Messiah. Why would you believe him? Lots of people have come and gone who claimed to be the Messiah. Why would you believe this one?

Jesus, I think, was sensitive to this. Sincere Jews had to have sufficient reason to transfer their belief from the Law to the Messiah. And the one asking them to do so appeared to be so ordinary on the outside. Why would *you* do it? What would be sufficient for *you* to make such a decision?

The answer? Miracles. Jesus claimed to be the light of the world, then He healed a blind man. He claimed to be the bread of life, then He fed the five thousand. He claimed to be the resurrection and the life, then He raised Lazarus from the dead.

John 6:1–15 describes how Jesus miraculously fed five thousand men (plus women and children) by multiplying a few fishes and loaves of bread. The next day when the crowd wished for a repeat feeding (6:26–34) Jesus' response was, "I am the bread of life" (6:35); that is, He was their necessary food, essential to true life.

In John 8:12 Christ said "I am the light of the world." The Bible portrays the world as being in darkness, which symbolizes evil, sin, and ignorance (Isa. 9:2; Matt. 4:16; 27:45; John 3:19). *Light* often represents God and His holiness (Acts 9:3; 1 John 1:5). Jesus proclaimed Himself to be "*the* Light," not merely a light among many lights (compare with John 1:9). By this Jesus meant that He alone was the genuine light that could distinguish between truth and falsehood and provide spiritual direction. In 9:5 Christ repeated, "While I am in the world, I am the light of the world." Immediately afterward, He restored the sight of a man who had been blind from birth as an outward, physical representation of His ability to enlighten those in spiritual darkness (9:6–7).

To Martha, grieving over the death of her brother Lazarus, Jesus declared: "I am the resurrection and the life; he who believes in Me shall live even if he dies; and everyone who lives and believes in Me shall never die" (John 11:25–26). By this Jesus indicated that He embodied the resurrection life that could overcome death. He authenticated this claim by proceeding to raise Lazarus from the dead.

Paul tells us that the apostles' miracles were related to proving their authority (2 Cor. 12:12) as they taught the new message of God made flesh and wrote the New Testament. Although God can perform a miracle whenever He chooses, miracles as recorded in the Bible began phasing out as the message of the gospel began to become established (Heb. 2:3–4).

Summary: Miracles occurred primarily in *three* concentrated times in history.

REVIEW:

Miracles occurred primarily in _____ concentrated times in history.

---

4. The Seven Signs of John's Gospel

Of the many signs performed by Jesus, John selects seven (not counting the resurrection or the miraculous fish catch described in John 21) to prove that Jesus was God's Son. Seven is the biblical number of completeness, and each sign revealed some specific characteristic of Jesus' power and person. They are, in order:

a. The Changing of Water into Wine (2:1–11)

Jesus showed Himself to be the master of *quality* by instantly accomplishing a change that the vine and the winemaking process produce over several months.

b. The Healing of the Nobleman's Son (4:46–54)

Jesus' healing of a boy more than twenty miles away revealed His mastery over *distance*, or space.

c. The Healing of the Impotent Man (5:1–9)

Disease becomes more difficult to cure the longer it afflicts a person. Jesus' instant healing of a man who had been ill for thirty-eight years demonstrated His mastery over *time*.

d. The Feeding of the Five Thousand (6:1–14)

By multiplying a boy's lunch of five loaves of bread and two fishes into sufficient food to feed five thousand men plus women and children, Jesus proved Himself to be the master over *quantity*.

e. The Walking on the Water (6:16–21)

By this miracle Jesus showed Himself to be master over *natural law*.

f. The Healing of the Man Born Blind (9:1–12)

Jesus healed this man in response to the question as to why this man should have been so afflicted, thus indicating His mastery over *misfortune*.

g. The Raising of Lazarus (11:1–16)

This miracle proved Jesus' mastery over *death*.

As Merrill C. Tenney summarizes in *John: The Gospel of Belief* (p. 31):

Quality, space, time, quantity, natural law, misfortune, and death circumscribe humanity's world. Daily existence is a struggle against their limitations. Christ's superiority over them as revealed by these events called signs was proof of His deity.

Summary: Jesus demonstrated, in the Gospel of John, His superiority over the *limitations* of this life.

REVIEW:

Jesus demonstrated, in the Gospel of John, His superiority over the _____ of this life.

Review

1. Miracles are events that run contrary to what we know of nature and are *possible* if God exists.

2. Miracles *validate* the authority and message of the divine messenger.

3. Miracles occurred primarily in *three* concentrated times in history.

4. Jesus demonstrated, in the Gospel of John, His superiority over the *limitations* of this life.

Self-Test

1. Miracles are events that run contrary to what we know of nature and are _____ if God exists.

2. Miracles _____ the authority and message of the divine messenger.

3. Miracles occurred primarily in _____ concentrated times in history.

4. Jesus demonstrated, in the Gospel of John, His superiority over the _____ of this life.

TWENTY-THREE

MESSIANIC PROPHECIES

 It is a pretty amazing thing when someone can tell the future. There is something very compelling about prophecy since the future is unknown to us. It is so compelling, in fact, that when a person appears to tell the future occasionally, that person often receives great notoriety. An American woman named Jeane Dixon offered predictions that sometimes came true and sometimes didn't. Her predictions often appeared in the tabloid newspapers at grocery-store checkout stands, particularly in December, when she gave her predictions for the new year.

She was undaunted by her predictions that don't come true. She claimed her ability was from God and her accurate predictions were from God. The ones that didn't come true, well, she must have gotten mixed up and, because of her own faulty understanding, uttered something that was not of God. Through this convoluted thinking, she claimed complete accuracy!

In the Old Testament, the test of a prophet was wonderfully effective: If anyone claimed to prophesy for God and his prophecy did not come true, he was stoned to death. Jeane Dixon would have been stoned many times under that system. She was not a prophetess of God.

Still, predicting the future is very compelling. If anyone can do it, it is very convincing.

The New Testament appeals to two main lines of evidence to prove that Jesus is the Messiah, the Son of God. The first is Jesus' resurrection, which will be discussed in chapter 25. The second type of evidence is Christ's fulfillment of hundreds of prophecies contained in the Old Testament regarding the Messiah. The fulfillment of these detailed prophecies, written hundreds of years before Jesus was born, validates His credentials as the Messiah.

1. The Importance of Messianic Prophecy

God's true divinity is demonstrated by His ability to reveal events in advance of their occurrence (see, for example, Isa. 48:3, 5). God placed more than three hundred references to the Messiah in the Old Testament, and they were fulfilled by Jesus Christ in order to help the Jews recognize their Messiah when He came.

Despite this help, Christ's disciples and contemporaries did not immediately understand how He fulfilled all of the prophecies. For example, in one of his post-resurrection appearances Christ joined two disciples as they walked to a village called Emmaus, located seven miles from Jerusalem. The disciples, who were supernaturally kept from recognizing Him, were dismayed over the death of Jesus, whom they had hoped would be the Messiah. Jesus responded:

> "How foolish you are, and how slow of heart to believe all that the prophets have spoken! Did not the Christ have to suffer these things and then enter his glory?" And beginning with Moses and all the Prophets, he explained to them what was said in all the Scriptures concerning himself. (Luke 24:25–27 NIV)

Later that same day Jesus appeared to the apostles and those with them and said: "'This is what I told you while I was still with you: Everything must be fulfilled that is written about me in the Law of Moses, the Prophets and the Psalms.' Then he opened their minds so they could understand the Scriptures" (Luke 24:44–45 NIV).

Once the disciples thoroughly understood these things, Christ's fulfillment of the Old Testament messianic prophecies became central to their presentation of the gospel. Paul wrote the Corinthians that the gospel was "that Christ died for our sins *according to the Scriptures,* that he was buried, that he was raised on the third day *according to the Scriptures*" (1 Cor. 15:3 NIV, emphasis added).

Summary: The ability to predict events before they occur demonstrates God's *power*.

REVIEW:

The ability to predict events before they occur demonstrates God's _____.

---

2.   Key Messianic Prophecies Fulfilled by Jesus

Sixty-one major prophecies in the Old Testament were fulfilled by Jesus. Some of the key prophecies include:

Descendant of Abraham

Prophesied—Genesis 12:3:

And I will bless those who bless you, / And the one who curses you I will curse. / And in you all the families of the earth shall be blessed.

Fulfilled—Matthew 1:1:

"The book of the genealogy of Jesus Christ, the son of David, the son of Abraham."

From the Tribe of Judah

Prophesied—Genesis 49:10:

The scepter shall not depart from Judah, / Nor the ruler's staff from between his feet, / Until Shiloh comes, / And to him shall be the obedience of the peoples.

Fulfilled—Luke 3:33:

"The son of Amminadab, the son of Admin, the son of Ram, the son of Hezron, the son of Perez, the son of Judah."

Heir to the Throne of David

Prophesied—Isaiah 9:7:

There will be no end to the increase of His government or of peace, / On the throne of David and over his kingdom, / To establish it and to uphold it with justice and righteousness / From then on and forevermore. / The zeal of the LORD of hosts will accomplish this.

Fulfilled—Luke 1:32:

"He will be great, and will be called the Son of the Most High; and the Lord God will give Him the throne of His father David; and He will reign over the house of Jacob forever; and His kingdom will have no end."

Born in Bethlehem

Prophesied—Micah 5:2:

But as for you, Bethlehem Ephrathah, / Too little to be among the clans of Judah, / From you One will go forth for Me to be ruler in Israel. / His goings forth are from long ago, / From the days of eternity.

Fulfilled—Luke 2:4–5, 7:

"And Joseph also went up from Galilee, from the city of Nazareth, to Judea, to the city of David, which is called Bethlehem, because he was of the house and family of David, in order to register, along with Mary, who was engaged to him, and was with child. . . . And she gave birth to her first-born son; and she wrapped Him in cloths, and laid Him in a manger, because there was no room for them in the inn."

Triumphal Entry

Prophesied—Zechariah 9:9:

Rejoice greatly, O daughter of Zion! / Shout in triumph, O daughter of Jerusalem! / Behold, your king is coming to you; / He is just and endowed with salvation, / Humble, and mounted on a donkey, / Even on a colt, the foal of a donkey.

Fulfilled—Mark 11:7, 9, 11:

"And they brought the colt to Jesus and put their garments on it; and He sat upon it. . . . And those who went before, and those who followed after, were crying out, "Hosanna! / BLESSED IS HE WHO COMES IN THE NAME OF THE LORD." . . . And He entered Jerusalem and came into the temple; and after looking all around, He departed for Bethany with the twelve, since it was already late."

Betrayed by Close Friend

Prophesied—Psalm 41:9:

Even my close friend, in whom I trusted, / Who ate my bread, / Has lifted up his heel against me.

Fulfilled—Luke 22:47–48:

"While He was still speaking, behold, a multitude came, and the one called Judas, one of the twelve, was preceding them; and he approached Jesus to kiss Him. But Jesus said to him, 'Judas, are you betraying the Son of Man with a kiss?'"

Betrayed for Thirty Pieces of Silver
Prophesied—Zechariah 11:12:

And I said to them, "If it is good in your sight, give me my wages; but if not, never mind!" So they weighed out thirty shekels of silver as my wages.

Fulfilled—Matthew 26:14–15:

"Judas Iscariot went to the chief priests, and said, "What are you willing to give me to deliver Him up to you?" And they weighed out to him thirty pieces of silver."

Forsaken by God
Prophesied—Psalms 22:1:

My God, my God, why hast Thou forsaken me? / Far from my deliverance are the words of my groaning.

Fulfilled—Matthew 27:46:

"And about the ninth hour Jesus cried out with a loud voice, saying, 'ELI, ELI, LAMA SABACHTHANI?' that is, 'MY GOD, MY GOD, WHY HAST THOU FORSAKEN ME?'"

Summary: Sixty-one major prophecies in the Old Testament were *fulfilled* by Christ.

REVIEW:

Sixty-one major prophecies in the Old Testament were _____ by Christ.

---

3.   Objections

There are those who suggest that the prophecies that Jesus fulfilled were done so deliberately or by coincidence. However, the odds against that happening are so remote as to make it impossible. For example, Josh McDowell, in his book *Evidence that Demands a Verdict*, includes a convincing quote from *Science Speaks* by Peter Stoner:

> The following probabilities are taken from Peter Stoner in *Science Speaks* to show that coincidence is ruled out by the science of probability. Stoner says that by using the modern science of probability in reference to eight prophecies . . . "we find that the chance that any man might have lived down to the present time and fulfilled all eight prophecies is 1 in 10^{17}." That would be 1 in 100,000,000,000,000,000. In order to help us comprehend this staggering probability, Stoner illustrates it by supposing that "we take 10^{17} silver dollars and lay them on the face of Texas. They will cover all of the state two feet deep. Now mark one of these silver dollars and stir the whole mass thoroughly, all over the state. Blindfold a man and tell him that he can travel as far as he wishes, but he must pick up one silver dollar and say that this is the right one. What chance would he have of getting the right one? Just the same chance that the prophets would have had of writing these eight prophecies and having them all come true in any one man, from their day to the present time, providing they wrote them in their own wisdom.
>
> "This means these prophecies were either given by inspiration of God or the prophets just wrote them as they thought they should be. In such a case the prophets had just one chance in 10^{17} of having them come true in any man, but they all came true in Christ."

Summary: The *fulfilled* prophecies suggest overwhelmingly that Jesus is the Messiah.

REVIEW:

The _____ prophecies suggest overwhelmingly that Jesus is the Messiah.

---

4. The Purpose of Prophecy

The purpose of prophecy is not to satisfy our curiosity but to change our lives. Prophecy is always given to get us to live properly. In chapter 3 of his second letter, the apostle Peter, after announcing some rather stunning prophecies about the end of the world, then said, "Since all these things are to be destroyed in this way, what sort of people ought you to be in holy conduct and godliness" (v. 11). His purpose in telling them about things in the future was to purify their lives now. It is not wrong to be interested in prophecy. However, it is possible to study prophecy the way some people study academic subjects. I have even witnessed some heated arguments over differences in prophetic interpretations. These are out of line. We should never let prophecy allow us to act unbiblically. Just the opposite should be true.

Summary: The purpose of prophecy is not to satisfy our curiosity but to *purify* our lives.

REVIEW:

The purpose of prophecy is not to satisfy our curiosity but to _____ our lives.

Review

1. The ability to predict events before they occur demonstrates God's *power.*

2. Sixty-one major prophecies in the Old Testament were *fulfilled* by Christ.

3. The *fulfilled* prophecies suggest overwhelmingly that Jesus is the Messiah.

4. The purpose of prophecy is not to satisfy our curiosity but to *purify* our lives.

Self-Test

1. The ability to predict events before they occur demonstrates God's _____.

2. Sixty-one major prophecies in the Old Testament were _____ by Christ.

3. The _____ prophecies suggest overwhelmingly that Jesus is the Messiah.

4. The purpose of prophecy is not to satisfy our curiosity but to _____ our lives.

TWENTY-FOUR

PASSOVER AND THE LORD'S SUPPER

 In her marvelous little book, *Tramp for the Lord*, Corrie ten Boom wrote of the time she was speaking to a group of young people about Jesus. Afterward the students joined her for coffee:

One student said to me, "I would love to ask Jesus to come into my heart, but I cannot. I am a Jew."

I said, "You cannot ask Jesus into your heart because you are a Jew? Then you do not understand that with the Jew (Jesus) in your heart, you are a double Jew."

He said, "Oh, then it is possible?"

"On the divine side, He was God's Son. On the human side He was Jew. When you accept Him you do not become a Gentile. You become even more Jewish than before. You will be a completed Jew."

With great joy the boy received the Lord Jesus as his Savior. (p. 186)

The link between Judaism and Christianity is much stronger than many people realize. Christianity is merely Judaism extended to its logical conclusion. "Judaism and Christianity are as inseparable as seed and flower, or tree and fruit. Nowhere can the organic relationship between the two be observed more clearly than in the Passover of the Jews and the Last Supper as ordained by our Lord, when He and His twelve disciples sat around the Passover table" (*The Gospel in the Feasts of Israel*, p. 1). Paul emphasized this crucial connection when he identified Christ as the true Passover Lamb by writing to the Corinthians that "Christ, our Passover lamb, has been sacrificed" (1 Cor. 5:7 NIV).

185

1.   The Old Testament Significance of the Passover

This festival (usually occurring in March or early April) commemorates God's deliverance of Israel from its Egyptian captivity, the central point in Jewish history and worship. The last of the ten plagues by which God judged Egypt was the death of each firstborn son (Ex. 11:5). Exodus 12:13 explains the name of the festival: God would "pass over" the Hebrew houses that displayed a sacrificial lamb's blood on the sides and top of their door frames. The Old Testament contains a number of regulations that define in detail such matters as the date, time, and duration of the festival, the manner of eating the Passover lamb, and who could participate in the festival (Ex. 12; Num. 9:12, 14).

The Passover in Jesus' day had a twofold significance. First, it looked back in commemoration of Israel's deliverance from Egyptian oppression (Ex. 12:14, 17). Second, it looked forward in anticipation to the coming of the Messiah to establish His kingdom. The rabbis believed the Messiah was most likely to come on the night of the Passover. Therefore, it was customary for each family to set a place at its Passover table for Elijah, the forerunner of the Messiah (Mal. 3:1; 4:5–6), in case Elijah should arrive to announce the joyful news that the Messiah had come.

The Passover represented a new birth, or new beginning, for the nation of Israel. When they fled from Pharaoh the Israelites had to forsake the beliefs and attitudes of Egypt. The Passover prepared them to enter into a new covenant with God at Sinai, which would establish them as a kingdom of priests and a holy nation (Ex. 19:6).

The significance of the Passover is seen in the fact that it changed Israel's reckoning of time. God commanded the Israelites to count the month of their deliverance as the first month of their religious year (Ex. 12:2). (By tradition the Jewish people celebrate their fiscal New Year in the fall, in the seventh month of the Jewish calendar.) It was as though God were saying, "The Passover is so significant that you are to rearrange your calendar on account of it." (In a similar fashion, today we reckon time B.C. and A.D., before and after the coming of the Christ.)

Summary: The Old Testament significance of the Passover is that it looked back on Israel's deliverance from slavery in Egypt and looked forward to ultimate spiritual deliverance through the *Messiah*.

REVIEW:

The Old Testament significance of the Passover is that it looked back on Israel's deliverance from slavery in Egypt and looked forward to ultimate spiritual deliverance through the _____.

---

2. Christ's Observance of Passover with His Apostles (The Lord's Supper)

"The Lord's Supper" is an expression found only once in the New Testament (1 Cor. 11:20), where it refers not only to the breaking of the bread and the drinking from the cup, but also to the common meal that accompanied it. The Lord's Supper began with the last supper Christ had with His disciples before His death. This supper, also known as *communion* or the *Eucharist*, is a religious ritual Christians are to observe regularly. The Synoptic Gospels indicate that the ritual of the Last Supper grew out of Christ's celebration of the Passover meal with His disciples. However, John has been understood to indicate that the Last Supper was "just before the Passover Feast" (13:1 NIV; see also John 13:2, 21–30). Jesus, as the ultimate Passover sacrifice, was put to death simultaneously with the slaying of the Passover lambs (compare with John 18:28; 19:12–14).

The best harmonization of this apparent conflict grows out of a recent recognition that there were apparently two dates for celebrating the Passover in Jesus' day. By observing it on the earlier day Jesus could observe this special Jewish religious holiday with His closest friends before bringing it to an end by His death on the official Passover date. In this way Jesus could show His disciples the full symbolic meaning of the Passover memorial. This is the context in which Christ's institution of the new Christian meal should be understood.

Summary: Jesus observed the Passover with His disciples the night before His death, not only in faithfulness as a Jew, but also in *prophetic* symbolism of His own forthcoming crucifixion.

> **REVIEW:**
>
> Jesus observed the Passover with His disciples the night before His death, not only in faithfulness as a Jew, but also in _____ symbolism of His own forthcoming crucifixion.

3. The Passover as Object Lesson

Again and again the Israelites were told by God to remember His deliverance of them as an encouragement to their continued faith in Him (for example, Deut. 5:15; 6:11–12; 8:2). How could all the Israelites, young as well as old, literate as well as illiterate, best remember God's deliverance? God commanded an annual reenactment of the first Passover. Through this object lesson God had His people employ all five senses (seeing, hearing, smelling, tasting, and touching) to powerfully remember the story of their deliverance. The head of the household would recount in great detail the story of Israel's deliverance and explain the significance of all the aspects of the Passover observance. The following description will clarify the significance of some of the more important elements of the Passover ceremony.

a. The object lesson began with the Passover lamb

Each family was to select from its flock the most attractive and healthy male, year-old lamb. A four-day period of close observation around the house followed to make sure the animal was healthy and perfect in every way. At the end of four days the entire family (especially the children) would have become fond of the frisky, young lamb. The sacrificial death of the lamb, which they would eat as part of the Passover meal, taught a painful lesson: God's holiness requires that sin be judged, and the price is a costly one. However, in His mercy God provides a way of escape or redemption.

Ceil and Moishe Rosen point out several ways in which the death of the innocent Passover lamb parallels the death of the One who would ultimately provide redemption from the penalty of sin (*Christ in the Passover*, pp. 26–27). First, the Passover lamb was marked for death. Isaiah 53:7–8 records the prophecy that the Messiah would be led like a lamb to the slaughter and that He would die for the people's transgressions. Jesus

Christ was chosen before the creation of the world to die as a sacrifice for sin (1 Pet. 1:19–20).

Second, the Passover lamb was carefully scrutinized to make certain it was perfect. Deuteronomy 15:21 reveals that a flawed animal was not an acceptable sacrifice for sin. Through His three-and-one-half-year public ministry Jesus demonstrated to the Jewish nation that He was perfect in heart and deed. Even the Roman governor Pilate could find no fault in Him. Hebrews 4:15 declares that Jesus had been tempted (or tested) "in every way, just as we are—yet was without sin" (NIV). First Peter 1:19 describes Jesus as "a lamb without blemish or defect" (NIV).

Third, the Passover lamb was roasted with fire. In Scripture fire is often symbolic of God's judgment. Isaiah 53 foretold that the Messiah would bear God's judgment for the sins of others and be numbered among the transgressors. Second Corinthians 5:21 proclaims of Jesus that "God made him who had no sin to be sin for us, so that in him we might become the righteousness of God" (NIV). As a result of His identification with our sin Jesus suffered God's judgment on the cross, leading Him to cry out: "My God, my God, why have you forsaken me?" (Matt. 27:46 NIV).

Fourth, none of the Passover lamb's bones were to be broken (Ex. 12:46; Num. 9:12). John 19:32–36 tells us the Roman soldiers did not break Jesus' legs as they did the two men crucified beside Him.

b. God instructed the Israelites to eat the Passover lamb with bitter herbs (Exodus 12:8)

On one level the bitter herbs represent the bitterness of the bondage Israel had experienced in Egypt. Bitterness is often symbolic of death in the Bible. The bitter herbs would serve to remind them that the Hebrew firstborn males only lived as a result of the sacrifice of the Passover lambs. Christians receive new life through their identification with the death of the ultimate Passover lamb, Jesus Christ. Finally, bitterness is often associated with mourning. In Zechariah 12:10 God speaks of a future time when the Israelites will look upon the Messiah, "the one they have pierced, and they will mourn for him as one mourns for an only child, and grieve bitterly for him as one grieves for a firstborn son" (NIV).

c. Unleavened bread was also part of the Passover meal (Exodus. 12:8)

Unleavened bread does not contain yeast and thus does not rise. While such bread was appropriate in view of the haste of the Hebrews' departure from Egypt, it has a deeper, symbolic significance. With the exception of Matthew 13:33, where it represents growth and expansion, leaven is a symbol of sin in the Bible. Thus Paul urged the Corinthian believers: "Get rid of the old yeast that you may be a new batch without yeast—as you really are. For Christ, our Passover lamb, has been sacrificed. Therefore let us keep the Festival, not with the old yeast, the yeast of malice and wickedness, but with bread without yeast, the bread of sincerity and truth" (1 Cor. 5:7–8 NIV).

The bread without yeast has a twofold symbolic reference. First, it represents the sinless Messiah. The father would take the middle matzo of the three unleavened cakes, break it, pronounce a blessing, and distribute half of the broken matzo among the members of his family while hiding the other half until the end of the meal. The breaking of the matzo symbolized the "breaking" of the Messiah's body (for example, see Matt. 26:26).

Second, the putting away of all leaven or yeast represented the Hebrews' breaking the cycle of sin and starting out as a new nation as they left Egypt. Similarly, Paul's exhortation is for the Corinthians to put away leaven/sin because they are the redeemed people of the Lord.

d. The Hebrews were to place the sacrificial lamb's blood on the door (Exodus 12:7)

The Passover lamb was killed right by the door where its blood was to be applied to the frame. The blood from the slaughtered lamb would run into the basin (Ex. 12:22), the container in the ditch dug just in front of the doorway, to avoid flooding of the house. A hyssop "brush" would be dipped into the basin, and the blood would be painted onto the door frame. The blood would first be applied to the top of the door frame, then to the two side posts. In doing this the Israelite would go through the motion of making a bloody cross, symbolic of the Passover sacrifice by Christ more than fourteen hundred years later.

It is important to note that the Israelite firstborns were not saved from divine judgment simply by the Hebrews' knowing about God's provision for their deliverance. No house was spared from judgment apart from personal application of the sacrificial blood. Similarly, a person receives no benefit from the sacrificial death of Christ apart from personal application through faith in His provision.

e. The Passover celebration concluded with the singing of Psalms 113–118. The Hallel Psalm (118:21–24) states:

> I will give you thanks, for you answered me;
>   you have become my salvation.
> The stone the builders rejected
>   has become the capstone;
> the LORD has done this,
>   and it is marvelous in our eyes.
> This is the day that the LORD has made;
>   let us rejoice and be glad in it. (NIV)

These were likely the very words sung by Christ and the disciples at the close of the Passover feast: "When they had sung a hymn, they went out to the Mount of Olives" (Matt. 26:30 NIV). In God's providence, each Passover celebrant sang these words that applied to Christ (Matt. 21:42). Jesus was the capstone or foundation the builders rejected, but upon which God would build His kingdom. So Passover and the Lord's Supper merge into one complete story of deliverance and salvation.

Summary: The Passover was an object lesson of sacrifice and atonement for *sin*.

REVIEW:

The Passover was an object lesson of sacrifice and atonement for _____.

---

4. The Significance of the Lord's Supper

The Lord's Supper has a fivefold significance. First, the Lord's Supper is a *memorial to Christ*, who said, "Do this in remembrance of Me" (1 Cor. 11:24). We are to look back, not just to His death, but to His life and resurrection. Rather than on the Sabbath as in the Jewish religion, the Christians met for worship and broke bread together on the first day of the week, resurrection day (Acts 20:7). We are to honor Jesus as the one who lives forever and is always present with His own (Matt. 28:20).

Second, the Lord's Supper is a *pledge of the new covenant.* The cup symbolizes the blood shed by Christ to ratify the new covenant, thus securing our forgiveness. Christ said, "This cup is the new covenant in my blood, which is poured out for you" (Luke 22:20 NIV). This covenant provides for the believer the forgiveness of sins (Heb. 10:16–18), and it is a better covenant than the old Mosaic one it supersedes (2 Cor. 3:6–18; Heb. 7:22; 12:24). So, partaking of the bread and the cup reminds us of our perfect forgiveness in Christ.

Third, the Lord's Supper is a *proclamation of Christ's death.* In 1 Corinthians 11:26 Paul wrote, "For whenever you eat this bread and drink this cup, you proclaim the Lord's death until he comes" (NIV). Christians proclaim both the fact and the significance of Christ's death when they partake of communion together.

Fourth, the Lord's Supper is a *prophetic reminder* of Christ's return. We are instructed to practice this ordinance until Christ comes again (1 Cor. 11:26). This ceremony not only looks back at Christ's death, but also looks forward to His return for His own. At the Last Supper, Jesus proclaimed to His disciples, "I will not drink of this fruit of the vine from now on until that day when I drink it anew with you in my Father's kingdom" (Matt. 26:29 NIV). Sharing in the Lord's Supper reminds believers of the joyful reunion and unending delight that await us when the Lord returns and we join Him in the wedding supper of the Lamb (Rev. 19:9).

Finally, the Lord's Supper is a *time of fellowship with Christ and other believers.* The redeemed gather together for a special time of fellowship around the Lord Jesus Christ. Christ is present in our midst as we partake of the elements symbolizing His body and blood. The early church ate a common meal together, "the love feast," before communion. The Lord's Table should remind us of Christ's humility and our responsibility to serve one another. For example, at the Last Supper Christ washed His disciples' feet, an act of humility, devotion, and love that He said was an example of how we should act (John 13:14–15).

Summary: The Lord's Supper is the New Testament *fulfillment* of the Passover, symbolizing Christ's fulfillment of the Old Testament promises.

REVIEW:

The Lord's Supper is the New Testament _____ of the Passover, symbolizing Christ's fulfillment of the Old Testament promises.

Review

1. The Old Testament significance of the Passover is that it looked back on Israel's deliverance from slavery in Egypt and looked forward to ultimate spiritual deliverance through the *Messiah*.

2. Jesus observed the Passover with His disciples the night before His death, not only in faithfulness as a Jew, but also in *prophetic* symbolism of His own forthcoming crucifixion.

3. The Passover was on object lesson of sacrifice and atonement for *sin*.

4. The Lord's Supper is the New Testament *fulfillment* of the Passover, symbolizing Christ's fulfillment of the Old Testament promises.

Self-Test

1. The Old Testament significance of the Passover is that it looked back on Israel's deliverance from slavery in Egypt and looked forward to ultimate spiritual deliverance through the

   _____.

2. Jesus observed the Passover with His disciples the night before His death, not only in faithfulness as a Jew, but also in _____ symbolism of His own forthcoming crucifixion.

3. The Passover was an object lesson of sacrifice and atonement for _____.

4. The Lord's Supper is the New Testament _____ of the Passover, symbolizing Christ's fulfillment of the Old Testament promises.

TWENTY-FIVE

THE RESURRECTION OF JESUS CHRIST

The resurrection of Jesus is the pivotal event in the history of the world, to say nothing of being the main event of redemption. Paul went so far as to assert that the Christian faith and the salvation it promises stand or fall with the resurrection: "And if Christ has not been raised, your faith is futile; you are still in your sins. Then those also who have fallen asleep in Christ are lost. If only for this life we have hope in Christ, we are to be pitied more than all men" (1 Cor. 15:17–19 NIV). If Christ was raised from the dead, then everything He said can be trusted. If He didn't, nothing He said can be trusted. It's true: Everything stands or falls on the resurrection.

It is not surprising, then, that critics of Christianity have zeroed in on the resurrection of Jesus Christ. If they can bring down the resurrection, they know they can bring everything crashing down. But, as best-selling author Paul Little once said, "After 2000 years, no one is going to ask a question that will bring Christianity crashing."

In fact, the attempt has backfired in a number of cases, with the intended assassins coming to a personal faith in Jesus as a result of their study. The evidence for His resurrection from the dead is overwhelming. For example, attorney Frank Morrison planned to write a book to show the error of the resurrection. However, his research compelled him to the opposite conclusion. Morrison's book *Who Moved the Stone?* is a powerful argument for the reality of the resurrection. Similarly, General Lew Wallace was researching the background for a historical novel about a

Jewish contemporary of Christ. After being overcome by the evidence for the resurrection, Wallace placed his faith in Christ and wrote *Ben Hur*, a compelling fictional story that supports the resurrection. As C. S. Lewis recounted in his autobiography, *Surprised by Joy*, the evidence for Christ's resurrection brought a reluctant Lewis kicking and screaming to faith in Christ.

If you apply the same tests to the resurrection as you would to any other historical event, you come away concluding that the resurrection of Jesus actually happened. Only those who do not want to believe it come to another conclusion, and they must twist the arm of historical research to do it.

There are three common attempts to explain away the resurrection.

1.   The Theft Theory

The earliest attempt to explain away Christ's resurrection involved the assertion that His body was stolen. Some way had to be found to explain the empty tomb. Thus, the Jewish leaders bribed the Roman guards to report that Jesus' body had been stolen by His disciples while the soldiers had slept (Matt. 28:11–15).

This story was so clearly false that Matthew did not bother to disprove it. As Paul Little observed in *Know Why You Believe* (p. 52), "What judge would listen to you if you said that while you were asleep your neighbor came into your house and stole your television set? Who knows what goes on while he's asleep? Testimony like this would be laughed out of any court."

The testimony that Jesus' body was stolen, the very thing the Roman guards had been posted to prevent, was ridiculous for other reasons as well. How likely is it that *all* the Roman soldiers fell asleep when the ordinary punishment for sleeping while on duty was death? If they had fallen asleep, would none of them have been awakened by the sound of the stone being rolled away from the mouth of the tomb?

In addition, the theft theory requires behavior by the disciples that is foreign to what we know of their character. Would they have deliberately perpetrated a lie that ultimately led to the deaths of countless people, including many of them? People are sometimes willing to die for what is false because they believe it to be true. But would the disciples face torture and death for what they *knew* to be a lie? How likely would it be that none of the alleged conspirators would ever recant his story, even on his deathbed? Even if the disciples had stolen Jesus' body, how can we explain the post-resurrection sightings, including one by more than five hundred people at one time (1 Cor. 15:6)?

As Professor E. F. Kevan summarized,

> The enemies of Jesus had no motive for removing the body; the friends of Jesus had no power to do so. It would have been to the advantage of the authorities that the body should remain where it was; and the view that the disciples stole the body is impossible. The power that removed the body of the Savior from the tomb must therefore have been Divine. (Quoted by Josh McDowell in *Evidence That Demands A Verdict*, p. 239)

Summary: The Theft Theory states that the *disciples* stole the body of Jesus from the tomb after He died.

REVIEW:

The Theft Theory states that the _____ stole the body of Jesus from the tomb after He died.

---

2. The Swoon Theory

This theory asserts that Christ did not really die on the cross. Rather, Christ appeared to be dead but had only swooned from exhaustion, pain, and loss of blood. He revived when laid in the cool tomb. After leaving the tomb He appeared to His disciples, who mistakenly concluded He had risen from the dead.

It should be pointed out that this theory first appeared at the end of the eighteenth century, which makes it a "Johnny-come-lately" in the extreme. None of the attacks made on Christianity in ancient times challenged the fact that Jesus had died on the cross. One of the responsibilities of the Roman soldiers who assisted with His execution was to make certain He died. We are told that Jesus had already died before He was removed from the cross. However, to make doubly certain, one of the soldiers thrust a spear into His side (probably piercing His heart) (John 19:33–34).

Jesus had suffered much even before He was nailed to the cross. He had undergone the horrible ordeal of a Roman scourging in which His back was shredded by being cut with pieces of glass and metal at the end of the whip. The governor's soldiers had struck Him on the head repeatedly. He had been forced to carry the cross from the governor's headquarters toward His place of execution until, due to Jesus' weakened state, another man was compelled to carry the cross the remainder of the way.

But suppose for a minute that the Roman executioners were wrong and Jesus had somehow survived and was buried alive. How likely would He have been to have endured another thirty-six hours in a cold, damp tomb without food, water, or medical attention? Would He have survived being bound (similar to embalming) in heavy, spice-laden grave clothes weighing an estimated seventy pounds? Would He have had the strength to free Himself from the grave clothes, role away the heavy stone sealing the mouth of the tomb, overpower the Roman guards, and then walk several miles on feet that had been pierced with nails?

Even the now-deceased German critic David Strauss, who did not believe in the resurrection, recognized the absurdity of this theory. Strauss said:

> It is impossible that One who had just come forth from the grave half dead, who crept about weak and ill, who stood in the need of medical treatment, of bandaging, strengthening, and tender care, and who at last succumbed to suffering, could have ever given the disciples the impression that he was the Prince of Life. This lay at the bottom of their future ministry. Such a resuscitation could only have weakened the impression which he had made upon them in life and death—or at the most, could have given an elegiac voice—but could by no possibility have changed their sorrow into enthusiasm or elevated their reverence into worship. (Quoted by Paul Little in *Know Why You Believe*, p. 54)

One final objection to this theory should be noted. If Jesus had somehow recovered from a deathlike swoon, He would have been guilty of glaring deception and falsehood. Would a person of the integrity revealed in the Gospels have encouraged His followers to preach and base their lives on a lie?

Summary: The Swoon Theory states that Jesus did not die on the cross, but merely went into a death-like *coma* from which He revived after being laid in the cool tomb.

REVIEW:

The Swoon Theory states that Jesus did not die on the cross, but merely went into a death-like _____ from which He revived after being laid in the cool tomb.

---

3. The Subjective Vision or Hallucination Theory

According to this theory the disciples so longed for their dead master that they imagined that they saw Him and heard Him speak to them. Whether the disciples' experiences are called hallucinations, illusions, or visions, they are believed to be completely subjective, taking place only in the excited minds of the disciples.

This theory is unacceptable for several reasons. First, generally only people who are very imaginative and nervous hallucinate. Many people of varied dispositions, including hard-headed fishermen like Peter, claimed to see the resurrected Jesus.

Second, because hallucinations are highly subjective and individual, no two people have the same experience. But Christ appeared to groups as well as to individuals. For example, 1 Corinthians 15:6 reports an appearance to more than five hundred people at once, most of whom were still living at the time this was written by Paul.

Third, hallucinations typically occur only at particular times and places that are associated with the imagined events. However, Christ appeared in a variety of settings, such as: (1) early morning to the women at the tomb (Matt. 28:9–10), (2) one afternoon to two disciples on the road to Emmaus (Luke 24:13–33), (3) early one morning to His disciples by the Sea of Tiberias (John 21:1–23), and (4) on a mountain in Galilee to more than five hundred believers (1 Cor. 15:6).

Most importantly, hallucinations of this type always "happen as the climax to a period of exaggerated wishful thinking" (John R. W. Stott, *Basic Christianity*, p. 55). However, the disciples were not optimistically looking for Jesus' resurrection. Instead, they disbelieved or doubted when they were told of His rising and even when they themselves saw the risen Lord (Matt. 28:17; Mark 16:8, 11, 14; Luke 24:11, 37; John 20:24, 25).

> **Summary**: The Hallucination Theory states that the disciples of Jesus had a *common* hallucination that Jesus rose from the dead.

REVIEW:

The Hallucination Theory states that the disciples of Jesus had a _____ hallucination that Jesus rose from the dead

---

4. The Resurrection as History

The positive case for the historical accuracy of the resurrection is overwhelming and will be briefly sketched below. First, is the New Testament historically valid? In other words, does it offer a reliable picture of Jesus' claims and actions? The New Testament clearly passes the three tests generally employed in the studies of history and literary criticism: the bibliographical, internal-evidence, and external-evidence tests.

The bibliographic test is simply that since we do not have the original documents, can we reconstruct them well enough to see what they claimed Jesus said and did? The New Testament documents are *by far* the best attested from antiquity in terms of both the number of existing copies and the shortness of the time span between the oldest copies and the original manuscripts. For example, shortly before his death Sir Frederic Kenyon, former director and principal librarian of the British Museum, concluded:

> The interval, then, between the dates of original composition and the earliest extant evidence becomes so small as to be in fact negligible, and the last foundation for any doubt that the Scriptures have come down to us substantially as they were written has now been removed. Both the authenticity and the general integrity of the books of the New Testament may be regarded as finally established. (Frederic Kenyon, *The Bible and Archaeology*, pp. 288–289)

The second test involves a consideration of the document's internal evidence. John Warwick Montgomery explains, "This means that one must listen to the claims of the document under analysis, and not assume fraud or error unless the author disqualifies himself by contradictions or known factual inaccuracies" (*History and Christianity*, p. 9). The New Testament authors frequently claim to have written as eyewitnesses or from firsthand knowledge (for example, Luke 1:1–3; John 19:35; and 2 Peter 1:16).

The test of external evidence seeks to determine whether other historical materials support or deny the internal testimony provided by the documents themselves. Careful examination of literature written at the same time as the Bible confirms the historical trustworthiness of the New Testament accounts. For example, after years of archeological and geographical investigation, Sir William M. Ramsay concluded, "Luke's history is unsurpassed in respect of its trustworthiness." More recently, Oxford history professor A. N. Sherwin-White wrote of the Gospel of Luke's companion volume, Acts, that "any attempt to reject its basic historicity even in matters of detail must now appear absurd. Roman historians have long taken it for granted" (*Roman Society and Roman Law in the New Testament*, p. 189).

The New Testament documents unanimously portray a Jesus who claimed to be divine and who was raised from the dead. If Jesus was not divine, there are only three remaining ways to interpret the New Testament data:

a. Jesus claimed to be God's Son but knew He was not. Jesus was a liar.

b. Jesus thought He was God's Son, but was not. Jesus was a lunatic.

c. Jesus never claimed to be God's Son. This means the disciples, who attributed the false claim to Jesus, were themselves liars, lunatics, or naive exaggerators.

Would Jesus, despite His own noble ethical teachings and personal character, have lied concerning His own identity and purpose? Could such a great moral teacher have been psychotically confused over His own identity? C. S. Lewis concluded that, if Christ were not a liar or a lunatic, He must be Lord—that is, the Son of God as He claimed. But is there not a third way to avoid this conclusion? Could not Jesus' followers have painted a false picture of Him?

As John Warwick Montgomery details in *History and Christianity* (pp. 66–67), such an interpretation falls down on three decisive counts:

> First, all types of Jewish messianic speculation at the time were at variance with the messianic picture Jesus painted of himself, so he was a singularly poor candidate for deification. Second, the apostles and evangelists were psychologically, ethically and religiously incapable of performing such a deification. Third, the historical evidence for Christ's resurrection, the great attesting event for his claims to deity, could not have been manufactured.

If the resurrection did not occur, how can one account for the transformation of Jesus' discouraged and defeated band of followers into dynamic, joyful people willing to suffer and die to preach a risen Savior? Why did none ever save themselves by recanting the story or salve their conscience by a death-bed confession of the deception? How did this message gain so many adherents among people who had contact with the events spoken of and thus would have detected falsehood? (For example, in 1 Cor. 15:6 Paul refers to the more than five hundred people who saw the risen Jesus and were still living more than twenty years later).

In his autobiography, *Surprised by Joy*, C. S. Lewis recounts a powerful story about the evidence for the resurrection. Shortly before Lewis's unwilling conversion from atheism to Christianity:

> The hardest boiled of all the atheists I ever knew sat in my room on the other side of the fire and remarked that the evidence for the historicity of the Gospels was really surprisingly good. "Rum thing," he went on. "All that stuff of Frazer's about the Dying God. Rum thing. It almost looks as if it had really happened once." To understand the shattering impact of it, you would need to know the man (who has certainly never since shown any interest in Christianity). If he, the cynic of cynics, the toughest of the toughs were not—as I would still have put it—"safe," where could I turn? Was there then no escape? (pp. 223–224)

To repeat, if you apply the same tests to the resurrection as you would to any other historical event, you come away concluding that the resurrection of Jesus actually happened. Only those who do not *want* to believe it come to another conclusion, and must twist the arm of historical research to do it.

Summary: The Resurrection as History position states that Jesus *rose* from the dead, as He said He would.

REVIEW:

The Resurrection as History position states that Jesus
_____ from the dead, as He said He would.

Review

1. The Theft Theory states that the disciples *stole* the body of Jesus from the tomb after He died.

2. The Swoon Theory states that Jesus did not die on the cross, but merely went into a death-like *coma* from which He revived after being laid in the cool tomb.

3. The Hallucination Theory states that the disciples of Jesus had a *common* hallucination that Jesus rose from the dead.

4. The Resurrection as History position states that Jesus *rose* from the dead, as He said He would.

Self-Test

1. The Theft Theory states that the disciples _____ the body of Jesus from the tomb after He died.

2. The Swoon Theory states that Jesus did not die on the cross, but merely went into a death-like _____ from which He revived after being laid in the cool tomb.

3. The Hallucination Theory states that the disciples of Jesus had a _____ hallucination that Jesus rose from the dead.

4. The Resurrection as History position states that Jesus _____ from the dead, as He said He would.

TWENTY-SIX

DISTINCTIVENESS OF CHRISTIANITY

 There used to be only three television networks; now there are scores of them. There used to be the "Big Three" automakers in Detroit; now there are many car manufacturers throughout the world. There used to be one telephone company; now there are many. We live in an age of increasing options.

Wherever you look, there are more and more options, more and more beliefs, more and more opportunities. Religious options are increasing too. Of the more than fifteen hundred religious groups in America today, more than six hundred are non-Christian. By matching 1990 census data with polling results by Gallup, there are estimates that 17.5 million adults in the United States claim a non-Christian religion as their own (Terry C. Muck, *Those Other Religions in Your Neighborhood*). A check of the local phone book's yellow pages will confirm a growing variety of religious options in most communities.

> As a result, there has been a switch from absolute values to relative values. Many Americans have no clear conviction of what is right and what is wrong; instead they hold to a philosophy of what's right or wrong for me is different from what's right or wrong for you. This is the ultimate expression of American individualism and independence. (Leith Anderson in *Dying for Change*, p. 32)

Sometimes it is asserted that all religions are fundamentally the same anyway. They are simply different ways to the same god. Life is like climbing a mountain. As long as one reaches the top, it is argued, why does it matter what path one takes to get there?

You have probably heard the poem by John Godrey Sacks about the blind men who went to see an elephant. Of course, they could only "see" it by touching it. When asked to describe an elephant, one grabbed the elephant by its trunk and concluded, "An elephant is like a snake." A second man, who grabbed the elephant's thick leg, determined, "No, an elephant is like a tree trunk." A third man, after he had grabbed one of the elephant's tusks, said, "You are both wrong; an elephant is smooth, cold, and hard." Another described the elephant as a fan because he grabbed the ear, and so on. Although all the men were trying to describe the same animal, their descriptions were quite different.

Thus we are left with a fundamental question: Are all (or even some) of the world's religions essentially the same? Or is Christianity distinctive in crucial ways from other religions? We will first examine several areas of commonality among different religions, then consider how they differ. We will close with suggested principles for proclaiming the truth in a pluralistic world.

1. Similarities between Christianity and Other Religions

Terry C. Muck (*Those Other Religions in Your Neighborhood*) points out three areas of similarity among all religions. First, they address the same human need. All persons (unless they have been educated or conditioned to deny it) have an innate sense that something is wrong, that they do not measure up to some standard (see Rom. 2:14–15). Thus they recognize a need for something beyond themselves.

Second, all religions are equally sincere. One could also argue that religions, as manmade attempts to find God, are equally insincere and doomed to failure. Some include institutional Christianity in this evaluation. No one genuinely seeks God, it is argued (for example, in Romans 3:10–11 Paul quotes the Old Testament that, "There is no one righteous, not even one; / there is no one who understands, / *no one who seeks God*" [NIV, emphasis added]). True Christianity is not so much a religion as a God-initiated relationship; for instance, note Christ's description of His own purpose: "For the Son of Man came to seek and to save what was lost" (Luke 19:10).

Third, all religions teach essentially the same moral code. There is a remarkable similarity between the principles of behavior taught by the major world religions. C. S. Lewis called the apparently universal code of morality that undergirds these various religions the *Tao*. For example, the foundation of religious life for Buddhists is the *pancasilia*, five rules of morality that disallow killing, stealing, lying, sexual unfaithfulness, and consumption of intoxicating substances. Confucius taught, "What you do not want done to yourself, do not do to others," a negatively stated form of the Christian Golden Rule ("Do unto others as you would have them do unto you").

However, it is a fundamental fallacy to identify the essence of Christianity with a code of ethics. Rather, Christianity is God's decisive interaction in human history through the incarnation, substitutionary death, and resurrection of Jesus Christ.

> **Summary**: Christianity has *similarities* with other religions that must be recognized.

REVIEW:

Christianity has _____ with other religions that must be recognized.

---

2. Differences between Christianity and Other Religions

A Christian perspective on reality differs in many specific ways from perspectives held by Hindus, Buddhists, New Age thought, etc. Two of the most crucial areas of difference between Christianity and other religions include, first, that religions offer different answers to the nature of humanity's basic problem and, therefore, the answer to that problem.

In *Buddhism* all pain and suffering are said to result from desire. The goal is to extinguish desire by following the Buddha's "Eightfold Path to Enlightenment." Success results in *nirvana*, a state of total nothingness in which the self is annihilated.

Nirvana is also the goal in *Hinduism*, where it is understood as reunion with God achieved through a continuous cycle of birth, life, death, and rebirth. Whether one is reborn in a higher form (and thus moves closer to eventual nirvana) or in a lower form depends upon how morally one has lived.

In *Islamic* thought, heaven (where, ironically, one may indulge in wine, women, and song) is achieved by a virtuous life of renouncing alcohol and sexual immorality as well as keeping the "Five Pillars of Islam": repeating the creed, traveling to the sacred city of Mecca, giving gifts to the poor, praying five times each day, and fasting each year during Ramadan.

The common denominator among these three religions and all non-Christian religions is that achievement of the ultimate salvation depends upon the adherent's good works. In contrast, the Bible teaches that salvation is a result of God's grace and that good works are the natural response to God's love (compare with Eph. 2:8–10). Because salvation depends on what God has done for us, Christians can have an assurance of salvation. How could adherents of any "works religion" be confident that their good works were sufficient to merit salvation? (For instance, Isaiah 64:6 states that "all our righteous acts are like filthy rags" in the sight of a holy God.)

Second, the various religions differ greatly in their conception of God. The Bible reveals God to be a Spirit who is infinite, or unlimited, in respect to knowledge (omniscience), space (omnipresence), power (omnipotence), and time (eternality). God is both transcendent, which means other than us and our world, and immanent, which means present with us. God is sovereign; nothing is beyond His interest, control, and authority. God's goodness is expressed in His holiness, or absolute righteousness, and His love. God is personal, not merely force, energy, or substance. Like us, God knows that He exists, thinks, and acts. Finally, in Christianity (not Judaism) God is revealed to be a Trinity. That is, "within the one essence of the Godhead we have to distinguish three 'persons' who are neither three gods on the one side, nor three parts or modes of God on the other, but coequally and coeternally God" (*Evangelical Dictionary of Theology*, p. 1,112). The three persons of the Godhead are God the Father, God the Son (Jesus Christ), and the Holy Spirit.

In contrast, the Buddha never claimed deity and professed agnosticism as to whether God even existed. Even if God did exist, according to the Buddha, He could not help an individual achieve enlightenment.

Hindus are pantheists, that is, they believe everything is "God"; God and the universe are identical. Actually, the material world is seen as illusion (*maya*), and all reality is spiritual. Thus God, or *Brahman*, is a principle or force underlying creation rather than a person. God is the universe's underlying "Force," and has a "dark side" as well as a light or good side. However, ultimately Brahman is beyond good and evil, and these categories are illusions.

Islam and Judaism proclaim views of God that are much closer to the Christian conception. Both religions acknowledge God as personal and as separate from His creation.

Mohammed taught that, while Jesus was, indeed, a prophet, he (Mohammed) was Allah's (God's) greatest prophet. The Koran, the Islamic scriptures, portrays Allah as capricious and totally separate from human beings. The total lack of identification between Allah and human beings makes the incarnation and substitutionary death of Jesus as the God-man inconceivable to Muslims.

The Jewish concept of God is inadequate because of its failure to accept that Jesus Christ is God's Son. To Jews who claimed God as their Father (John 8:41), Jesus responded, "If God were your Father, you would love me, for I came from God. . . . He who belongs to God hears what God says. The reason you do not hear is that you do not belong to God" (John 8:42, 47).

Christianity is unique in that Jesus Christ claimed to be God.

Summary: Christianity has *differences* from other religions that make it distinctive.

REVIEW:

Christianity has _____ from other religions that make it distinctive.

---

3. Christ as the Only Way to God

The Bible asserts that Jesus Christ is the only way to God. Jesus, unlike other great religious teachers, made belief in His divine identity the focal point of His teaching. For example, Jesus proclaimed:

No one knows the Father except the Son and anyone to whom the Son chooses to reveal Him. (Matt. 11:27 NIV)

Whoever believes in him is not condemned, but whoever does not believe stands condemned already because he has not believed in the name of God's one and only Son. (John 3:18 NIV)

The work of God is this: to believe in the one he has sent. (John 6:29 NIV)

If you do not believe that I am the one I claim to be, you will indeed die in your sins. (John 8:24 NIV)

I am the way and the truth and the life. No one comes to the Father except through me. (John 14:6 NIV)

The clear, unequivocal teaching of the apostles was that "Salvation is found in no one else, for there is no other name under heaven given to men by which we *must be saved*" (Acts 4:12, emphasis added). Indeed, "No one who denies the Son has the Father; whoever acknowledges the Son has the Father also" (1 John 2:23). Sir Norman Anderson wrote, "It is unmistakably clear from the New Testament that Jesus of Nazareth was proclaimed by the apostles as Lord and Savior, and that the very basis of the apostolic message was his death and resurrection" (*Christianity and World Religions*, p. 46). Christ's identity as the God-man is critical because "it is only the fact of who Christ was that gave his sacrificial death its redemptive and atoning significance" (Anderson, pp. 29–30). Anderson properly asks (pp. 139–140):

For if God could have adequately revealed himself in any other way, how can one possibly believe he would have gone to the almost unbelievable length of the incarnation? . . . And if God could have dealt with the problem of evil in any other way whatever, how can one possibly believe that he would, in Christ, himself have taken the sinner's place and borne the sinner's guilt—with all the agony (to say nothing of the mystery) expressed in that cry of dereliction from the cross: "My God, My God, why hast Thou forsaken Me?" (Mark 15:34).

To summarize, *"For the human sickness there is one specific remedy, and this is it. There is no other"* (Stephen Neil quoted by Anderson, p. 143; emphasis added).

As Kenneth Boa and Larry Moody point out in *I'm Glad You Asked*, there are three major objections to the truth of Christianity's exclusivity as a way to God, each of which is based on a false assumption.

(1) The first major objection to Christianity's claim of exclusivity is that it eliminates many sincere people who are seeking God through other religions. The faulty assumption behind this argument is that sincere people cannot be wrong. Probably all of us have been sincerely wrong before.

(2) The second major objection to Christianity's claim of exclusivity is that, even though Christianity may be right for some people, it may not be right for everybody. The assumption is that truth is determined by one's beliefs or lack of beliefs. The error is that, while subjective preferences (for example, favorite food) do vary, not all truth is subjectively determined. For instance, the law of gravity is true regardless of one's individual preferences on the subject! Similarly, the truth of Christianity must be determined on objective grounds.

(3) The third objection to Christianity's exclusivity is the false belief that anything so narrow must be wrong. While tolerance is admirable in personal relationships, truth is intolerant of error. As Paul Little comments in *Know Why You Believe* (p. 152):

> If two plus two is four, the total at the same time cannot be twenty-three. But one is not regarded as intolerant because he disagrees with *this* answer and maintains that the only correct answer is *four*.
>
> The same principle applies in religious matters. One must be tolerant of other points of view and respect their right to be held and heard. He cannot, however, be forced in the name of tolerance to agree that all points of view, including those that are mutually contradictory, are equally valid. Such a position is nonsense.

The Bible presents a unique perspective on reality as well as God's unique provision for our reconciliation through the substitutionary death of Jesus Christ. How can we "speak the truth in love" (see Eph. 4:15) about God and His provision in our pluralistic world? The next section offers a number of suggestions in this regard.

Summary: Christianity's primary distinction is that *Christ* is the only way to God.

> **REVIEW:**
>
> Christianity's primary distinction is that _____ is the only way to God.

4. Principles of Proclaiming the Truth

First, understand well your own faith. You must be able to articulate your faith to yourself before you can fully explain it to others.

Second, recognize truth in other religions. Probably all other religions have some truth in them, and to deny this is to deny factual accuracy and intellectual honesty.

Third, consider your motives. When we proclaim God's truth we must beware of the following motivations and behaviors: (1) *scalp hunting*, being focused on getting "a decision" (perhaps, in part, to glorify ourselves) and forgetting that we are but one link in the chain of transformation (see 1 Cor. 3:5–7); (2) *manipulation*, using high-pressure salesmanship instead of the simple, honest sharing of the gospel message; and (3) *arrogance*, forgetting God's grace in reaching out to us, and that we, too, are sinners.

Fourth, set limited goals for the discussion. We should aim for clear communication and understanding. We cannot argue someone into the kingdom; the Holy Spirit must produce the response of faith. Be positive and focus on proving Christianity rather than disproving others' religion. We share the message of salvation in an attitude of prayer and reliance on the Holy Spirit to work in us and the hearer, leaving all the results with God. Only He can save.

Summary: There are certain principles that should guide us in *proclaiming* the truth.

> **REVIEW:**
>
> There are certain principles that should guide us in _____ the truth.

Review

1. Christianity has *similarities* with other religions that must be recognized.
2. Christianity has *differences* from other religions that make it distinctive.
3. Christianity's primary distinction is that *Christ* is the only way to God.
4. There are certain principles that should guide us in *proclaiming* the truth.

Self-Test

1. Christianity has _____ with other religions that must be recognized.
2. Christianity has _____ from other religions that make it distinctive.
3. Christianity's primary distinction is that _____ is the only way to God.
4. There are certain principles that should guide us in _____ the truth.

TWENTY-SEVEN

DIFFERENT LITERARY FORMS IN THE BIBLE

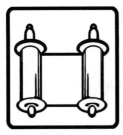 You cannot read history and poetry the same way. History is very factual. Poetry is very symbolic and figurative. If you take everything literally in poetry, you destroy the art. If you take everything figuratively in history, you lose the facts. For example, the following lines make acceptable poetry:

Barn Swallow . . . Barn Swallow . . . Hmmmm, well, I'll be.
What can explain this small bird that I see,
That flits in the air like a well-confused flier,
Swooping down low and then sweeping up higher?

Why was it given the name that it follows?
Why are they not called, say, Slicers, not Swallows?
What could they swallow? A fly or a moth?
They couldn't swallow a small table cloth!

The name doesn't fit; if it's true to my hunch,
That bird could not eat a *shed* for its lunch.
I've finally concluded it must be a yarn;
That size of a bird couldn't swallow a barn.

But while these thoughts make acceptable poetry they make terrible ornithology (the scientific study of birds)! This poem is inaccurate from beginning to end in its assumptions and purpose.

So, in education, it makes a difference what kind of literature you are studying as to how you treat it. In poetry, you look for art, symbolism, hidden meaning, etc. In history, biology, physics, etc., you look for accuracy.

The same principle is true of the Bible. When trying to understand a particular biblical book or passage, the reader must understand what kind of literature he or she is reading. This characterization of literature is called its "literary form."

Understanding literary form is vital to proper interpretation. The various forms must be studied and interpreted differently. Earlier, in chapter 21, we examined the literary form of the parable as employed by Jesus. In this chapter, we will overview five other kinds of writing that appear in the Bible and examine how they should be interpreted. While God also used other literary forms to communicate His message, these five (along with parables) are the most important.

1. The Didactic Form (Exposition)

Didactic or expository literature teaches truth in a relatively direct manner. The argument or explanation usually moves from point to point in a logical, highly organized fashion. Because the author employs comparatively few figures of speech, the meaning of a didactic passage is often easy to understand. The more difficult challenge becomes obediently applying the truth in one's own life.

Paul's epistles are clear examples of the didactic form. For example, in Romans Paul offers a tightly reasoned explanation and justification for the gospel. He frequently uses transitional and connective words such as *for, therefore, and,* and *but.* Paul employs many rhetorical questions to advance his argument (for example, Rom. 2:17–21, 26; 3:1, 3, 5; 4:1, 3, 9).

The meaning lies close to the surface in didactic literature. For this reason most didactic books are very good starting points for people who are just beginning to study the Bible. However, the truths taught in the didactic literature are profound enough to warrant detailed analysis even by experienced Bible students. What are some principles that will help us in understanding and applying this type of biblical material?

The most important guideline is to study the logical development of the argument. Pay attention to the structure and the terms employed. This is more difficult in some cases (such as James and 1 John) than in others (such as 1 Corinthians and Hebrews).

A second principle is to study the situation behind the statements. This will enable you to better understand both the argument of the book and the way in which the teachings of the passage apply in our present cultural context. For example, in this culture we greet one another with a "holy handshake" rather than the holy kiss described five times in the New Testament. As an additional example, one must understand the principle behind Paul's command not to eat meat sacrificed to idols (an issue he discusses in 1 Cor. 8:1–13 and 10:14–22) if one is to correctly apply the injunction today.

Biblical examples of didactic literature include: Paul's letters; Hebrews; James; 1 and 2 Peter; 1, 2, and 3 John; and Jude.

Summary: Didactic literature *teaches* truth in a relatively direct manner.

REVIEW:

Didactic literature _____ truth in a relatively direct manner.

---

2.   The Narrative Form

Narrative literature emphasizes stories. One reason for the Bible's enduring popularity is its abundance of compelling stories. For instance, the Bible's first book (Genesis) tells such stories as God's creation of the world, the Flood, the tower of Babel, how God began His plan to bless all nations through the family of Abraham, and how He worked in the lives of Abraham, Isaac, Jacob, and Joseph. Exodus picks up the story of this family, which has now become the Jewish nation, by telling how Moses led it out of captivity in Egypt. The Book of Joshua tells how Joshua led the next generation of Israelites out of the wilderness and back into the Promised Land. The narrative books include all the books from Genesis through Ezra, the four Gospels, and Acts.

How are we to understand the narrative sections of the Bible? What truths are the stories intended to convey? In what ways are these truths significant today?

Begin with a close reading of the text, focusing on the narrative flow and the plot. Determine how the story progresses. Is the movement of the book physical, spiritual, relational, or political? Look at the book as a whole, then analyze individual stories. What has changed by the end of the book, and why?

Who are the characters, and how are they presented? Note how the characters interact with one another and with God. Do they succeed or fail, and why?

Study the effect of the setting (geographical, temporal, or social) on the plot. An awareness of the prevailing social customs will greatly enhance your understanding of many of the biblical stories.

Note how the author uses literary devices such as repetition to emphasize certain elements of the narrative. Realize that the narrative sections express theological truths seen in living relationships, and consider what lesson(s) they illustrate. How might these truths be expressed in the lives of people in our time and culture?

Summary: Narrative literature tells a *story*.

REVIEW:

Narrative literature tells a _____.

---

3. The Poetic Form

Poetry appeals to our emotions and our imagination. The tremendous appeal of the Book of Psalms grows out of the depth and variety of the emotions the psalms convey. The books of the Bible that are mainly poetic are Job, Psalms, Proverbs, Ecclesiastes, and the Song of Solomon.

Hebrew poetry varies in important ways from English poetry. First, most of the psalms were composed to be sung rather than read. Thus, even though we do not have the music to which they were sung, it is even more important than for poetry in general that you listen to how they sound. Second, as was explained in chapter 13, Hebrew poetry makes extensive use of parallelism.

What are some principles that will help you properly interpret the poetic passages in Scripture?

First, recognize that each psalm has a controlling topic or theme and that the stanza patterns can assist you in discerning the flow of thought. For example, in the penitential Psalm 51,

David pleads for forgiveness and cleansing (vv. 1–2), confesses his guilt (vv. 3–6), prays for pardon and restoration (vv. 7–12), resolves to praise God (vv. 13–17), and prays for Jerusalem's continued prosperity (vv. 18–19). Newer translations help the reader by inserting a blank line between the stanzas, or *strophes.*

Second, group parallel lines and try to identify which type of parallelism is being used (for assistance, see the discussion of parallelism in chapter 13).

Third, be alert to the frequent use of figurative language (see the discussion of figures of speech in chapter 13). For instance, Hebrew poets frequently made their point by using *hyperbole,* a literary device that uses extreme or exaggerated language for emphasis.

Fourth, when possible, identify the historical background of the psalm. Knowing that David wrote Psalm 51 after being confronted regarding his sin with Bathsheba helps us understand the depth of David's spiritual agony and repentance. Likewise, the earnestness of David's desire for God and his trust in the Lord despite present circumstances become more striking when we realize that Psalm 63 was written while he was fleeing for his life from his son Absalom. Whether or not you can identify the historical setting, try to identify the poet's spiritual and psychological mood at the time of the psalm's composition.

Fifth, study the messianic psalms (2, 8, 16, 22, 40, 45, 69, 72, 89, 102, 109, 110, and 132) first in the light of their immediate historical purpose at the writer's time (primarily referring to David's situation). Then consider which elements, because of what they involve, must ultimately refer to the Messiah.

Although the prologue (1:1–2:13) and epilogue (42:7–17) of Job are in prose, the rest of the book is poetry. Here are some suggestions to help you get the most out of studying Job: Examine the complete statements made by each of the main characters (Job, Eliphaz, Bildad, Zophar, and Elihu). Identify each person's basic assumptions and evaluate his arguments. Study God's declarations and how they reflect on each of the characters. Identify the basic questions the book poses and the answers offered for them.

Context is crucial in interpreting Ecclesiastes. Virtually the entire book is a discourse on the meaninglessness and futility of life (see 1:2 and 12:8). Although there are more positive statements, at times the author seems to deny the validity of a pious life (see 2:15; 3:19; 5:16; and 8:14). The key to interpretation is the "theological commentary" found in the book's epilogue (12:9–14). Ecclesiastes 12:13 summarizes, "Now all has been heard; here is the conclusion of the matter: Fear God and keep His commandments, for this is the whole duty of man." This verse indicates that the entire book was written to demonstrate the meaninglessness of a life lived apart from God and the wisdom of living in reverence to God. The seemingly negative verses must be understood and interpreted in the light of this larger context.

Summary: Poetic literature presents poetry and must be *interpreted* in light of key principles.

REVIEW:

Poetic literature presents poetry and must be _____ in light of key principles.

---

4. The Proverb

This distinctive literary form concisely states a moral truth, frequently reducing life to black-and-white categories. As does poetry, proverbs often use parallelism to make their point. Metaphors and similes are two other frequently employed literary devices. Although individual proverbs do appear in other books of the Bible, the book known as Proverbs is the only place where proverbs are the major literary form.

The key to interpretation of proverbs is to realize that a proverb is a general guideline that offers wise advice rather than establishing a strict, invariable rule by which God works. For example, Proverbs 16:3 declares, "Commit to the LORD whatever you do, / and your plans will succeed" (NIV). At first glance this might appear to be a "blank check." However, as Fee and Stuart state in *How to Read the Bible for All It's Worth*, "A hasty marriage, a rash business decision, an ill-thought-out vocational decision—all can be dedicated to God but can eventually result in misery" (p. 198). Many proverbs employ hyperbole. In addition, "success" must be understood in the light of God's will, which often contradicts worldly values. Any proverb is a general statement which must be understood in accord with the totality of scriptural teaching on the topic.

Second, consider whether the context is important. This is the case in Proverbs 1–9 and 30–31 since each of these sections has a lengthy discourse style. The remainder of the book is primarily a collected series of proverbs where context is less important. For Proverbs 10–29 you should first examine each proverb on the basis of its parallelism, then collate the proverbs according to topic and interpret the similar proverbs together.

Third, extract the timeless principles embodied in the proverbs from their ancient cultural context and apply them to current situations. For example, Proverbs 11:1 ("The LORD abhors dishonest scales, / but accurate weights are his delight" [NIV]) refers to the ancient practice of using scales to weigh goods so that their value may be determined. Thus, the present-day significance of the proverb is to call us to honest business practices—for example, don't pad your expense account.

> **Summary**: Proverbial literature concisely states a moral truth as a general *guideline*.

> **REVIEW:**
>
> Proverbial literature concisely states a moral truth as a general
> _____ .

5. The Prophetic and Apocalyptic Forms

Much of the Bible is prophetic. Although we often think of prophecy as a prediction of the future, this is only part of the biblical conception of prophecy. Prophecy is not just the *foretelling* of the future; it is also the *forthtelling* of God's message (whether encouragement, admonition, or warning) to the people. Sometimes God would have the prophet make a prediction of what would happen in the near future so that the event's occurrence would validate the rest of the prophet's message.

The Old Testament books from Isaiah to Malachi are prophetic. The New Testament Book of Revelation is the primary example of a special category of prophetic literature known as *apocalyptic.* Apocalyptic literature focuses on the cataclysmic events having to do with the end of the world and God's ultimate triumph over evil. Apocalyptic literature makes especially heavy use of symbolism and vivid imagery. Large sections of apocalyptic material occur in the books of Daniel, Zechariah, and Revelation; other books have smaller amounts.

Interpretation of the prophetic literature can be particularly challenging. What are some principles that will help you to understand biblical prophecy?

First, as with any literary form in the Bible, study the passage in terms of its history, context, and literal meaning. Study the historical circumstances of both the prophet and the people involved in the particular prophecy. Carefully consider both the immediate (that is, what precedes and what follows the passage) and broad (such as parallel passages) context. For example, one's comprehension of the Book of Revelation is enhanced by an understanding of the Book of Daniel. Take the words in their normal sense unless it is evident that a figure of speech or a symbol is being used.

Second, identify exactly to whom or to what the passage refers. Is the passage didactic (forthtelling) or predictive (foretelling)? If it is didactic, note how the people responded. If it is predictive, consider two additional questions. Was the prophecy *conditional* or *unconditional?* For instance, in Jeremiah 18:5–10 God declares that He will turn aside (1) promised judgment when a nation repents and turns from its evil ways, and (2) promised blessing when a nation turns to evil. It is in this light that we should understand God sparing Nineveh after Jonah's preaching led to its repentance (see Jonah 3:10). The second question is: Has the prophecy been *fulfilled,* or is it still *unfulfilled?* In the former case, study the writings that tell about the fulfillment. If the prophecy has not been fulfilled, study it carefully and humbly. Unfulfilled prophecy is often enigmatic because of its use of symbolism.

Third, distinguish between *direct predictions* and *types.* Direct prediction refers to a prophecy that has a single fulfillment. For example, Micah 5:2 states that the Messiah would be born in Bethlehem. Christ's fulfillment of this prophecy is seen in Matthew 2:5–6. A type is "a preordained representative relationship which certain persons, events, and institutions bear to corresponding persons, events, and institutions occurring at a later time in salvation history" (Henry Virkler, *Hermeneutics,* p. 184). For example, Jesus referred to the events in Numbers 21:4–9 when He stated, "Just as Moses lifted up the snake in the desert, so the Son of Man must be lifted up, that everyone who believes in him may have eternal life" (John 3:14–15 NIV). Jesus identified two corresponding resemblances: (1) the lifting up of both the servant and Himself, and (2) life for those who looked upon the object lifted up (that is, who responded in faith to God's provision).

Finally, always take care to remember that the main purpose of prophecy is not to inspire debate or dogmatism about the future but to encourage faith in God and holy living in the present. This is more obviously true in the didactic or forthtelling passages where the prophet encourages, exhorts, warns, etc. However, even in the predictive passages God's primary intent is not to satisfy our curiosity about the future but to change our lives.

For example, Paul introduces his discussion of the rapture (1 Thess. 4:13–18) by saying that he did not want the Thessalonian believers to be ignorant or to grieve as those who have no hope. In contrast to false teachers who evidently were teaching that their loved ones who died before Christ's return would not be raised to new life, Paul proclaimed that "the dead in Christ will rise first" (v. 16), and all believers "will be with the Lord forever. Therefore encourage each other with these words" (vv. 17–18).

A second example is found in 2 Peter 3, where the apostle speaks of a future "day of judgment and destruction of ungodly men" (v. 7). As an additional result of God's judgment the present heaven and earth will be destroyed and replaced by a new heaven and earth. Peter exhorts, "Since everything will be destroyed in this way, what kind of people ought you to be? You ought to live holy and godly lives as you look forward to the day of God" (vv. 11–12). And again, "So then, dear friends, since you are looking forward to this, make every effort to be found spotless, blameless and at peace with him" (v. 14).

Remember that the "blessed hope" of the believer is Christ's imminent, personal return to receive His own unto Himself, regardless of when that event will occur. God's desire is that the promise of Christ's return have a motivating and purifying effect on the personal life and service of Christians (compare Titus 2:11–14), not that its timing should become a source of division.

Thus, when studying biblical prophecy (or any other type of biblical literature), always ask yourself, "How does God intend this truth to change my life?"

Summary: Prophetic literature proclaims the Word of God and sometimes tells the *future*, often in highly figurative and symbolic language.

REVIEW:

Prophetic literature proclaims the Word of God and sometimes tells the _____, often in highly figurative and symbolic language.

Review

1. Didactic literature *teaches* truth in a relatively direct manner.
2. Narrative literature tells a *story*.
3. Poetic literature presents poetry and must be *interpreted* in light of key principles.
4. Proverbial literature concisely states a moral truth as a general *guideline*.
5. Prophetic literature proclaims the Word of God and sometimes tells the *future*, often in highly figurative and symbolic language.

Self-Test

1. Didactic literature _____ truth in a relatively direct manner.
2. Narrative literature tells a _____.
3. Poetic literature presents poetry and must be _____ in light of key principles.
4. Proverbial literature concisely states a moral truth as a general

   _____ .

5. Prophetic literature proclaims the Word of God and sometimes tells the _____, often in highly figurative and symbolic language.

TWENTY-EIGHT

HOW TO BE PROPERLY RELATED TO GOD

 In ancient Persia, if you came into the presence of the king unbidden, it could cost you your life. The chasm between monarch and mortal has always been difficult and dangerous to cross. If so with kings, how much more so with God? How then does one approach God? On what basis might we be accepted into His presence and establish a relationship with Him? How can we be properly related to God?

God is, in a sense, a monarch, and there are certain rules that apply in our ability to approach Him. Yet, unlike most monarchs, God earnestly desires our fellowship. He encourages us to come to Him. Billy Graham, in his book *How to Be Born Again*, tells an interesting story that captures this fact so well.

> Picture a courtroom. God the Judge is seated in the judge's seat, robed in splendor. You are arraigned before Him. He looks at you in terms of His own righteous nature as it is expressed in the moral law. He speaks to you:
>
> God: John (or Mary), have you loved Me with all your heart?
>
> John/Mary: No, Your Honor.
>
> God: Have you loved others as you have loved yourself?
>
> John/Mary: No, Your Honor.
>
> God: Do you believe you are a sinner and that Jesus Christ died for your sins?
>
> John/Mary: Yes, Your Honor.

God: Then your penalty has been paid by Jesus Christ on the cross and you are pardoned. . . . Because Christ is righteous, and you believe in Christ, I now declare you legally righteous.

Can you imagine what a newspaperman would do with this event?

SINNER PARDONED—

GOES TO LIVE WITH JUDGE

> It was a tense scene when John and Mary stood before the Judge and had the list of charges against them read. However, the Judge transferred all of the guilt to Jesus Christ, who died on a cross for John and Mary.
>
> After John and Mary were pardoned, the Judge invited them to come to live with Him forever.

The reporter on a story like that would never be able to understand the irony of such a scene, unless he had been introduced to the Judge beforehand and knew His character.

Pardon and Christ's righteousness come to us only when we totally trust ourselves to Jesus as our Lord and Savior. When we do this, God welcomes us into His intimate favor. Clothed in Christ's righteousness we can now enjoy God's fellowship.

Faith is the key to a relationship with God. If we believe in Him, He adopts us as His spiritual children (Eph. 1:5), and the relationship we might imagine existing between a model earthly father and his children is a picture of the spiritual relationship we then have with God.

The Program of God

God's strategy in developing His relationship with man has been consistent throughout the ages. The four main principles of the program of God are:

1. Revelation from God
2. Requirement of Faith
3. Reward of Blessing
4. Redemption of Others

1.   Revelation from God: God reveals truth to man

In the earliest days, He did this directly, through direct contact, dreams and visions, angels, etc. Now His primary means of revelation is the Bible.

2.   Requirement of Faith: God asks man to believe and obey the revelation, living by faith

Many of the things God asks of man in the revelation take man in the opposite direction of his natural inclinations. Therefore, man will only respond if he believes God! Such is the nature of faith. You believe something you can't see! You act on something that is unnatural! You subordinate your own instincts to someone you believe has greater wisdom.

3.   Reward of Blessing: God blesses "living by faith"

As man lives for God by faith, trusting God and obeying Him as best he knows how, God blesses that man and gives him a quality of life that makes his life of faith deeply satisfying.

4.   Redemption of Others: Others are drawn to faith in God

Finally, when others look at the "child of God" and see the blessing that comes to him through his relationship with God, a thirst is created in some lives to want to know God also.

How these principles worked themselves out was quite different in the Old Testament than it is in the New Testament. We are now going to look at each of these principles (revelation, faith, blessing, and redemption), and see how they are worked out in the Old and New Testaments.

The Old Testament: The Fruit of the Vine

1.   Revelation from God: God reveals truth to man

God revealed Himself to the people in the Old Testament in many different ways. In the earliest days it was entirely through miraculous means, since none of the Bible was written. Later, as the Old Testament was being recorded, they had the benefit of that Scripture.

This revelation asked the Old Testament people to act in ways that departed from the normal behavior. For example, they were not to amass horses to themselves as military resources. God would fight for them and protect them from all enemies as long as Israel remained righteous.

They were to refrain from labor or commerce every seventh day. Every seventh year, they were to let their land lie fallow for the entire year. God promised to bless their business and agricultural pursuits to such an extent that they would have plenty.

They were to give almost 30 percent of their income in tithes and offerings for national taxes and for the functioning of the sacrificial and priestly system. God promised to prosper them economically if they would obey these commands.

2. Requirement of faith: God asks man to believe and obey the revelation, living by faith

If you believed that an invisible God would protect you from enemies, you would be willing to forego the development of a cavalry-and-chariot warfare. If you did not trust God to protect you, you would disobey and raise all the horses you could to protect yourself.

If you believed that an invisible God would prosper your farming to such an extent that you could actually not plant a crop one year out of seven and spend that year in praise to the Lord, you would obey and forego planting in the seventh year. If you did not trust God to prosper you, you would disobey and raise all the crops you could to supply yourself.

If you believed that God would prosper you financially, so that you could afford to give 30 percent of your money for national and religious purposes, you would obey and tithe your income. If you didn't trust God to prosper you, you would disobey and keep the money for yourself.

These are just three examples of how God's revelation took man in the opposite direction from his natural inclinations. His natural inclinations are to protect himself, supply himself, and fund himself. Instead, faith requires that we believe God and do things His way.

3. Reward of Blessing: God blesses "living by faith"

If the Israelites would trust God to meet their needs and obey His commandments, God promised to give them, not just subsistence, but abundance in every area of their national life.

> Now it shall be, if you will diligently obey the LORD your God, being careful to do all His commandments which I command you today, the LORD your God will set you high above all the nations of the earth.

> And all these blessings shall come upon you and overtake you, if you will obey the LORD your God.

> Blessed shall you be in the city, and blessed shall you be in the country.

> Blessed shall be the offspring of your body and the produce of your ground and the offspring of your beasts, and the increase of your herd and the young of your flock.

> Blessed shall be your basket and your kneading bowl.

> Blessed shall you be when you come in, and blessed shall you be when you go out.

> The LORD will cause your enemies who rise up against you to be defeated before you; they shall come out against you one way and shall flee before you seven ways.

> The LORD will command the blessing upon you in your barns and in all that you put your hand to, and He will bless you in the land which the LORD your God gives you.

> The LORD will establish you as a holy people to Himself, as He swore to you, if you will keep the commandments of the LORD your God, and walk in His ways.

> So all the people of the earth shall see that you are called by the name of the LORD, and they shall be afraid of you. (Deut. 28:1–10)

God put His word on the line in unambiguous terms. Marvelous blessing was theirs if in faith they were obedient from the heart to His commandments.

4.   Redemption of Others: Others are drawn to faith in God

God did not choose the nation of Israel to the exclusion of all the other people in the world. He chose Israel in order to reach all the other people in the world. God's idea was to so bless Israel that the other nations of the world would see the "thumb print" of God on their national life, and desire to know their God because of the quality of life He had given Israel.

This is stated in Psalm 67 as succinctly as anywhere in the Bible:

> God be gracious to us and bless us,
> And cause His face to shine upon us—
> That Thy way may be known on the earth,
> Thy salvation among all nations.
> Let the peoples praise Thee, O God;
> Let all the peoples praise Thee.
> Let the nations be glad and sing for joy;
> For Thou wilt judge the peoples with uprightness,
> And guide the nations on the earth.
> Let the peoples praise Thee, O God;
> Let all the peoples praise Thee.
> The earth has yielded its produce;
> God, our God, blesses us.
> God blesses us,
> That all the ends of the earth may fear Him. (Ps. 67:1–7)

There it is in black and white: God blesses Israel, that all the ends of the earth may fear Him. *Fear* here does not mean "fright or terror"; rather it means respect or reverence.

But God's blessing is always tied to obedience to His commandments, which is the evidence of faith. Israel was never successful at living righteously for very long. The longest sustained period of righteousness for the nation overlapped David's reign and the first part of Solomon's reign. There was a period of perhaps as long as sixty years of sustained righteous national living. As a result, this was the period of greatest blessing on them as a nation. It was stupendous, and its effect on the surrounding nations was observable.

We read in 1 Kings 10 that word of the splendor of Israel was spreading. Even the queen of Sheba heard of the glory of Jerusalem and the wisdom of Solomon. So fascinated was she by the reports of Israel's grandeur that she came for a closer look. Solomon displayed to her his palace, the city of Jerusalem, and the temple, one of the most glorious buildings ever built.

After the queen had seen everything, the Bible says in 1 Kings 10:5 that "there was no more spirit in her." She swooned! Then she began to babble. "It was a true report which I heard in my own land about your words and your wisdom. Nevertheless, I did not believe the reports, until I came and my eyes had seen it. And behold, the half was not told me. You exceed in wisdom and prosperity the report which I heard" (vv. 6–7). Then she broke out in spontaneous eulogy to God. "Blessed be the Lord Your God" (v. 9).

This was the way it was designed to work. The people of the world see the splendor of Israel, and their attention is drawn to God.

The New Testament: The Fruit of the Spirit

God's dealings with the nation of Israel were very much physical, and were designed to picture or foreshadow the spiritual truths that would be presented in the New Testament. The Old Testament sacrificial system was intended to picture, in literal terms, the spiritual work that would be done by Christ on the cross in the New Testament. The beauty of the temple was designed to picture the glory of God. The physical blessing of protection and food was designed to picture the spiritual protection and nourishment that is ours in Christ.

While God's strategy of developing His relationships with man is the same in the New Testament as it was in the Old Testament, the principles are worked out differently. The blessings in the Old Testament were conspicuously material and physical— the fruit of the vine. The blessings in the New Testament are conspicuously spiritual—the fruit of the Spirit.

1.   Revelation from God: God reveals truth to man

The revelation from God in the New Testament is quite different from the Old Testament. Christ said that He came to fulfill the law. Now that He has come and died for our sins and has risen again from the dead, there is no longer any need for the sacrificial system. There is no need to observe the Mosaic

Law. We no longer have to worry about not planting the seventh year, and so on, because whereas Israel was a physical kingdom designed to picture the coming spiritual kingdom, now the spiritual kingdom is here. If Jesus' kingdom were of this world, we would have to be concerned about some of those things. But it isn't, so we don't.

Nevertheless, the nature of the revelation remains the same. It asks us to function in a way contrary to our natural inclinations. If we would keep our life, we must lose it; if we want to be great, we must become a servant. If we are to be strong, we must be gentle. It is better to give than to receive. Pursue the kingdom of God first, and all our material needs will be met. Reality in the New Testament is that which is *not* seen, while that which is seen is a counterfeit. We must live for the next world instead of this one.

2. Requirement of Faith: God asks man to believe and obey the revelation, living by faith

All of this, going against our natural inclinations, is most unnatural—just as unnatural as the commands in the Old Testament. And faith is required just as much in the New Testament as in the Old. It all boils down to the same thing: If we believe God, we obey the commands. If we don't believe, we don't obey. The opposite of obedience is not disobedience. It is unbelief. Our disobedience is linked to lack of faith.

3. Reward of Blessing: God blesses "living by faith"

In the Old Testament, God blessed the Israelites with material abundance. In the New Testament, the material blessings are no longer necessarily operative. God blesses the Christian with spiritual abundance. If we live in faith, trusting and obeying God, He gives us, rather than the fruit of the vine, the fruit of the Spirit: love, joy, peace, patience, kindness, goodness, faithfulness, gentleness, self-control (Gal. 5:22–23). If you ask anyone what he wants out of life, he will say, "I just want to be happy." The blessing that is promised to the faithful child of God in the New Testament is greater than that. It is inner peace, genuine love, and deep joy.

4. Redemption of Others: Others are drawn to faith in God

In the Old Testament, God promised to raise Israel higher than the other nations of the world by bestowing material abundance. In the New Testament, He promised to raise individual Christians higher than the world by bestowing spiritual abundance. "Let your light shine before men in such a way that they may see your good works, and glorify your Father who is in heaven" (Matt. 5:16). "Do all things without grumbling or disputing; that you may prove yourselves to be blameless and innocent, children of God above reproach in the midst of a crooked and perverse generation, among whom you appear as lights in the world" (Phil. 2:14–15). It is our inner spiritual abundance, not our outer material abundance, that reveals God to the world.

When we live as we ought, it calls attention to the Lord and encourages others to become Christians. "A new commandment I give to you, that you love one another, even as I have loved you, that you also love one another. By this all men will know that you are My disciples, if you have love for one another" (John 13:34–35). And, as Christ is accurately portrayed and proclaimed to the world, people will be drawn to Him to become Christians.

Consequences

We see, then, that to be properly related to God, faith is the central issue. Faith is critical, because it is the *only* way to establish a relationship with God (Eph. 2:8–9), and living by faith is the only way to receive the blessings of that relationship.

By faith, we become His spiritual children (John 1:12) and by faith, as we read His revelation and believe it, we respond accordingly. In doing so, we are eligible for His spiritual blessing, which has three primary consequences:

1. God is glorified

As we respond in faith, trusting and obeying God, striving to live according to the Scriptures, our lives gradually begin to take on the character of God Himself. When this happens, the world begins to get an accurate picture of who God really is, because they begin to see Him in us. The value and worth of God begin to be known publicly, and in this way, God is glorified.

2. Man is satisfied

In addition, we who are living by faith, His spiritual children, experience the pleasure of the life that God grants to us. Peace, love, and joy become ours in increasing measure, and we are satisfied.

3. Others are evangelized

Others see the quality of life available to the children of God. Some will be drawn to faith in God. Because of what they see of Him in the lives of those who are living by faith, others are evangelized.

Summary: The Program of God and Its Consequences

God wants to have a personal relationship with us. Our relationship with Him is established by faith.

Revelation from God

God has made His revelation known to us in His Word, the Bible.

Requirement of Faith

The Bible asks us to do some things that we would not naturally be inclined to do. If we trust God and believe in Him, we live by faith and obey them. If we don't believe, we don't obey.

Reward of Blessing

If we believe God and live by faith, striving from the heart to obey the Bible, He blesses us with spiritual abundance (peace, love, and joy), and we begin to take on the character of God in our lives.

Redemption of Others

Seeing the spiritual blessings of God's character in our lives, others are drawn to Him for relationship.

When man responds in faith to the revelation from God, the consequences of the rewards of blessings continue in full circle as others are drawn to Him for redemption and relationship: God is glorified, man is satisfied, others are evangelized.

Review

(Fill in the blanks of the four main principles of the program of God.)

1. **R**_____ from God.

2. **R**_____ of Faith.

3. **R**_____ of Blessing.

4. **R**_____ of Others.

TWENTY-NINE

HOW TO BE PROPERLY RELATED TO SELF

I went to a professional dog show once and, in observing the relationship between man and dog, made some comparisons with the relation of God and man, and on meaning and purpose in life.

The obedience trials that took place within a large, square green of closely mowed grass were particularly interesting. Several tests of obedience were displayed.

1. One at a time, the dogs had to start, stop, change direction, sit, stay, and return to their master, following a prescribed course that took them all over the lawn, without any verbal commands . . . only hand signals.

2. The dogs had to select, out of a pile of "dumbbells," the one wooden dumbbell their master had handled. The dumbbell was identical to all the others except for its identification number.

3. On command, the dogs had to jump back and forth over a high, solid-wood hurdle; again, only hand signs were used.

4. The dogs were required to lie down in the center of the lawn and, upon being told to "stay," were required to remain there for a number of minutes while being totally ignored by their master, who was out of sight behind a canvas.

Two dogs in particular stood out. One was a large, white German shepherd. He was an eager, grinning, tongue-lolling, fun-loving dog, but not fully trained. While enduring one of the early "sit-stay" commands, he spied a cottontail rabbit hopping at leisure around the back edge of the lawn. The large, well-muscled paragon of canine virtue began trembling like a white jell-o statue, eyes riveted in utter absorption on this tasty treasure.

As though deliberately baiting him, the rabbit began cavorting playfully around the base of a mesquite bush, gamboling about in utter ecstasy under the inflamed scrutiny of the shepherd.

One final tantalizing hop was more than the white powder keg could endure and, as though shot out of a cannon, the shepherd exploded in the direction of the rabbit. Both disappeared quickly into the brush, not to be seen in public again. While entertaining to watch, the dog was a failure, an embarrassment to its owner. Untrained, he had not yet attained that marvel of harmony and communication that exists between skillful trainer and well-trained dog.

In contrast to the white German shepherd was a glorious, silky golden retriever. The retriever's excellence was as great as the shepherd's failure. Obedience to every command was instantaneous and perfect. Before, during, and after each command, the eyes of the retriever were, rather than roaming the horizon for signs of life, fixed devotedly . . . no, adoringly, on the young girl who was his owner and trainer. After each drill the dog would return to her side and, with head up and tongue hanging out, panting, he would stare into her eyes for the next command.

After all the dogs had gone through the trials, all the trainers and canines lined up for the awards. Fourth prize went to a Springer spaniel, third to a German shepherd, second to a black Lab. All during this time, the golden retriever sat obediently beside his master, looking up into her eyes.

Finally, first prize went to this marvelous dog and the girl who trained him. A polite ripple of applause washed through the audience. Then crowd and contestants began to disperse. As they did, a marvelous thing happened. The girl wheeled to face her dog, squealed with delight, and began clapping her hands together excitedly. At this, the dog lunged up toward the girl's face in a desperate attempt to lick her in the mouth. She laughed and pushed him back. He tried again. She began running toward her car, laughing, clapping in unbridled joy as her dog barked and jumped and circled around her all the way, sharing completely in her joy.

Chills played up and down my spine as I watched in undisguised admiration the joy, the intimacy, the trust, the devotion, and the adoration that flowed between dog and girl.

The intelligence, athletic ability, courage, and personality latent within this dog were developed to a higher degree and displayed more effectively than in any other dog I have ever seen. I thought, "This is the highest good to which I have ever seen canine life elevated." He was a marvel, a tribute to himself and his master. But everyone knew that the skill, intelligence, insight, patience, and personality of the owner were also on display. A lesser trainer could not have gotten so much from her charge. Glory for the dog! Glory for the owner!

Had that dog been left to his own world, he would have been just a dog, an ignorant slave of his basic instincts to eat and bark.

There were surely times in the training process when the dog was unhappy. Surely he had occasionally wanted to quit, to run away. There were times when the owner wondered if he would ever learn. Before the training process was completed, the dog would gladly have been dismissed. But after the training process, the dog was happier and more fulfilled at its master's side than anywhere else in the world. The dog received what it most wanted out of life and from its relationship with its master.

How like God and man this is! If we cast ourselves in utter devotion on our "heavenly Master," He will enlarge, expand, and develop us so that we achieve our highest good as a human being—to the satisfaction of man and the glory of God.

Man's Motivation in Life—
Two Basic Needs

God created man with certain basic inner needs that must be fulfilled for him to have satisfaction in life. Man's two primary needs are for (1) meaning or purpose in life, and (2) meaningful relationships, to love and be loved.

1. Meaning: Purpose in life

Rabbi Harold Kushner wrote, in *When All You Ever Wanted Isn't Enough,* "Our souls are not hungry for fame, comfort, wealth, or power. Those rewards create almost as many problems as they solve. Our souls are hungry for meaning, for the sense that we have figured out how to live so that our lives matter, so that the world will be at least a little bit different for our having passed through it." One of the basic motivations in our lives is to do something so that our lives will have mattered.

2. Relationships: To love and be loved

We also long for meaningful relationships. There are those who have accomplished significant things with their life, but died hollow and unfulfilled because they had no one to share them with. If we can do something we consider significant with our life, and if we can love and be loved, then we feel fulfilled, and a basic motivation in life is satisfied.

It is not wrong to feel these needs. They are gifts from God. God's strategy was to implant those needs within our souls and then meet these needs Himself. They can only fully and permanently be met in Him.

Fulfilling the Needs

It is a man's thoughts, what he believes, that determine his actions, and his actions determine his life consequences. If a man wants to change his life consequences, he must go back to the beginning and change his beliefs. On that basis, he can change his actions, and thereby his life consequences.

Beliefs

MAN'S WAY:	GOD'S WAY:
The fall has confused man and now he believes that truth is what he can determine through his intellect and his five senses.	This is not true, of course. Truth is revealed in the Bible, and sometimes it goes contrary to man's reasoning.

Man's confused beliefs put him at odds with God.

Actions

MAN'S WAY:	GOD'S WAY:
Therefore, since by nature man believes he must meet those two needs himself, he attempts to control people and circumstances to win for himself the significance and the relationships he craves.	He does this rather than to believe and obey the Lord who promises to give him what he longs for: a sense of purpose and meaningful relationships.

Man's misguided efforts are never fully satisfying.

Consequences

MAN'S WAY:	GOD'S WAY:
We cannot control people and circumstances long enough to bring permanent satisfaction, and if we are counting on that, we are bound to have a marginally satisfying life at best and an utterly unsatisfying one at worst.	God intends for us to give up trying to get our basic needs met by controlling people and circumstances. He has promised that if we live for Him He will satisfy us with the fruit of the spirit: love, joy, and peace.

We get our satisfaction in life from living for and with our heavenly Master, just as the golden retriever got its satisfaction from its relationship with its master.

"Man was created to know God," the Westminster Confession states, "and to enjoy Him forever." God created man with deep longings for meaning and love. Then God planned to meet those longings, fully and eternally, Himself. We are pulled to sin when we try to meet those longings outside of what God has properly given us. So, in being rightly related to yourself, you must understand who you are. You have been created for God. Your longings can only be met in relationship with Him. All that you want is found as you pursue Him. You can then be at peace not only with God but also with yourself.

Summary: Fulfilling the Needs of Man

MAN'S WAY: GOD'S WAY:

Beliefs

lead to . . .

Actions

lead to . . .

Consequences

result in . . .

Frustration   **Satisfaction**
(Inner Turmoil)   (Inner Peace)

Review: Fulfilling the Needs of Man

(Fill in the blanks.)

MAN'S WAY: GOD'S WAY:

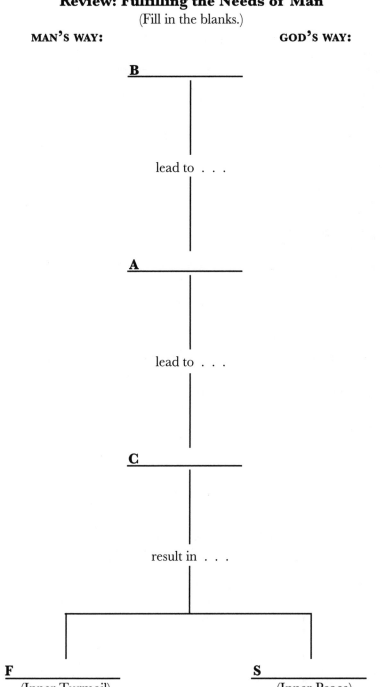

B _____

lead to . . .

A _____

lead to . . .

C _____

result in . . .

F _____   **S** _____
(Inner Turmoil)   (Inner Peace)

HOW TO BE PROPERLY
RELATED TO OTHERS

> When I was young, I admired clever people.
> Now that I am old, I admire kind people.
>
> Abraham Joshua Herschel

Love is central to human relationships, and human relationships are central to life. The man who said he was a rock and an island was a fool. He died a lonely man. No one ever had a meaningful life without meaningful relationships. God does not want us to live alone. In fact, He made us so that we cannot make it alone. We need other people. On his death bed, no one ever said, "I wish I had spent more time on my business." But many have said, "I wish I had spent more time with those I loved. I wish I had told them more often that I loved them."

C. S. Lewis once wrote:

> To love at all is to be vulnerable. Love anything, and your heart will certainly be wrung and possibly be broken. If you want to make sure of keeping it intact, you must give your heart to no one, not even to an animal. Wrap it carefully round with hobbies and little luxuries; avoid all entanglements; lock it up safe in the casket or coffin of your selfishness. But in that casket—safe, dark, motionless, airless—it will change. It will not be broken; it will become unbreakable, impenetrable, irredeemable. . . . The only place outside Heaven where you can be perfectly safe from all the dangers . . . of love is Hell.

This is reflected in the most dramatic and startling poem I have ever read: "Richard Cory" by Edward Arlington Robinson.

Whenever Richard Cory went downtown,
We people on the pavement looked at him;
He was a gentlemen from soul to crown,
Clean favored, and imperially slim.

And he was always quietly arrayed,
And he was always a human when he talked.
But still he fluttered pulses when he said,
    "Good morning,"
And he glittered when he walked.

And he was rich—yes richer than a king,
And admirably schooled in every grace.
In fact, we thought he was everything,
To make us wish that we were in his place.

So on we worked and waited for the light;
And went without meat and cursed the bread.
And Richard Cory, one calm summer night,
Went home and put a bullet through his head.

A rich, full life is a life lived *with* other people and *for* other people. We are all part of one another, and the more deeply we learn to love and accept love, the more life becomes what we hoped it would be.

Jesus understood this well. That is why He said so much about love.

A new commandment I give to you, that you love one another, even as I have loved you, that you also love one another. (John 13:34)

You shall love your neighbor as yourself. (Matt. 22:39)

God made us and knows what we need. He commanded us to love because He knows we need love.

Throughout the Bible, love is one of the dominant themes.

Husbands, love your wives. (Eph. 5:25)

Encourage the young women to love their husbands, to love their children. (Titus 2:4)

Let us love one another. (1 John 4:7)

Walk in love. (Eph. 5:2)

But probably the most complete passage in the Bible on love is commonly referred to as the "love passage," 1 Corinthians 13:4–8:

> Love is patient, love is kind, and is not jealous; love does not brag and is not arrogant, does not act unbecomingly; it does not seek its own, is not provoked, does not take into account a wrong suffered, does not rejoice in unrighteousness, but rejoices with the truth; bears all things, believes all things, hopes all things, endures all things. Love never fails.

If we were all to begin manifesting this kind of love, we would need no armies, no police, no criminal lawyers, no jails, no locks. We would begin experiencing the deepest, most meaningful relationships imaginable. It would be a taste of heaven on earth.

God Himself sets the example for us. In Christ, He has demonstrated infinite love for each of us. Then He calls us to the same kind of love.

In his book, *Release from Phoniness,* Arnold Prater writes:

> A man I knew who stood behind the second chair in the barber shop was a friend of mine, but this fellow in the second chair, a man about sixty-five years of age, was the vilest, most vulgar, profane, wicked-talking man I had ever known. He must have had some kind of fixation on preachers, because it seemed to me that every time I came in the shop, he doubled his output. One day when I went in, he was gone. I asked my barber friend where he was, and he said, "Oh, he's been desperately ill. For a while they despaired of his life."

> Perhaps six weeks later, I was entering the post office when I heard my name, and I turned and saw the profane man. He was seated in a car so he could see the people walking in and out of the post office. He was a mere shadow of a man, and his face was the color of death itself. He crooked a long, bony finger at me, and I walked over to where he was. He said in a voice so weak I had to lean over to hear it. "Preacher, I want to tell you something. I was in a coma down at the hospital. And I could hear the doctor tell my wife, 'I don't think he can last another hour.'" Then his voice trembled and it was a moment before he could continue. Then he said, "Preacher, I ain't never prayed in my entire life . . . but I prayed then. I said, 'Oh, God,

if there is a God, I need you now.' And when I said that . . . I don't know how to put it in words, but He was there. He came."

Then tears welled up in his reddened eyes, and then he said, "Oh, preacher, just imagine. I kicked Him in the face every day of my life for sixty years, and the first time I called His name, He came."

Stories of men loving the way God loves become some of the most meaningful stories we hear. In Chuck Colson's book, *Loving God*, he tells the story of Senator Bill Armstrong, who shows his love for God by loving his fellow man.

Jack Swigert, pilot of the Apollo 13 lunar mission, lay in a hospital bed, critically ill from cancer. With him, sitting where he had sat almost every night, was Bill Armstrong, senator from Colorado and chairman of the Senate subcommittee handling Washington's most difficult issue, Social Security. He was there, not because he was a powerful politician. He was there as a deeply committed Christian, and as Jack Swigert's friend, fulfilling a responsibility he would not delegate or shirk, even though he disliked hospitals.

As Colson told it, this night Bill leaned over the bed and spoke quietly to his friend.

"Jack, you're going to be all right. God loves you. I love you. You're surrounded by friends who are praying for you. You're going to be all right." The only sound was Jack's tortured and uneven breathing.

Bill pulled his chair closer to the bed and opened his Bible. "Psalm 23," he began to read in a steady voice. "The Lord is my shepherd, I shall not want . . ."

Time passed. "Psalm 150," Bill began, then his skin prickled. Jack's ragged breathing stopped. He leaned down over the bed, then called for help. As he watched the nurse examining Jack, Bill knew there was nothing more he could do. His friend was dead.

Politicians are busy people, especially Senate subcommittee chairmen. Yet it never occurred to Bill Armstrong that he was too busy to be at the hospital. Nothing dramatic or heroic about his decision—just a friend doing what he could.

Being properly related to others is just a matter of loving them. Usually, it is nothing spectacular. But it is letting others know we love them, that they matter, that we care. It is meeting their needs, if we can. It is letting them meet our needs. As we give our lives for the sake of others, trusting God to meet our own deep longing for love, it frees others to be able to give love too. And often that love is returned to us, and our needs are met in the context of love, unity, and harmony.

Forgiveness, kindness, compassion, love. Those are the things of which meaningful relationships are made.

In a beguilingly simple little poem, Henry Wadsworth Longfellow wrote:

> Kind hearts are the gardens,
> Kind thoughts are the roots,
> Kind words are the flowers,
> Kind deeds are the fruits.
> Take care of your garden,
> And keep out the weeds.
> Fill it with sunshine,
> Kind words and kind deeds.

Summary

God has created in us a need to love and be loved. The Bible gives us a good deal of insight on what it means to love, and our observations of life can augment that understanding. As we consistently reach out to others, making them feel loved and accepting love in return, we become "rightly related" to others and experience the joy and fulfillment of meaningful relationships.

Loving Others

1. Love is the basis of all meaningful relationships.
2. Love gives.
3. Love receives.

Review

(Fill in the blanks.)

1. **L**_____ is the basis of all meaningful relationships.

2. Love **g**_____.

3. Love **r**_____.

My hat goes off to you! You are finished! *Congratulations!* Your completed copy of *30 Days to Understanding the Bible* stands as a permanent tribute to your commitment and perseverance. It is my earnest hope that it has made an important contribution to your life.

APPENDIX

Story of the Bible

ERA	FIGURE	LOCATION	STORY LINE SUMMARY
Creation	*Adam*	*Eden*	Adam is created by God, but he *sins* and *destroys* God's original *plan* for man.
Patriarch	*Abraham*	*Canaan*	Abraham is *chosen* by God to "father" a *people* to *represent* God to the world.
Exodus	*Moses*	*Egypt*	Through Moses God *delivers* the Hebrew people from *slavery* in Egypt and then gives them the *Law*.
Conquest	*Joshua*	*Canaan*	Joshua leads the *conquest* of the *Promised Land*.
Judges	*Samson*	*Canaan*	Samson and others were chosen as *judges* to *govern* the people for *four hundred* rebellious years.
Kingdom	*David*	*Israel*	David, the greatest king in the new *monarchy*, is followed by a succession of mostly *unrighteous* kings, and God eventually *judges* Israel for her sin, sending her into exile.
Exile	*Daniel*	*Babylonia*	Daniel gives *leadership* and encourages *faithfulness* among the *exiles* for the next seventy years.

ERA	FIGURE	LOCATION	STORY LINE SUMMARY
Return	*Ezra*	*Jerusalem*	Ezra *leads* the people back from *exile* to rebuild *Jerusalem*.
Silence	*Pharisees*	*Jerusalem*	Pharisees and others *entomb* the Israelites in *legalism* for the next *four* hundred years.
Gospels	*Jesus*	*Palestine*	Jesus comes in fulfillment of the Old Testament *prophecies* of a savior and offers *salvation* and the true kingdom of God. While some accept Him, most *reject* Him, and He is crucified, buried, and resurrected.
Church	*Peter*	*Jerusalem*	Peter, shortly after the *ascension* of Jesus, is used by God to *establish* the *Church*, God's next major plan for man.
Missions	*Paul*	*Roman Empire*	Paul *expands* the Church into the *Roman* Empire during the next two *decades*.

Arc of Bible History

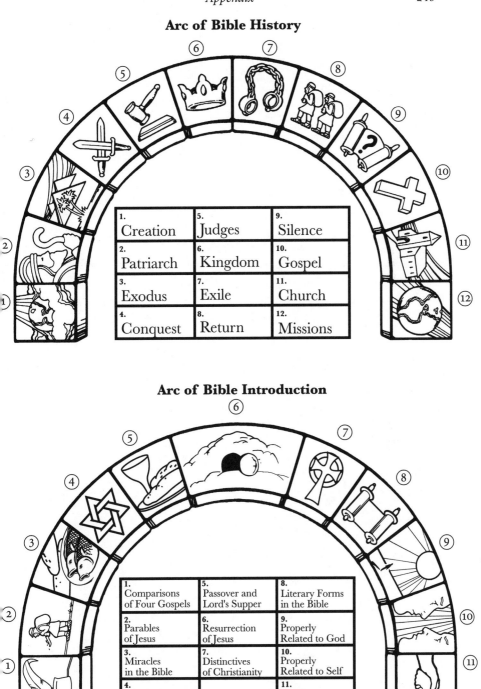

1. Creation	**5.** Judges	**9.** Silence
2. Patriarch	**6.** Kingdom	**10.** Gospel
3. Exodus	**7.** Exile	**11.** Church
4. Conquest	**8.** Return	**12.** Missions

Arc of Bible Introduction

1. Comparisons of Four Gospels	**5.** Passover and Lord's Supper	**8.** Literary Forms in the Bible
2. Parables of Jesus	**6.** Resurrection of Jesus	**9.** Properly Related to God
3. Miracles in the Bible	**7.** Distinctives of Christianity	**10.** Properly Related to Self
4. Messianic Prophecies		**11.** Properly Related to Others

The Story of the Bible in 1,000 Words

The Old Testament begins when God created Adam and Eve in a perfect paradise. They later sinned and were driven out of the Garden of Eden, forced to live "by the sweat of their brow" in an imperfect world. As their offspring multiplied, sin also multiplied. Eventually, humanity became so sinful that, as judgment, God destroyed the earth with a universal flood, preserving only Noah and his immediate family on the ark to repopulate the earth.

Sin kept its hold over humanity, however, and once again people forgot God. As the years passed, God revealed Himself to Abraham (two thousand years before Christ), promising him a nation, many descendants, and a blessing that would ultimately extend to everyone on the earth. Abraham believed God and became the father of the Hebrew people. Abraham had a son, Isaac, and Isaac had a son, Jacob. The promises God made to Abraham were passed down through Isaac and Jacob. Jacob had twelve sons, and the promises were passed to all twelve sons, who became the fathers of the twelve tribes of Israel.

Jacob and his family of about seventy people were living in the land of Canaan (1) when a famine hit. They were forced to migrate to Egypt (2) to get food. In time, they became so numerous that they were perceived as a threat by the Egyptian people, and the Egyptians enslaved the Hebrew people for nearly four hundred years. Finally (approximately fifteen hundred years before Christ), God raised up Moses to lead them out of Egypt. With many astounding miracles, including the crossing of the Red Sea, they escaped Egypt and went to Mt. Sinai (3), where they received the Ten Commandments. Then they rebelled against God again and, as a judgment, wandered in the wilderness for forty years. When their time of judgment was up, they were allowed to enter the promised land (4). Moses died, and Joshua led in the conquest of the land.

Israel lived in the promised land in a loose governmental system, ruled by judges, for the next four hundred years. Samson and Samuel were the most famous judges. Then Israel insisted on establishing a monarchy (approximately one thousand years before Christ), and the Hebrews were ruled by kings for the next four hundred years. Saul, David, and Solomon were the first three kings, who ruled over a united monarchy for 120 years (forty years each). When Solomon died, the nation divided over the issue of taxation. There was now a northern kingdom, which kept the name Israel, because a majority (ten) of the tribes were loyal to the north, and a southern kingdom, which was called Judah, because Judah was by far the larger of the two southern tribes.

Because of the accumulating sin of Israel, Assyria, a nation to the northeast, came and conquered Israel (5) and scattered many of the people throughout that part of the world (6). About one hundred fifty years later, because of the accumulating sin of Judah, Babylonia came and conquered Judah (7), destroyed Jerusalem, and took many of the people into captivity in Babylonia (8).

About seventy years later, Persia defeated Babylonia, who had previously defeated Assyria. Thus Persia now ruled the entire part of the world from the eastern shores of the Mediterranean Sea to the borders of India. The king of Persia allowed the Israelites living in captivity in Babylonia to return to Jerusalem (9) to rebuild it. Fifty thousand people returned (approximately five hundred years before Christ), rebuilt the city, rebuilt the temple, and restored ceremonial worship of God. They continued to live that way for the next four hundred years. During that time, Persia fell to Greece, and Greece in turn fell to Rome. Rome was ruling that part of the world when Jesus was born.

The ministry of Jesus was preceded by the ministry of His cousin, John the Baptist, who warned the Jews to get ready for the coming of the Messiah. Jesus was born in Bethlehem, near Jerusalem, in fulfillment of Old Testament prophecy. Then Jesus and His parents, Mary and Joseph, moved back to their hometown in Nazareth, in the northern part of the country, just west of the Sea of Galilee. There Jesus lived an apparently normal childhood until the age of thirty, when all teachers, by Jewish custom, began their ministry. Jesus began His ministry in Jerusalem and in the surrounding area of Judea. His ministry was highlighted by authoritative teaching and remarkable miracles.

Because of mounting opposition to His ministry on the part of the Jewish religious leaders, Jesus went north to the area around the Sea of Galilee, making Capernaum on the north shore His home base. Much of His three-year ministry was conducted in the area around Capernaum, though many events did not actually take place in Capernaum. Eventually, He returned to Jerusalem and, because of the jealousy of the religious leaders, was soon crucified. Three days later He rose from the dead, and He showed Himself to His disciples several times over the next forty days. Then, with His disciples gathered around Him on the Mount of Olives, just outside Jerusalem, He visibly ascended into heaven.

He had commissioned His disciples to take the new message of salvation through Christ to Jerusalem, Judea, and Samaria (the surrounding regions), and to the uttermost parts of the earth. The church was established in Jerusalem, and the first Christians were Jews. The church there was overseen by Jesus' apostles. The spread of the gospel to the surrounding area and uttermost parts of the earth focused primarily on the apostle Paul, who conducted missionary journeys into areas of Asia Minor and Greece (10). Finally, Paul was arrested and taken to Rome, where he was eventually executed for his faith. There were enough disciples, however, not only in Jerusalem, but also in Asia Minor, Greece, and Rome, that the message not only lived on, but it grew until it became the dominant world religion.

TEACHING PLAN

Introduction

The book *30 Days to Understanding the Bible* is an excellent tool for people who want to learn more about the Bible and its life-transforming message. The book features such learning helps as maps, charts, tables, review exercises, and self-tests to encourage reader interaction with the material in order to increase learning and comprehension.

Group study of *30 Days* adds another dimension to the learning process. In a group, students can interact with the teacher as well as one another to deepen their insights into the nature and purpose of the Bible. The following teaching suggestions are designed to help you lead an effective group study of this important book.

Your students will be expected to read the book on their own. But they will attend the group study to process what they are learning, discuss their ideas with others, clarify the insights and facts to which they are being exposed, and perhaps even celebrate with one another the blessings which come with greater understanding of God's Word.

Preview of the Study

The thirty chapters of *30 Days to Understanding the Bible* will be covered in the following twelve sessions:

Session 1: Structure of the Bible, Old Testament Geography, and Historical Books   (Chs. 1–3)

Session 2: The Old Testament Story, Creation—Conquest (Chs. 4–7)

Session 3: The Old Testament Story, Conquest—Silence (Chs. 8–12)

Session 4: Poetical and Prophetical Books (Chs. 13 and 14)

Session 5:   New Testament Geography and Structure
              (Ch. 15)

Session 6:   Gospel/Church Eras (Chs. 16 and 17)

Session 7:   Missions Era/Epistles (Chs. 18 and 19)

Session 8:   Gospels Comparison/Parables (Chs. 20 and 21)

Session 9:   Miracles/Prophecies (Chs. 22 and 23)

Session 10:   Passover–Lord's Supper/Resurrection
              (Chs. 24 and 25)

Session 11:   Distinctiveness/Literary Forms (Chs. 26 and 27)

Session 12:   Properly Related to God, Self, and Others
              (Chs. 28–30)

Transparency Masters

At the back of this book (see pp. 0000) you will find nineteen graphic drawings, maps, and charts which may be enlarged on a copy machine and converted into transparencies for use on an overhead projector. Picked up from various places throughout this book, these transparency masters will be used in various sessions throughout this study. For your convenience, here's a complete list of these nineteen transparency masters. (Details on how to use these transparencies appear in the individual session plans below.)

- Old Testament Books/New Testament Books
- The Three Kinds of Books in the Old Testament
- The Three Kinds of Books in the New Testament
- Work Map: Locations of the Old Testament
- Map: State of Texas/Land of the Bible
- Overview of Old Testament History
- Arc of Bible History
- Bodies of Water in the Gospels
- The Geography of Acts
- Overview of New Testament History
- Time Line of the New Testament
- Arc of Bible Introduction

- Map of Palestine
- Map of the New Testament World
- Self-Test for Session 8
- Self-Test for Session 9
- Self-Test for Session 10
- Self-Test for Session 11
- Fulfilling the Needs of Man

General Preparation for the Study

In order to lead students in this study of the Bible, you must be well prepared yourself. Here are some practical steps you can take to make sure you are ready before the time for Session 1 rolls around.

1. Read this book thoroughly at least once. Take time to complete the written exercises in the book. This will give you a good idea of the challenges and rewards your students will face in the study of the material.

2. Look over the teaching plans for all twelve sessions. Note especially those sessions that suggest that you give advance assignments to students. Make a note on the students whom you will ask to do these extra tasks. Begin now to enlist students in advance for these assignments.

3. Pull together a selection of reference books that might be helpful to students who agree to do these extra assignments. Bible dictionaries, Bible handbooks, and books which overview the entire Bible should be especially helpful.

4. Prepare the room by arrangimg the chairs in circular fashion in order to generate dialogue and discussion among the students. Collect equipment and learning aids you will need—overhead projector, chalkboard or poster board, pencils or pens, felt-tip pens, etc.

5. Pray that the Lord will bless your teaching and that the students will be open and receptive to truths and insights presented during this study.

6. Remember, these lesson outlines are guides, not straightjackets. Feel free to amend them so they meet your needs. You may have to add or subtract material based on your students' previous knowledge or the amount of time you have. You may want

to cover the material in six sessions or sixteen rather than twelve. The procedures offered here assume a class session of 45 minutes to one hour.

NOTE: Before the first class, have the students read Chapter 1–3, but they should not fill in the blanks in their books.

Session 1:
Structure of the Bible, Old Testament Geography, and Historical Books

Overview: This session covers the material in Chapters 1–3.

Before the Session

1. Make the transparencies of the following items from the back of this book and have them ready to display on an overhead projector during this session:

- Old Testament/New Testament Books
- The Three Kinds of Books in the Old Testament
- The Three Kinds of Books in the New Testament
- Work Map: Locations of the Old Testament
- Map: State of Texas/Land of the Bible
- Overview of Old Testament History

2. Review Chapters 1–3 to call to mind the content to be covered in this session. Be sure to complete all the self-tests, writing the answers to the questions in your book.

3. Read carefully the article "The Story of the Bible in 1,000 Words" in the Appendix, while looking at the "Geography of the Old Testament" map to be sure you have the big picture of the story in your mind.

4. Prepare a poster with the titles of all twelve sessions of this study (see "Preview of the Study" above). Place this poster in a prominent place in the room. Leave this poster up throughout the study as a visible reminder to the students of the progress they are making. You might even place a check mark on each session as it is completed, and remind them at the beginning of each session of the lessons they have already completed.

During the Session

1. Open with prayer that this will be a profitable and encouraging study for everyone.

2. As an icebreaker, have the students break into pairs (assuming they do not know each other), introduce themselves to one another and chat for two or three minutes. Then ask them to introduce their partners to the rest of the group, telling their name and other information such as family, employment, hobbies, etc.

3. Direct the students' attention to the wall poster with an outline of all twelve sessions of the study, commenting on the scope of this challenging learning opportunity. Remind students that they will be expected to complete the reading for each session in their books before they come to class, but they will not fill in the blanks. This will be done in class after a review of the material. If they want to take the quiz at home when they read the chapter, have them write the answers on another sheet of paper.

4. Display the "Old Testament Books/New Testament Books" transparency. Review the information, then have them close their books and ask them how many books are in the Old Testament, in the New Testament, and the whole Bible.

Finally, have them write the answers in their books.

NOTE: This patterns of orally drilling the students until they seem to know the answers, then having them fill in the blanks in their books, will be used frequently throughout the book.

5. Display the "The Three Kinds of Books in the Old Testament" transparency, followed by "The Three Kinds of Books in the New Testament" transparency. Review the information on these transparencies, then drill the students until they can give you the responses readily. Then, have them complete the self-tests on pages 11–12. Remind them that you will learn more about these books and the categories of literature to which they belong in later sessions of this study.

6. Have one or more persons read aloud "The Story of the Bible in 1,000 Words." On the map of the Old Testament, draw the arrows for each number in the story that show the movement of the story.

7. Display the "State of Texas/Land of the Bible" transparency. Explain that the entire territory known as the "Old Testament World" is approximately the same size as the state of

Texas. Most students are surprised to learn that the Old Testament world was no larger than this. Ask, "How does this compare with what you had previously thought about the size of the Old Testament world?"

8. Display the "Work Map: Locations of the Old Testament" transparency. Point out the locations A through G, and 1–8 on this map, commenting briefly on the significance of each. Then point at each of these places again, asking the students to provide the correct name. Next, have the students do the same for their partners, and the partners for the students. Finally, ask them to complete the self-test.

9. Display the "Overview of Old Testament History" transparency, explaining that this chart is a convenient summary of all the material covered in Chapter 3 in their books. More than 2,000 years of biblical history are represented by this chart.

Cover the entire transparency with a sheet of paper so that none of the information shows. Then ask students to search Chapter 3 in their books and find the following information. As they locate and call out the information, uncover it so it is visible on the transparency:

- The nine eras of Old Testament history
- The major figure or biblical personality of each era
- The primary geographic location of the events in these nine different eras
- The story lines which summarize these nine eras, their personalities, and their locations.

10. If time permits, divide the students into teams of two. Ask them to work together to complete the remaining self-tests in chapters 1–3. If time does not permit, you can tell them the answers to complete all the remaining self-tests.

11. Close with prayer.

Looking Ahead to the Next Session

Remind the students that the next session will cover chapters 4–7. They should read the material, but not fill in the blanks in their books. This will be done in class.

Session 2
The Old Testament Story (Creation–Conquest)

Overview: This session covers the material in Chapters 4–7.

Before the Session

1. Make transparencies of the following items from the back of the book and have them ready to display on an overhead projector during this session:

- Overview of Old Testament History
- Arc of Bible History

2. Gather materials needed to create a "map" on the floor, so that as you review the Old Testament story, Creation–Conquest, you can point/walk to the place on the floor map where the event occurred. Use the Old Testament Work Map as your guide. The floor map only needs to approximate the accuracy of a real map, especially since you can have the real map showing on an overhead projector as you lay out the floor map. You will need:

- Cord/string/rope long enough to use as the coastline for the Mediterranean Sea.
- Shorter cord/string/rope for the Jordan, Tigris, and Euphrates Rivers.
- Small paperback book (or anything else) to represent the Sea of Galilee.
- Two larger books (or anything else) to represent the Dead Sea.
- Styrofoam/plastic cups on which you can, with a felttip marker, write the names of cities, countries, etc.

Make the map as large as feasible for your room. Then, as you tell the story, you can walk or point to the appropriate place on the floor map.

3. Prepare a 15–30 minute (depending on how long your session is) presentation of the story of the Old Testament, Creation–Conquest. Follow the story in the book. Be sure to highlight

the information called for in the self-test material. It is desirable for you to supplement the book material with your own knowledge and to be able to answer questions. If you need help preparing, consult a Bible handbook, Bible atlas, and other material. *Reader's Digest* has published *Great People of the Bible and How They Lived*, which can also be a good source of historical, geographical, and cultural information (though you may not always agree with some of their theological or spiritual comments).

4. Read Chapters 4–7 and complete the self-tests and learning exercises. Remember, a good teacher should always be at least a step or two ahead of his or her students!

During the Session

1. Open with prayer for God's guidance and blessing during this session.

2. As a review for students, display the "Overview of Old Testament History" transparency which you used last session. Lead them to identify the nine eras of Old Testament history.

3. Diplay the "Arc of Bible History" transparency, pointing out that the first four eras of Old Testament history (Creation—Conquest) are represented by the first four icons on the chart (the last five represent the last five eras in Old Testament history, and the final three icons represent New Testament history). Point to each icon and ask the students to name these four eras. Ask the students to drill each other in teams of two until they readily identify the era by pointing to the icon. They can use their books for this review.

4. Talk through the history of Creation–Conquest, walking through the map as you do. After you have gone through it in depth once, go through it quickly a time or two as review. After you have finished with the events in a given era, point to the icon on the "Arc of Bible History" transparency to reinforce the era with the events.

5. If time permits, have the partners help each other as they fill in all the self-test material. If time does not permit, talk them through the answers yourself.

6. Close with a prayer of thanksgiving for the peole of Old Testament times who obeyed God and passed His message on

to succeeding generations, and who helped us understand how to live by faith.

Looking Ahead to the Next Session

Remind the students to read chapters 8–12 before the next session.

Session 3
The Old Testament Story (Conquest–Silence)

Overview: This session covers the material in Chapters 8–12.

Before the Session

Make the same preparations for this session (Conquest–Silence, Chapters 8–12) as you did for the last session.

During the Session

Use exactly the same procedures for this session as you did for the last session, but relating the information on Conquest–Silence, found in Chapters 8–12.

Looking Ahead to the Next Session

Remind the students to read Chapters 13 and 14 before the next session.

Session 4
Poetical Books and Prophetical Books

Overview: This session covers the material in Chapters 13 and 14.

Before the Session

1. Make transparencies of the following items from the back of this book and have them ready to display on an overhead projector during this session:

- The Three Kinds of Books in the Old Testament
- Work Map: Locations of the Old Testament

2. Enlist a student in your class to do research on "The Poetic Books of the Old Testament" and to be prepared to present a five-minute report on this topic during Session 4. (If this does not fit your circumstances, prepare the report yourself.)

3. Enlist another student to do research on "The Prophets of the Old Testament" and to be prepared to present a five-minute report on this topic during Session 4 (or do it yourself).

4. Review Chapters 13 and 14 to call to mind the content to be covered in Session 4. Be sure to complete the self-tests on pages 98 and 103, writing the answers to these questions in your book.

5. Enlist a student to read a short psalm from the book of Psalms and to lead the class in prayer at the beginning of the session, if appropriate. If your class is geared to seekers or young/new Christians, be cautious of embarrassing them.

During the Session

1. Call on the student whom you have enlisted to read a short psalm and lead the class in prayer.

2. Remind the students that this psalm read at the beginning of the class is from the book of Psalms—one of the great poetic books of the Old Testament. Then state that you will be studying the poetic and prophetic books of the Old Testament during this session.

3. Display "The Three Kinds of Books in the Old Testament" transparency to show that poetic books make up one of the major categories of Old Testament literature.

4. Call on the student whom you have enlisted to give the report on "The Poetic Books of the Old Testament." Ask the other students to open their books to pages 97–98 while this report is being presented and to compare the student report with this printed information. They might jot down in the margins of their books on these pages any important information covered by the student report.

5. After the student report, drill the students on the self-test. Then have them review the material with their partner. Finally, let the students complete the self-test on page 98.

6. Display "The Three Kinds of Books in the Old Testament" transparency again. Ask, Which of these books are known

as the *major prophets* and which are called the *minor prophets?* What do these two terms mean—*major prophets* and *minor prophets?*

7. Call on the student whom you have enlisted to give a report on "The Prophets of the Old Testament." Then ask the class to turn to the information on "Structure of the Prophetical Books" (pp. 102–103). Point out that the prophetical books were addressed to many different regions of the Old Testament world under many different situations and conditions.

8. Display the "Map: Locations of the Old Testament" transparency. Ask students to locate on this map the different nations and regions to which the prophetical books of the Old Testament were addressed.

9. Drill the students on the self-test for the prophetical books. Then have them review with their partners. Finally, have them complete the self-test on page 103.

10. Ask a student to lead the closing prayer, if appropriate, expressing special thanks for the poetic and prophetic books of the Old Testament. If your students are unaccustomed to praying in public, close with prayer yourself.

Looking Ahead to the Next Session

1. Remind the class to read Chapter 15 of their books before the next class meeting—Session 5.

Session 5:
New Testament Geography and Structure

Overview: This session covers the material in Chapter 15.

Before the Session

1. Make transparencies of the following items from the back of this book and have them ready to display on an overhead projector during the session:

- Bodies of Water in the Gospels
- The Geography of Acts
- Overview of New Testament History
- Arc of Bible History

2. Review Chapter 15 to call to mind the content to be covered in this session. Be sure to complete the self-test on page 112, writing the answers in the blanks in your book.

3. Pray for the Holy Spirit's guidance as you prepare to lead the class in this important session on an introduction to the New Testament.

During the Session

1. Begin with a prayer of thanks to God for the two grand divisions of the Bible—the Old Testament and the New Testament. Ask for God's insight and guidance in this introductory study on the New Testament.

2. Call attention to the poster with titles of all twelve sessions of this study of the Bible. Remind the students that you have now completed all sessions on the Old Testament and that this session marks the beginning of your studies of the New Testament. Use the following questions to generate interest and discussion about the New Testament and its relationship to the Old Testament.

- What's your favorite section of the Bible—the Old Testament or the New Testament? Why?
- What's the major difference between the Old Testament and the New Testament?
- Which is more important—the Old Testament or the New Testament?
- Which is easier to understand—the Old Testament or the New Testament?

3. Display the "Bodies of Water in the Gospels" transparency, asking students to identify these bodies of water in the New Testament world and to write these names in their books (p. 109).

4. Ask the students to open their books to pages 111–112 while you display "The Geography of Acts" transparency. Mention each of these sites and its significance, pointing out its location on the transparency. Then divide the class into teams of two and let them work together on learning these names and

their locations, completing the blank map on page 113 of their books.

5. Display the "Overview of New Testament History" transparency. Then flash the "Overview of Old Testament History" transparency briefly, followed by the New Testament transparency. Note that Old Testament history features nine different eras covering about 2,000 years, while New Testament history has only three different eras covering about 100 years. Reinforce this truth by displaying the "Arc of Bible History" transparency, which shows all twelve eras of biblical history together.

6. Ask the students to turn to page 114 in their books. Then lead them to complete the exercises on page 114 and 116–119 and to write the answers in their books. Take time to answer questions or provide information as needed to broaden their understanding about the geography and structure of the New Testament.

7. Close with prayer.

Looking Ahead to the Next Session

1. Remind the class to read Chapters 16 and 17 of their books before the next class—Session 6.

Session 6
Gospel/Church Eras

Overview: This session covers the material in Chapters 16 and 17.

Before the Session

1. Make a transparency of the map of Palestine from the back of this book and have it ready to display on an overhead projector during this session.

2. Review Chapters 16 and 17 to call to mind the content to be covered in this session. Be sure to complete the self-tests on pages 123 and 131, writing the answers to these questions in your book.

3. Gather materials needed for a floor map of the New Testament area.

4. Write the following outline on the chalkboard or a large sheet of poster paper, leaving adequate space after each point for writing in major events from the life of Jesus:

MAJOR EVENTS IN JESUS' LIFE

1. Early Life: Childhood to Baptism

2. Early Ministry: Initial Acceptance

3. Later Ministry: Growing Rejection

4. Death and Resurrection: Final Rejection

Note that this outline comes from pages 122–123 of the book.

During the Session

1. Lead in a prayer of thanksgiving for the life and ministry of Jesus and His saving power, and ask for His blessings on the session.

2. Remind the students that today's study will focus on the life and ministry of Jesus and the beginning of the church. State, Jesus' ministry lasted only about three years and it was conducted in an area only about thirty miles wide by ninety miles long.

3. Display the transparency of the map of Palestine, pointing out the relatively small size of Palestine. Ask the students to identify in the life of Jesus the significance of each of these five places on the map:

- Bethlehem
- Egypt
- Nazareth
- Capernaum
- Jerusalem

4. Using the same materials as for the Old Testament, lay out a map of the New Testament area on the floor of the room. Direct the students' attention to the outline, "Major Events in Jesus' Life," which you have posted in the room. Ask them to help you fill in this outline by recalling major events in His life and ministry under each point on the outline. Write in these events as they are recalled by the class. As they are identified, trace the geographical movement on the floor map. Here are a few major events, just in case you don't get any help from your students (Be sure you know where all these events took place):

(1) Early Life
    Birth in Bethlehem
    Flight into Egypt
    Presentation as an infant in the temple
    Discussion with learned scholars in the temple
(2) Early Ministry: Acceptance
    Temptations in the wilderness
    Miracles of healing
    Sermon on the Mount
    Calling of His disciples
(3) Later Ministry: Rejection
    Clash with Pharisees and Sadducees
    Withdrawal with His disciples
    Teaching His disciples about His forthcoming death
    Peter's confession at Caesarea–Philippi
(4) Death and Resurrection
    Triumphal entry into Jerusalem
    Last Supper with His disciples
    Agonizing prayer in the Garden of Gethsemane
    Crucifixion
    Resurrection
    Post-resurrection appearances

5. Ask the students to turn to page 123 in their books and to review with their partner before they complete the self-test and other exercises.

6. Display the "Map of Palestine" transparency again and show on this map how the church spread from Jerusalem to Judea to Samaria after Jesus' ascension, in accordance with the promise and prediction of Jesus. Use a transparency marker to write "Judea" and "Samaria" on the map. Explain that this stage of the growth of the church is described in chapters 1—12 of the Book of Acts.

7. Close with a prayer of thanks for Jesus, the gospel, and the church.

Looking Ahead to the Next Session

1. Remind the class to read the text and complete the exercises in Chapters 18 and 19 of their books before the next meeting—Session 7.

Session 7
Missions Era/Epistles

Overview: This session covers the material in Chapters 18 and 19.

Before the Session

1. Make transparencies of the following items from the back of this book and have them ready to display on an overhead projector during this session:

- Time Line of the New Testament
- Map of the New Testament World

2. Enlist two students to do research and prepare two different five-minute reports on the apostle Paul for presentation during Session 7. One report should focus on "The Life and Missionary Travels of Paul," while the other should cover "The Epistles and Theological Contribution of Paul." If you have no volunteers, prepare them yourself.

3. Review Chapters 18 and 19 to call to mind the content to be covered in this session. Be sure to complete the self-tests on pages 137 and 150.

During the Session

1. Begin the class with prayer, asking the Holy Spirit to direct the class during the session as you focus on the exciting years of the expansion of the early church.

2. Display the "Map of the New Testament World" transparency. Ask the students to open their books to page 136. Explain that the person who took the lead in planting churches throughout the New Testament world during the first Christian century was the apostle Paul. Page 136 in their books gives an outline of the missionary travels of this great "apostle to the Gentiles."

3. Introduce the student whom you have enlisted to give a report on "The Life and Missionary Travels of Paul." Ask the other students to take notes during this student presentation, comparing the facts presented with the outline of Paul's travels on page 136 in their books. After this presentation, generate additional discussion on Paul with questions such as these:

- Why do you think Paul became the great "apostle to the Gentiles"? How was he uniquely qualified for his role as the first great missionary of Christianity?
- How did Paul support himself during his missionary travels?
- Who were some of the key helpers and companions who assisted Paul in his work?

4. After this discussion, ask students to turn to page 137 in their books and review with their partners before they complete the self-test on the major events in Paul's life.

5. Display the "Time Line of the New Testament" transparency. Ask the students to turn to page 143 in their books. Ask them to identify the twenty-year period during which the epistles of Paul were written by comparing these epistles with the time line. Point out that Paul was more than a great missionary in early Christianity; he was also a great theologian and letter writer who wrote thirteen of the twenty-seven books of the New Testament.

6. Ask the students to open their books to pages 144–146, which discusses Paul's epistles to churches and individuals. Then introduce the student whom you have enlisted to present a report

on "The Epistles and Theological Contribution of Paul." Ask them to fill in the blanks in their books regarding Paul's epistles as they listen to the student presentation on this subject.

7. Refer the students to the information about the general epistles on pages 146–147 of their books. Lead a discussion of these books, helping them to fill in the blanks in their books with the missing information about these epistles.

8. Call on a student, if appropriate, to close with a prayer of thanksgiving for the apostle Paul and his contribution to God's kingdom.

Looking Ahead to the Next Session

1. Remind the students to read the text and complete the exercises in Chapters 20 and 21 of their books before the next class meeting—Session 8. Tell them to be sure to bring their Bibles to the next session. You will be doing some group Bible search activities that will require them to use their Bibles.

Session 8
Gospels Comparison/Parables

Overview: This session covers the material in Chapters 20 and 21.

Before the Session

1. Make a transparency of the self-test for Session 8 from the back of this book. Also have ready the transparency on "The Three Kinds of Books in the New Testament" which you used in Session 1.

2. Review Chapters 20 and 21 to call to mind the content to be covered in this session. Be sure to complete the self-tests on pages 162 and 169, writing the information called for in the blanks in your book.

3. Prepare a five-minute lecture on "The Parables of Jesus," drawing from Chapter 21 of the book.

During the Session

1. Open the session with prayer.
2. Display "The Three Kinds of Books in the New Testament" transparency. Direct the students' attention to Matthew,

Mark, Luke, and John in the "Historical" column on this transparency, stating that these are the books you will study during this session. Generate interest and discussion on this subject with questions such as these:

- What exactly is a "Gospel"?
- Why do we have four individual Gospels with four different writers in the New Testament?
- How are these four Gospels similar? How do they differ?

3. Inform the students that there is a good discussion of these four Gospels on pages 154–161 of their books. Have them open their books to these pages.

4. Divide the class into four equal small groups. Let these four groups work together for about ten to fifteen minutes to compile a report or summary of the four Gospels—group one working on Matthew, group 2 on Mark, etc. They should use their books and their Bibles as resources in compiling these reports. Each group should elect a leader who is responsible for directing the discussion and compiling the report. After they finish their work, each group should present its report to the rest of the class.

5. Ask the students to open their books to Chapter 21 on "The Parables of Jesus." As you present a brief lecture on this subject, ask them to underline in their books any facts or insights about Jesus' parables which seem important or significant to them. When you finish the lecture, ask them to discuss any facts or insights that they underlined in their books.

6. Display the self-test transparency for Lesson 8. Have the students drill with their partners until they know the answers to the self-tests. Then have them complete the self-tests in their books (pages 162 and 169) while you serve as a resource person to direct their search and clarify their thinking. While they are working on the parables part of the self-test, ask them to recall one of their favorite parables of Jesus from the Gospels. Ask if they know where these "favorite parables" are found in the Gospels, and invite them to look these parables up in their Bibles.

7. Close the session by having a student read a parable from the Gospels after finding it in the Bible-search activity above.

Looking Ahead to the Next Session

1. Remind the students to read Chapters 22 and 23 of their books before the next class meeting—Session 9.

Session 9
Miracles/Prophecies

Overview: This session covers the material in Chapters 22 and 23.

Before the Session

1. Make transparencies of the following items from the back of the book and have them ready to display on an overhead projector during this session:

- Arc of Bible Introduction
- Self-test for Session 9

2. Review Chapters 21 and 22 to call to mind the content to be covered in this session. Be sure to complete the self-tests on pages 177 and 184, writing the answers to these questions in your book.

During the Session

1. Call on a student to lead in prayer, thanking God for the ministry of His Son Jesus, particularly His miracles, and asking for His blessing on the class.

2. Tell the students that Session 9 is a good time to pause and take stock of what you have covered up to this point in this series of studies. Direct their attention to the poster with an outline of all twelve sessions in the study. Ask, What have you learned so far that has contributed to your appreciation and understanding of the Bible?

3. Display the "Arc of Bible Introduction" transparency. Tell the students that this graphic is a handy summary of selected introductory matters about the Bible that you will be studying together during these final sessions. Inform them that the last session, Session 8, was actually the first of these studies on introductory matters about the Bible. Then direct them to the twelve-session overview

poster again, pointing out the subjects of Sessions 10, 11, and 12. Invite the class to ask any questions they might have about the direction of these studies in the series.

4. Display the "Self-test for Session 9" transparency. Remind the class that one chapter of the book covered by this session and the self-test is on miracles. Ask them to turn to pages 171–176 of their books for information on miracles. Generate student interaction and discussion with questions like these:

- What is a miracle?
- In your opinion, what is the greatest miracle in the Bible?
- In your opinion, what is the greatest miracle performed by Jesus?
- Does God still work miracles today?

5. Ask the class, after they have drilled with their partners, to complete the self-test in their books about miracles (p. 177).

6. With the "Self-test for Session 9" transparency still on display, ask the class to turn to the self-test on messianic prophecies in their books (p. 184). Ask, Why are the messianic prophecies about Jesus important? Ask them to examine Chapter 23 in their books to find some of the key messianic prophecies about Jesus.

7. Close with a prayer of thanks for Jesus, our Messiah and Savior.

Looking Ahead to the Next Session

1. Remind the students to read Chapters 24 and 25 before the next class meeting—Session 10.

Session 10:
Passover–Lord's Supper/Resurrection

Overview: This session covers the material in Chapters 24 and 25.

Before the Session

1. Make a transparency of the self-test for Session 10 from the back of this book and have it ready to display on an overhead projector during this session.

2. Review Chapters 24 and 25 to call to mind the content to be covered in this session. Be sure to complete the self-tests on pages 193 and 202, writing the information called for in the blanks in your book.

3. Check the three major theories on the resurrection of Jesus discussed on pages 195–202 of the book. Enlist three students in advance to do research on these three theories and to be prepared to present brief reports of about three minutes each on these theories during the upcoming session.

During the Session

1. Call on a student to lead in prayer.

2. Inform the class that the two major subjects to be covered in this session are (1) the Passover and the Lord's Supper and (2) the resurrection of Jesus.

3. Ask the students to open their books to pages 186–192, which discusses the Passover and the Lord's Supper. Invite them to look over these pages for answers to questions like these:

- What event in the Old Testament led to an annual observance known as the Passover?
- How was the Passover observed?
- How did Jesus and His disciples observe the Passover?
- What new meaning did Jesus give the Passover?
- How are the Jewish Passover and the Christian rite known as the Lord's Supper related?

4. Display the "Self-test for Lesson 10" transparency. Refer the students to page 193 of their books. Ask them, after drilling with their partner, to complete the first part of this self-test on the Passover and the Lord's Supper.

5. Instruct the students to open their books to pages 195–202. State, The resurrection of Jesus Christ is one of the most important teachings of the church. The church has kept alive an emphasis on the resurrection of our Lord, although the doctrine has been repeatedly attacked by unbelievers. Several theories have been advanced to explain the resurrection in rationalistic terms.

6. Introduce the three students whom you have enlisted to present the three major theories advanced by an unbelieving world to explain the resurrection. Ask, Why have believers rejected these theories and continued to insist that the resurrection of Jesus Christ is indeed an actual historical event? Draw from the information on pages 199–202 of the book ("The Resurrection as History") during this discussion.

7. Display the "Self-test for Session 10" transparency. Ask the students, after drilling with their partners, to complete the self-test on page 202 in their books. Encourage them to ask any additional questions they might have about the resurrection of Jesus.

8. Close with a prayer of thanks for the sacrificial death of Jesus on the cross and His victorious resurrection.

Looking Ahead to the Next Session

1. Remind the students to read Chapters 26 and 27 of their books before the next class meeting—Session 11.

Session 11:
Distinctiveness/Literary Forms

Overview: This session covers the material in Chapters 26 and 27.

Before the Session

1. Make a transparency of the "Self-test for Session 11" from the back of this book and have it ready to display on an overhead projector during the session.

2. Write the following two headings at the tops of two large sheets of poster paper or write them on two separate sections of the chalkboard, leaving plenty of space for writing under each heading:

SIMILARITIES BETWEEN CHRISTIANITY AND
OTHER RELIGIONS

DIFFERENCES BETWEEN CHRISTIANITY AND
OTHER RELIGIONS

3. Review Chapters 26 and 27 to call to mind the content to be covered in this session. Be sure to complete the self-tests on pages 211 and 221, writing the answers to these questions in your book.

During the Session

1. Begin with prayer, thanking God for the many insights into His Word which He has revealed to both teacher and students during this series of studies.

2. Ask the students to open their books to pages 203–211 on "Distinctiveness of Christianity."

3. Display the poster with the heading, "Similarities between Christianity and Other Religions." Ask the students to find the similarities discussed on pages 204–205 of their books. Write these similarities on the poster as they are called out by the students.

4. Display the poster with the heading, "Differences between Christianity and Other Religions." Ask the students to find these differences discussed on pages 205–207 of their books. Write these differences on the poster as they are called out by students.

5. Remind the students that we as Christians believe that God has revealed Himself supremely through His Son and that Jesus Christ is the only way to God. Ask them to find in their books the four principles of proclaiming the truth of Jesus Christ to others (p. 210). Write these four principles on the chalkboard as they are discovered by the students, and lead in a discussion of these principles.

6. Display the "Self-test for Session 11" transparency. Ask the students, after drilling with their partners, to complete the first part of this self-test by filling in the blanks on page 211 of their books.

7. Remind the students that the Bible is a book with many different types of literature. This subject is discussed in Chapter 27 of their books. Each type of literature in the Bible has its own unique guidelines for interpretation. Divide the class into five equal small groups. Each of these groups should compile a list of guidelines for interpreting one of the types of literature in the Bible, using the information on pages 213–221 as a resource. Let each group report on these guidelines and discuss them together in the large group, as time permits.

8. Close with prayer.

Looking Ahead to the Next Session

1. Remind the group that the next session, Session 12, will conclude this series of studies. Ask them to read Chapters 28, 29, and 30 in their books before the next and final class meeting in preparation for the conclusion of this study.

Session 12:
Properly Related to God, Self, and Others

Overview: This session covers the material in Chapters 28, 29, and 30.

Before the Session

1. Make a transparency of "Fulfilling the Needs of Man" from the back of this book and have it ready to display on an overhead projector during the session. Use small strips of paper to mask the key words until students have identified them.

2. The Arc of Bible History and the Ark of Bible Introduction are designed as tools to help students recall the elements covered in this study. Have these transparencies from Sessions 3 and 9 ready to use again.

3. Since this is the last session in this series of studies, plan a celebration activity for the last fifteen minutes or so of the session. Provide soft drinks and cookies as refreshments and let the students mingle and socialize to mark the closure of this important time of learning about the Bible.

4. Review Chapters 28, 29, and 30 to call to mind the content to be covered in this session. Be sure to complete the reviews on pages 232, 239, and 245, writing the answers to these questions in your book.

During the Session

1. Remind the class that this concluding session is on how to be properly related to God, self, and others. Ask questions like these to generate dialogue and discussion on this topic:

- What good does it do a person to study the Bible if he or she is not properly related to God, self, or others?

- Why does God want every person to come to know Him personally as Lord and Savior?
- Which is more important—to be properly related to God, to self, or to others?

2. Ask several students to give their personal testimonies about their daily walk as Christians and how they came to know Christ as Lord and Savior.

3. Display the "Fulfilling the Needs of Man" transparency with the key words masked. Lead the students, after drilling with their partners, to fill in the blanks on this self-test on page 239 of their books. Then call for students to identify the key words, unmasking them on your transparency as they are identified. Ask, "Do you know anyone who has experienced frustration because he sought to meet his personal needs by following man's way? What does it mean to meet our personal needs by following God's way?"

4. Display the "Arc of Bible History" transparency. Let individual students call out, in order, the twelve stages represented by the arc. Write the key words in the blanks with a grease pencil or erasable felt-tip marker.

5. Display the "Ark of Bible Introduction" transparency with the eleven key phrases already written in. Ask students to recall at least one fact related to each of these final eleven chapters in the book.

6. Ask the students to think back over this series of studies and what they have learned about the Bible. Ask questions like the following to generate interaction and discussion:

- What is the most important thing you have learned about the Bible through this series of studies?
- How will these new insights contribute to your personal growth as a Christian and your relationships with others?

7. Close with a prayer of thanksgiving for this series of studies and the Christian growth which has resulted among students in the class.

8. Adjourn to the celebration activity that you have planned for the group.

TRANSPARENCY MASTERS

On the pages which follow are nineteen masters designed to be used in producing transparency cells for an overhead projector. Suggestions for using each one of these transparencies are included in the Teaching Plan on pages 255-280. The masters are presented here in the order in which they are called for in the Teaching Plan. In each instance they are identified by the title of the master. You probably will want to produce all nineteen transparencies before you begin the first session.

Because this book (and therefore the masters which follow) is smaller than an 8 1/2" by 11" page, you may wish to enlarge the master on your copy machine to as much as 120 percent to maximize the image area on the screen.

Old Testament Books

Genesis	2 Chronicles	Daniel
Exodus	Ezra	Hosea
Leviticus	Nehemiah	Joel
Numbers	Esther	Amos
Deuteronomy	Job	Obadiah
Joshua	Psalms	Jonah
Judges	Proverbs	Micah
Ruth	Ecclesiastes	Nahum
1 Samuel	Song of Solomon	Habakkuk
2 Samuel	Isaiah	Zephaniah
1 Kings	Jeremiah	Haggai
2 Kings	Lamentations	Zechariah
1 Chronicles	Ezekiel	Malachi

New Testament Books

Matthew	Ephesians	Hebrews
Mark	Philippians	James
Luke	Colossians	1 Peter
John	1 Thessalonians	2 Peter
Acts	2 Thessalonians	1 John
Romans	1 Timothy	2 John
1 Corinthians	2 Timothy	3 John
2 Corinthians	Titus	Jude
Galatians	Philemon	Revelation

The Three Kinds of Books in the Old Testament

Historical	Poetical	Prophetical
Genesis	Job	Isaiah
Exodus	Psalms	Jeremiah
Leviticus	Proverbs	Lamentations
Numbers	Ecclesiastes	Ezekiel
Deuteronomy	Song of Solomon	Daniel
Joshua		Hosea
Judges		Joel
Ruth		Amos
1 Samuel		Obadiah
2 Samuel		Jonah
1 Kings		Micah
2 Kings		Nahum
1 Chronicles		Habakkuk
2 Chronicles		Zephaniah
Ezra		Haggai
Nehemiah		Zechariah
Esther		Malachi

The Three Kinds of Books in the New Testament

Historical	*Pauline*	*General*
Matthew	TO CHURCHES:	Hebrews
Mark	Romans	James
Luke	1 Corinthians	1 Peter
John	2 Corinthians	2 Peter
Acts	Galatians	1 John
	Ephesians	2 John
	Philippians	3 John
	Colossians	Jude
	1 Thessalonians	Revelation
	2 Thessalonians	
	TO INDIVIDUALS:	
	1 Timothy	
	2 Timothy	
	Titus	
	Philemon	

Work Map: Locations of the Old Testament

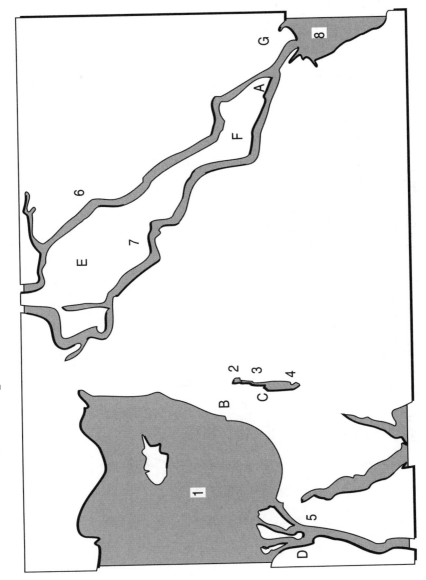

Map: State of Texas/Land of the Bible

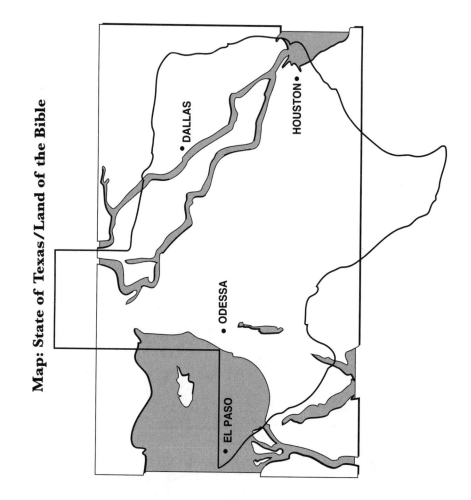

Overview of Old Testament History

ERA	FIGURE	LOCATION	STORY LINE SUMMARY
Creation	*Adam*	*Eden*	Adam is created by God, but he *sins* and *destroys* God's original *plan* for man.
Patriarch	*Abraham*	*Canaan*	Abraham is *chosen* by God to "father" a *people* to *represent* God to the world.
Exodus	*Moses*	*Egypt*	Through Moses God *delivers* the Hebrew people from *slavery* in Egypt and then gives them the *Law.*
Conquest	*Joshua*	*Canaan*	Joshua leads the *conquest* of the *Promised Land.*
Judges	*Samson*	*Canaan*	Samson and others were chosen as *judges* to *govern* the people for *four hundred* rebellious years.
Kingdom	*David*	*Israel*	David, the greatest king in the new *monarchy,* is followed by a succession of mostly *unrighteous* kings, and God eventually *judges* Israel for her sin, sending her into exile.
Exile	*Daniel*	*Babylonia*	Daniel gives *leadership* and encourages *faithfulness* among the *exiles* for the next seventy years.
Return	*Ezra*	*Jerusalem*	Ezra *leads* the people back from *exile* to rebuild *Jerusalem.*
Silence	*Pharisees*	*Jerusalem*	Pharisees and others *entomb* the Israelites in *legalism* for the next *four hundred* years.

Arc of Bible History

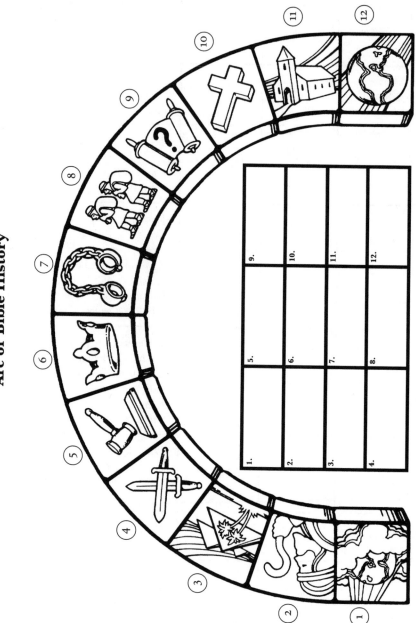

Bodies of Water in the Gospels

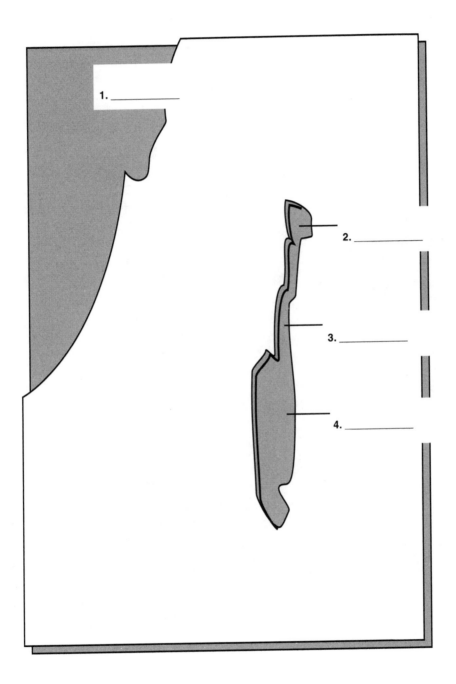

1. _____

2. _____

3. _____

4. _____

The Geography of Acts

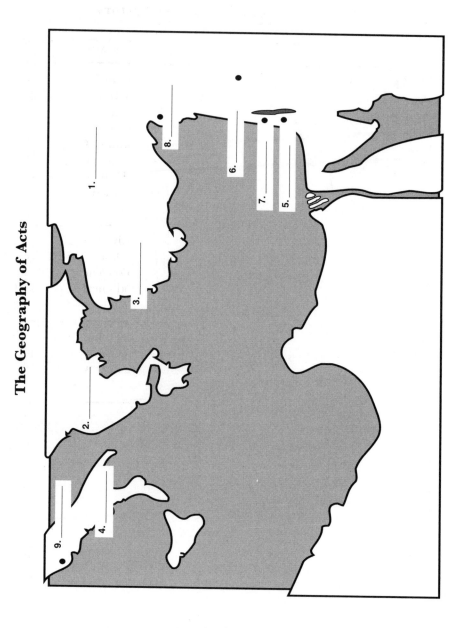

Overview of New Testament History

ERA	FIGURE	LOCATION	STORY LINE SUMMARY
Gospels	*Jesus*	*Palestine*	Jesus comes in fulfillment of the Old Testament *prophecies* of a savior and offers *salvation* and the true kingdom of God. While some accept Him, most *reject* Him, and He is crucified, buried, and resurrected.
Church	*Peter*	*Jerusalem*	Peter, shortly after the *ascension* of Jesus, is used by God to *establish* the *Church*, God's next major plan for man.
Missions	*Paul*	*Roman Empire*	Paul *expands* the Church into the *Roman* Empire during the next two *decades*.

Time Line of the New Testament

Historical Books

	Gospel–Acts					post–Acts		
A.D. **0**	A.D. **30**	A.D. **48**	A.D. **50**	A.D. **53**	A.D. **60**	A.D. **62**	A.D. **67**	A.D. **95**

Pauline Epistles

| | | Galatians | 1 Thessalonians
2 Thessalonians | 1 Corinthians
2 Corinthians
Romans | Ephesians
Colossians
Philemon
Philippians | 1 Timothy
Titus | 2 Timothy | |

General Epistles

| | | James | | | | 1 Peter
2 Peter | Hebrews
Jude | 1 John
2 John
3 John
Revelation |

Arc of Bible Introduction

1.	5.	8.
2.	6.	9.
3.	7.	10.
4.		11.

Map of Palestine

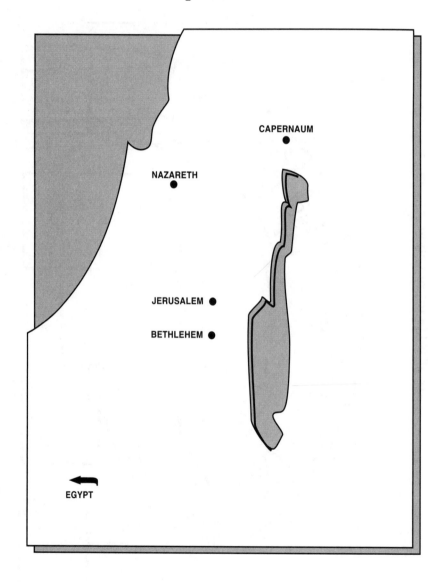

CAPERNAUM ●

NAZARETH ●

JERUSALEM ●

BETHLEHEM ●

EGYPT

Map of the New Testament World

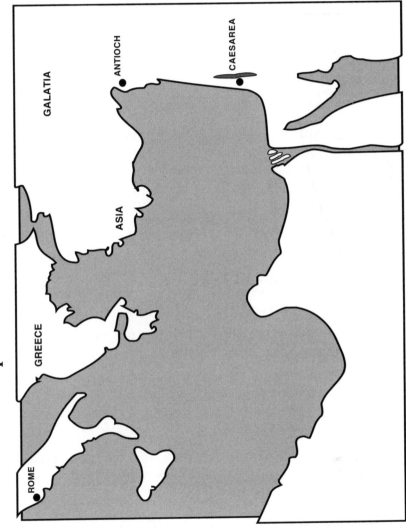

ROME

GREECE

GALATIA

ANTIOCH

ASIA

CAESAREA

Self-Test for Session 8

1. Overview:

a. The four Gospels record the life of Jesus, each from a different _____.

b. Three Gospels are called synoptic (literally, "seen together") because they present the life of Christ from basically the same _____ point of view. They are Matthew, Mark, and Luke.

c. John presents the life of Christ from a _____ viewpoint, highlighting seven miracles and seven "sayings" of Christ.

2. Gospels:

a. Matthew was a Jew, writing to an audience of Jews to convince them that Jesus was the Messiah, the _____ of the Jews.

b. Mark was a Jewish Christian, writing to Roman Christians, presenting Jesus as a perfect _____.

c. Luke wrote to a Greek audience to convince them that Jesus was the perfect Son of _____.

d. John wrote to a universal audience to convince them that Jesus was the Son of _____.

3. Parables:

a. A parable is a story intended to communicate a _____ truth, illustrating it with a familiar situation of common life.

b. Jesus taught in parables to _____ truth to the believers and to _____ truth from the unbelievers.

c. Parables must be interpreted in light of the _____ in which they are found.

d. Parables must be interpreted in light of the _____ setting in which they occur.

Self-Test for Session 9

1. Miracles are events that run contrary to what we know of nature and are _____ if God exists.

2. Miracles _____ the authority and message of the divine messenger.

3. Miracles occurred primarily in _____ concentrated times in history.

4. Jesus demonstrated, in the Gospel of John, His superiority over the _____ of this life.

5. The ability to predict events before they occur demonstrates God's _____.

6. Sixty-one major prophecies in the Old Testament were _____ by Christ.

7. The _____ prophecies suggest overwhelmingly that Jesus is the Messiah.

8. The purpose of prophecy is not to satisfy our curiosity but to _____ our lives.

Self-Test for Session 10

1. The Old Testament significance of the Passover is that it looked back on Israel's deliverance from slavery in Egypt and looked forward to ultimate spiritual deliverance through the _____.

2. Jesus observed the Passover with His disciples the night before His death, not only in faithfulness as a Jew, but also in _____ symbolism of His own forthcoming crucifixion.

3. The Passover was an object lesson of sacrifice and atonement for _____.

4. The Lord's Supper is the New Testament _____ of the Passover, symbolizing Christ's fulfillment of the Old Testament promises.

5. The Theft Theory states that the disciples _____ the body of Jesus from the tomb after He died.

6. The Swoon Theory states that Jesus did not die on the cross, but merely went into a death-like _____ from which He revived after being laid in the cool tomb.

7. The Hallucination Theory states that the disciples of Jesus had a _____ hallucination that Jesus rose from the dead.

8. The Resurrection as History position states that Jesus _____ from the dead, as He said He would.

Self-Test for Session 11

1. Christianity has _____ with other religions that must be recognized.

2. Christianity has _____ from other religions that make it distinctive.

3. Christianity's primary distinction is that _____ is the only way to God.

4. There are certain principles that should guide us in _____ the truth.

5. Didactic literature _____ truth in a relatively direct manner.

6. Narrative literature tells a _____.

7. Poetic literature presents poetry and must be _____ in light of key principles.

8. Proverbial literature concisely states a moral truth as a general _____.

9. Prophetic literature proclaims the Word of God and some-times tells the _____, often in highly figurative and symbolic language.

Fulfilling the Needs of Man

MAN'S WAY: GOD'S WAY:

Beliefs

lead to . . .

Actions

lead to . . .

Consequences

result in . . .

Frustration   **Satisfaction**
(Inner Turmoil)   (Inner Peace)

If you are interested in having Max Anders speak to your church, organization, or special event, please contact:

interAct Speaker's Bureau
P.O. Box 1022
Dickson, TN 37056
Telephone: (615) 446-2837
Facsimile: (615) 446-7818

Other Nelson books by Max Anders:

30 Days to Understanding What Christians Believe in 15 Minutes a Day. The essential truths of the Christian faith are presented in a clear, easy-to-grasp form. The major doctrines reviewed include the Bible, God, Christ, the Holy Spirit, sin, salvation, angels, man, the church, and the future. Also included are discussions of biblical principles regarding such issues as unity, money, suffering, and spiritual transformation. A third section interprets often misunderstood terms such as "regeneration" and "sanctification." A teaching plan and other helps are included for use in a small-group study. (0-7852-0999-9)

30 Days to Understanding the Christian Life in 15 Minutes a Day. Knowing what God expects of us is essential to living a life that is pleasing to Him. By helping his readers *understand* the Christian life, Dr. Anders helps them take some important first steps to *living* the Christian life. Along the way, he cautions about such dangers as spiritual snares and spiritual warfare. He also challenges his readers to engage in such spiritual disciplines as prayer, worship, using spiritual gifts, and sharing the good news. Also includes a teaching plan and overhead transparency masters for a small-group study in 12 weeks. (0-7852-0998-0)

The What You Need to Know Study Guide Series: individual titles dealing with:

God (0-8407-8485-6)	*Salvation* (0-7852-1191-8)
Jesus (0-8407-8486-4)	*Spiritual Growth* (0-8407-1936-1)
The Holy Spirit (0-8407-1925-6)	*Spiritual Warfare* (0-7852-1149-7)
The Bible (0-8407-1926-4)	*Bible Prophecy* (0-8407-1938-8)
The Church (0-7852-1153-5)	*Defending Your Faith* (0-7852-1192-6)

Each of 12 lessons in these ten guides can be completed by individuals or small groups in under an hour. Each guide is: *relevant*, applying Bible truth to everyday life with warmth and humor; *concise*, providing lessons that can be studied quickly and easily; *balanced*, explaining major views and encouraging you to embrace your own convictions; and *teachable*, offering easy-to-teach resources, including preview and summary features and plenty of questions for discussion. The series as a whole is also *complete*, forming a trustworthy core curriculum on the basics of Christianity, regardless of your level of experience with the Christian faith.